CRIMINAL JUSTICE, LAW ENFORCEMENT AND CORRECTIONS

CONSCIENCE OF JUDGES IN INTERNATIONAL CRIMINAL LAW

THE HEART OF JUDGEMENTS

Criminal Justice, Law Enforcement and Corrections

Additional books and e-books in this series can be found on Nova's website under the Series tab.

CRIMINAL JUSTICE, LAW ENFORCEMENT AND CORRECTIONS

CONSCIENCE OF JUDGES IN INTERNATIONAL CRIMINAL LAW

THE HEART OF JUDGEMENTS

FARHAD MALEKIAN

nova science publishers
New York

https://doi.org/10.52305/PTSU5114

Library of Congress Cataloging-in-Publication Data

ISBN: 978-1-68507-252-0

Published by Nova Science Publishers, Inc. † New York

CONTENTS

Conscience is not a set of rules but the
limit of the personal capacity of the judge
Punishment of an innocent is equal to
the punishment of the ethical morality of all men
The ethical face of a judge is only a façade
if a love for the truth is not present

Preface

The administration of criminal justice in any court in the world should be based on the truth. The fact is that we have created a number of regulations, rules, codes, and conventions regarding criminal procedures, and yet they are still not comprehensive enough. Therefore, there must be something wrong with our legislation and codes. We have been attempting to create a framework of judicial conscience through our policy of international criminal justice. However, we ignore the fact that more regulation means that there are more barriers to finding out the truth. The reality is that no civilisation can maintain successful regulations and codes if they are not based on the truth. If I speak about the truth, some may argue that I am threatening not only those who are working as academics in the field of criminal justice, but also the big political parties of the world–which may well be true.

Moreover, within the mechanisms of the international criminal justice of any international criminal court, ethical codes can already be found. However, the criteria for the application of those ethical codes are still under the control of those who work in the courts as judges. This means that whatever a code of conduct is and can be, it is still up to an individual to show what the code of conduct is and how it works for them. Although the codes are decisive and should be respected at all times by judges under oath, the interpretation of the rules of codes of ethics varies between judges based on their cultural backgrounds and personal experiences. Even when rules of ethics are codified by international criminal courts, the most practical part of the codes are in the possession of individual judges and dependent upon their understanding of the moral standard of criminal justice and the truth.

The truth may therefore be interpreted differently by different judges, although they can still reach a majority conclusion regarding a case. The fact remains that a judgement is part of the ethical code, and the ethical code represents judicial independence as dictated by the oath made by the judge. In other words, the interpretation of all ethical codes and the judicial conscience of judges are principally based on the naked truth. However, the history of criminal civilisation has proven that the naked truth has rarely been seen in the administration of criminal justice when it comes to the big criminals.

For the author of this book, law is that substance which combines legal and moral norms together with the norms of love, which do not discriminate between its subjects. Furthermore, a judge is a person with high morality and respect for their position. Additionally, a court does not have a roof, doors, regulations, branches, judges, prosecutors, or any part of the kingdom of law. Rather a court conjures the image of a place where we confront the whole truth, where every single individual, every judge and prosecutor, every victim and witness, and every accused person, offender, and the condemned, come together to reveal the naked truth. This therefore represents the nature of our criminal codes of ethics, the high morality of judges, and the ultimate intention of diverse cultures and pluralist interpretation.

Courts thus pose a challenge to the science of international criminal law and to the monopoly on legal knowledge which is held by the strong. Truth challenges the law of masters i.e., the established institutions of positive law which hide the truth behind criminal laws. The truth attempts to prevent politics from hindering international criminal law and justice. We should remember that, in reality, criminal justice systems represent the personal desires of judges or lawyers and not the actual law. That is why we must continue to fight for justice in the faculties of law.

The judicial conscience of criminal justice which integrates all aspects of ethical and moral recognition into itself, should be mindful that the judges of all criminal courts in the world can not only endanger the jurisprudence of criminal justice, but they can also harm the overall integrity of criminal justice. *We should try to avoid validating the expression that a good lawyer knows the law, but a great lawyer knows the judge.* If we would fight against this expression, there would be no impunity for big criminals within the International Criminal Court like we continue to see today. This means that the notion of international criminal responsibility found in the statutes of international criminal courts cannot be achieved as promised as long as discrepancies in the attribution of accountability to criminals exist.

I suppose that a critical inquiry into the true function of our criminal legal system is at least vital, if not welcomed. One can observe that our national, regional, and international norms, give priority to the validity of the law over the maintenance of justice and the truth. This is one of the serious issues plaguing our national and international criminal legislations. I refer here to the real cognition of the law, or our awareness of the reality of the existence of the law, including our methods of argumentation, reasoning, and delivering judgements based on the nature of the law. Thus, if the intent of criminal law is to protect justice, and if the intent of international criminal legislation is to preserve the value of human dignity, then criminal law must have been created to help the victims and humanity. Whilst protection of justice and the value of criminal legislation may differ from one another, the purpose of both is to reveal what is possible, and what violates the nature of criminal justice, criminal judicial conscience, codes of criminal ethics, and the power of the naked truth.[1]

For the author, the notion of justice has no father, mother, friend, nor guardian. Justice does not have a particular theoretical basis, political power, or any political authority. Justice is simply an impartial movement in which wise, rational, and honest individuals promote the truth. It is also

---

[1] Farhad Malekian, *Judgments of Love in Criminal Justice* (Switzerland: Springer, 2017, 2018), *Pp.*142-143. Consult *also* Farhad Malekian, *Trading Virginity of International Criminal Justice* (New York: Nova Science Publishers, 2020).

true that justice has to be strong and independent in order to preserve itself. In other worlds, water can wash everything but not itself. Storms move heavy objects, but not themselves. Fire can burn everything, but not itself. Roots hold up an entire tree, but not themselves. A good prosecutor, a good judge, and a good lawyer should banish themselves, but not the integrity of national or international criminal justice. I therefore wonder how many quality lawyers we have. Please if you find any, write their name in the soil of justice.

F. Malekian
Uppsala, Sweden
Spring/Autumn 2021
f.malekian.in.crim.l@telia.com
f.malekian.in.crim.l@gmail.com

About the Book

For the author, a judge is a person with high ethical and moral capacity who respects their position. When we think of a court, we think about a place where we confront the truth, where every single individual, every judge and prosecutor, every victim and witness, and every accused person, offender, and the condemned, come together to reveal the naked truth. The main objective of criminal proceedings is to uphold a pure juridical system with full ethical conscience in order to protect the rights of all individuals, including members of the general public. Judges of criminal courts are required to be independent in order to pursue the truth and uphold judicial conscience, which is itself an institution based on the professional values of criminal justice. A judge with ample judicial conscience should not be afraid of being attacked or losing their position if they work to uphold and uncover the truth. This implies the independent freedom of judicial justice. If justice is safe, then the safety of the victims and the accused will also be guaranteed. That is why confidence in the professional standards of the ethical requirements of judges of national criminal courts or of the International Criminal Court is heavily contingent upon their honesty, which in turn relates to their practical experiences and ought to be based on the knowledge of the essence of humanity. Professional ethics are particularly vital when evaluating diverse values and the very question of pluralist systems of national and international criminal justice which deal with core international crimes. The intention is to assess the way in which our administration of national and international criminal justice requires judges to be impartial, pursue the truth, and not be the puppets of politicians.

Chapter 1

PROFESSIONAL RESPONSIBILITY OF JUDGES

1.1. THE TRADITIONAL DEFINITION OF "JUDGE"

It would be very difficult to explain the historical role of judges in the administration of criminal justice here, especially since judges have played different roles in different nations.[2] In sum, the existence of criminal law goes back to the establishment of civilisation, and thus criminal law is one of the oldest laws governing the relations between people. In the past, all forms of social conflict were investigated under the provisions of criminal law, although this criminal law did not yet have any statute for its application. Many clans had and still have a number of customs and regulations concerning reparations. This means that no particular administration was established for the settlement of conflicts, and often wise men or elders took on the roles of judges and prosecutors in the clan forum. Any judgement made by these individuals would only be accepted by the victims and the accused if the clan was in agreement.

---

[2] See *infra*.

> Judges have performed diverse functions in criminal cases, and have not only served as judges, but also prosecutors, in that they were responsible for gathering all evidence relating to a given case. Beyond these duties, judges were not only legally liable for the procedure, judgement, and consequences of the outcome of proceedings; they were also morally responsible for the maintenance of justice under certain social and moral rules. Almost every judge in history has found it necessary to carry out their work by following the requirements of justice and of the institutional tradition. In addition to this task, judges have also been held criminally responsible for making bad decisions, for example if they applied biased justice during the court proceedings or if they harmed the spiritual nature or value of moral justice. In extreme cases, they have even been identified as being in intimidation of the court for issuing false ruling. These requirements which constitute an integral part of corpus juris of criminal justice, have served to strengthen the moral attitudes of prosecutors and judges in order to prevent them from delivering false rulings and to punish reckless behaviour.[3]

One of the most notable early criminal legislations was the Code of Hammurabi, which is one of the most famous codes in history. The Code had many regulations and was enforced by the judges of the administration of criminal justice. One may say that the judicious enforcement of the Code was much stronger than the Statute of the International Criminal Court is today based on the fact that the regulation of the Code was applicable to all, but the Statute of the ICC cannot be enforced if the parties do not submit themselves to the jurisdiction of the Court. The Code of Hammurabi was therefore a very effective and competent Code because of its strong enforcement and flexibility concerning the ruling proceedings of the Code. It is for this reason that the Code was greatly respected by civilisation at that time, and the Hammurabian courts were decisive in the application of their decisions. King Hammurabi stated himself:

---

[3] Farhad Malekian, *Conscience of Prosecutors in International Criminal Law, The Heart of the Matter* (New York: Nova Science Publishers, 2021), pp.1-2. See also *The Code of Hammurabi*, available online at http://www.sjsu.edu/people/james.lindahl/courses/Hum1A/s3/The-Code-of-Hammurabi.pdf (visited 20 September 2019). See also Farhad Malekian, *Corpus Juris of Islamic International Criminal Justice* (Cambridge Scholars Publishing, 2017 and 2018).

> The king who ruleth among the kings of the cities am I. My words are well considered; there is no wisdom like unto mine. By the command of Shamash, the great judge of heaven and earth, let righteousness go forth in the land: by the order of Marduk my lord, let no destruction befall my monument. In E-Sagil, which I love, let my name be ever repeated; let the oppressed, who has a case at law, come and stand before this my image as king of righteousness; let him read the inscription, and understand my precious words: the inscription will explain his case to him.[4]

The Code had certain rules concerning corrupt judges and their punishment. A judge could be punished for making a false judgement, not meeting certain criteria with their judgement, or for punishing an innocent person. The purpose was not really to punish the judge, but rather to emphasise that the sacred position of the administration of criminal justice and its imperative rule must be preserved.

Almost 4,000 years ago, Hammurabi promulgated justice on behalf of the state, and judges acted on his orders which aligned with the Code. Therefore, judges not only acted upon superior orders from the high judge for the administration of criminal justice in the land, but also in response to the ethical or moral requirements of cultural attitudes and their needs. Thus, citizens could submit their complaints or lawsuits to the relevant judges.[5] The Code offered clear examples of justice and outlined the duties of the judge. Some of the most interesting and imperative rules of the Code regarding the duties and function of judges and their judgements include:

> 5. If a judge try a case, reach a decision, and present his judgement in writing; if later error shall appear in his decision, and it be through his own fault, then he shall pay twelve times the fine set by him in the case, and he shall be publicly removed from the judge's bench, and never again shall he sit there to render judgement.

---

[4] https://avalon.law.yale.edu/ancient/hamframe.asp.

[5] Kathryn E. Slanski, *The Law of Hammurabi and Its Audience*, p.109, at The Law of Hammurabi and Its Audience.pdf.

9. If anyone lose an article, and find it in the possession of another: if the person in whose possession the thing is found say "A merchant sold it to me, I paid for it before witnesses," and if the owner of the thing say, "I will bring witnesses who know my property," then shall the purchaser bring the merchant who sold it to him, and the witnesses before whom he bought it, and the owner shall bring witnesses who can identify his property. The judge shall examine their testimony–both of the witnesses before whom the price was paid, and of the witnesses who identify the lost article on oath. The merchant is then proved to be a thief and shall be put to death. The owner of the lost article receives his property, and he who bought it receives the money he paid from the estate of the merchant.
12. If the witnesses be not at hand, then shall the judge set a limit, at the expiration of six months. If his witnesses have not appeared within the six months, he is an evil-doer, and shall bear the fine of the pending case.[6]

1.2. The Concept of Judicial Conscience

Judicial conscience constitutes a set of norms and values which regulates the ethical and moral standards of the identity of criminal jurisdiction. This may also be referred to as the influence of moral judgements on the outcome of judicial proceedings. Judicial conscience relates to the unspoken complex capacity of those involved in criminal proceedings to present scrutiny of moral judgements.[7] It is the conscience of judges that precedes the central questions of criminal justice. There is in fact an intrinsic clash between the rigid body of criminal law and the

---

[6] https://avalon.law.yale.edu/ancient/hamframe.asp.

[7] "*Moral scrutiny* refers to the idea that the essence of man should not be violated by any law in any way-- regardless of who was responsible for the drafting and adoption of the law. Without a doubt, this *moral scrutiny* is related to the very essential and substantial value of the dignity of man and their universal nature. In other words, although Hart was a positivist, he did not approve of the adoption of law which violated the moral basis of the relevant law. Again, in a broader aspect, he believed that we cannot enact a law in any country which violates the universal or collective united value of man. Nor can we adopt a law which ignores this universal essence of human dignity, i.e., *the law of somebodiness*." Farhad Malekian, *International Criminal Law, the Law of Somebodiness, the Law of Nobodiness* (New York: Nova Science Publishers, 2021), p.47. Hart *also* speaks about moral scrutiny. See L.A. Hart, The Concept of Law (Oxford University Press, 1961), p.206.

judicial conscience of judges who are involved in the interpretation of different issues. This clash is predominantly expressed in the collision of strict notions of justice and equity. In other words, the impressions of the equity of justice, judgements, and judges must be broadly seen. The intention of the judicial conscience of judges is therefore to differentiate between right and wrong. In addition, the main values in judicial conscience include the principle of independence, the principle of impartiality, and the principle of diligence. All these values are essential for the proper understanding of the procedures of criminal justice, and they are all equally important. If any of these main principles are not present, then there is an issue with the entire legal system since these principles are interrelated and cannot exist in isolation.

The principle of independence refers to the denunciation of any external conducts which can influence the judgements of international criminal courts. The principle of impartiality concerns the tendency of the judge to empower the fair and equal treatment of all parties involved in a criminal case. It implies the integrity, confidentiality, equality, competence, and propriety of justice and the judge's commitment to remaining unbiased. The principle of diligence concerns the faithful fulfilment of duties. All three principles represent the manner in which judicial conscience is interpreted. However, the entire situation is quite different when it comes to the practical interpretation of these principles, as certain interpretations can prevent deny liberty to someone if the judges violate these principles in their interpretations. This can in turn harm millions of victims and deny them justice.[8]

The judicial conscience of a judge becomes relevant following the prosecutor's completion of their work and the submission of a case to the court. The theory of judicial conscience in the office of a judge is not only significant for the process of good criminal justice, but it also constitutes the second heart of the machinery of criminal justice. This means that

---

[8] Moreover, "For some international criminal lawyers, money constitutes a combination of fragrant liquid provisions of the rules of criminal law made from the blood of the victims of genocide which has been extracted from their dead bodies and destruction of their houses." Farhad Malekian, *Conscience of Lawyers in International Criminal Law* (New York: Nova Science Publishers, 2021), p.96.

although the office of the prosecutor and the court are integral parts of the systems of national and international criminal justice, they carry out their duties independently and have their own procedures relating to the examination, investigation, and continuation or termination of a given case. Despite this, these two bodies are still dependent on one another and work together more often than they work separately.

These two legal bodies are populated by people who have studied law and work together to ensure that criminal justice remains empowered and effective. This book therefore explores what these pillars of justices are permitted to do, and what is prohibited in the interest of criminal justice. This is because one of the significant duties of judges is to determine whether the office of the prosecutor came to an accurate conclusion concerning the guilt or innocence of the accused.[9] Therefore, the ultimate act of condemnation remains in the hands of the judges, and it is their judgements which ultimately decide whether the accused will be punished, set free, or whether more evidence must be gathered before a decision can be reached.

1.3. Professional Ethical Conscience of Judges

Judges of all courts work under a particular guarantee of independence which emanates from their profession. Their function is based on judicial ethics, their correctness, and honesty. Judicial conscience is actually an institution based on professional values. The court is based on judges, and judges are based on the court, and together they present the same

---

[9] Moreover, "Detention of the accused in all cases must be founded in logic and be based on the fact that their freedom would result in harm to themselves, others, or the case. This means that when a person commits a minor offence, detention is not necessary and a fine is sufficient. Most questions of detention are based on the severity of the criminal case. If a conduct is not grave, like in the case of unintentional crimes, detention may not be an option. However, it is possible that prosecutors in certain situations decide that there is sufficient evidence to prove that the criminal conduct has been committed by the suspect, but the preliminary investigation come to a different conclusion. Again, in many countries, the suspect may admit guilt and ease the complication of the situation and thus accept their penalty without investigation." Malekian, *Conscience of Prosecutors in International Criminal Law, The Heart of the Matter*, note 3, pp.18-19.

professional institutional judiciary values as an integral part of the administration of a criminal court. Thus, the main objective of a criminal court is not to bring the accused to trial and apply appropriate punishment, but rather to represent a pure judicial system with full ethical conscience in order to protect the rights of all individuals including the victims, witnesses, the accused, the condemned, and the public.

The term "professional ethics" is defined as: a) Intending to justify moral values that should govern the work of professionals, b) Dealing with moral values that essentially guide groups of professionals. These values may be identified as principles in the codes of ethics directed by professional societies or as actual beliefs and actions of professionals, C) Referring to the study of professional ethics either through normative philosophical inquiries into the values needed for professionals to carry out their duties, or through descriptive searches into the actual beliefs and acts of groups of professionals.[10]

Judicial conscience encompasses the essential professional moral and legal ethics of judges which must be present in the administration of criminal justice in every nation.[11] These professional ethics are particularly essential and imperative in the case of international crimes such as crimes against humanity, war crimes, genocide, torture, and aggression. This ethical inspiration of judicial conscience is also crucial when evaluating diverse values or pluralist systems of national or international criminal justice. This ethical aspect of the function of the court, which manifests in the activities of its judges, is therefore necessary for the settlement of criminal disputes. In particular, a judge should not be afraid of being

---

[10] *The Cambridge Dictionary of Philosophy*, 2nd edition (Cambridge University Press 1995, 1999), p.749.

[11] The principle of morality constitutes one of the most fundamental principles of jurisdiction. Consult Farhad Malekian, *Classical Morality in International Peremptory Criminal Law* (Newcastle: Cambridge Scholars Publishing, 2018, republished 2021); K. Robert Vischer, *Martin Luther King Jr. and the Morality of Legal Practice: Lessons in Love and Justice* (2014); David Lyons, 'Moral Aspects of Legal Theory' in Kenneth Himma and Brian Bix (eds) *Law and Morality* (2005); A. R. C. Duncan, *Practical Reason and Morality* (Nelson, 1957); Luvios Lon Fuller, *The Morality of Law* (Yale Law University, 2nd ed., 1969); Joseph Raz, *Ethics in the Public Domain: Essays in the Morality of Law and Politics* (Oxford: Oxford University Press, 1994); K. Robert Vischer, *Martin Luther King Jr. and the Morality of Legal Practice: Lessons in Love and Justice* (2014).

attacked or losing their job while pursuing the truth—which is also guaranteed by the principle of professional ethics. In other words, judges have to carry out their duties professionally, and with clear minds and enlightened hearts in order to defend justice, which in turns protects the victims and the accused. As a result, the powers of criminal justice and its mechanisms which are entrusted to judges have strong connections to the values of honesty and justice. The freedom of judicial conscience, the freedom of professional ethics, and the freedom of the dignity of the administration of criminal justice are completely based on the truth. The professional standards of the ethical requirements of judges are connected to these corollary values and establish confidence in the mechanisms of criminal justice, in particular for international criminal courts. In connection to the American constitutional system, it has been correctly asserted that:

> There is no doubt that the business of judging in this constitutional system, in which the rule of law prevails, is difficult at best. It has never been easy to apply the law free from any personal, religious, or philosophical beliefs. Some have argued it cannot be done because it is a contradiction at its worst or a paradox at its best. However, a judge in our system must be able to set aside any and all of these factors in the decision-making process. If the judge cannot do this and, most importantly, knows that he or she cannot, resignation may be the only remaining option.[12]

The fact is that judges should avoid issuing paradoxical statements during criminal justice proceedings in both national and international courts. Judges of both types of court should carry out their work on behalf of the population which they represent. The population of the world expects that international courts and tribunals issue high-quality and independent jurisdictional criminal decisions within reasonable timeframes. The principles of proficiency, skill, adroitness, and efficiency

---

[12] Gene E. Franchini, 'Conscience, Judging, and Conscientious Judging', 2 *The Journal of Appellate Practice and Process* (2000), p.25.

are all internationally common requirements of judges, which are needed in order to discharge their obligations and responsibilities to the best of their ability. A judge of an international criminal court must attempt to maintain an extraordinary level of knowledge, which includes their moral and ethical experience. The word expertise also raises the question of the capacity of the judges of international criminal courts to mediate coherent decisions and rulings for all those involved in the case.[13] A judge of the court must guarantee that cases and other matters are heard appropriately and are taken into consideration without delay. All this also means that every judge must discharge their judicial duties accurately and appropriately.

1.4. Guaranteeing Access to Justice

Access to appropriate and authentic justice is an elementary value of the rule of law. This means that access to justice allows the possibility for everyone to speak their truth during an objective process of justice. The access to unbiased justice should be present in all countries, and should be regarded as one of the primary conditions for the independence of institutions of justice, as well as of constitutions. Access to justice allows those involved in a case to be heard by an objective court, which is particularly significant when gross violations of human rights law are involved. Access to justice is thus the core component in ensuring proper

---

[13] For a background of international criminal courts see Vespesian V. Pella. 'Plan d'un Code RépressifMondial', 6 *Rewe International de Droit Pénal* 1948 (1935); United Nations War Crimes Commssion, History of the United Nations War Commission and the Deveelopment of the Laws of War (1949), pp.443-50); A. Sowilet, Sowilet A., *The Problem of the Creation of a Permanent International Criminal Court* (1951); Quincy Wright, 'Proposal for an International Criminal Court', 46 *American Journal of International Law* (1952); Bienvenido C. Fannie Klein & Daniel Wilkes, 'United Nations Draft Statute for an International Criminal Court: An American Evaluation', in *International Criminal Law* 526 (Gerhard O.W. Mueller & Edward M. Wise eds., 1965); 'La Créationd'une Juridiction Pénale Internationale et la Coopération Internationale en Matière Pénale', 45 *Revue Internationale de Droit Penale* 435 (1974); Ferencz Benjamin, *International Criminal Court* (2 vols. 1980); M. Cherif Bassiouni & Daniel Derby, 'Final Report on the Establishment of an International Criminal Court for the Implementation of the Apartheid Convention and Other Relevant Instruments', 7 *Hofstra Law Review* 523 (1981).

justice. This means that the delivery of justice should be objective and non-discriminatory in all cases.

Ensuring access to appropriate justice is the duty of state authorities, the administration of criminal justice, and its prosecutors and judges. Consequently, when a case is submitted to a court, the judge of the court must be aware of the fact that the victims are seeking justice for unlawful violations and therefore require urgent assistance.[14] That is why judges are responsible for realising that their objectivity and the way in which they treat a case, have significant influence on the outcome of the case. These are the essential prerequisites for upholding the rule of law and ensuring that there is no delinquency in the administration of justice.

However, it must be noted that access to justice is not available to everyone in all countries due to a number of political and financial reasons. More importantly, access to justice may be denied in certain situations as a result of discrimination. Thus, for example, although many states in Europe speak about the rights of individuals, they fail to guarantee those rights, and as a result their words are empty. This can clearly be seen in the following statement made by a judge:

> Announcing rights without providing guarantees to enforce them is useless. It becomes a sterile formulation that sows expectations and produces frustrations. Therefore, guarantees must be established that permit: demanding that rights should be recognized, claiming them when they have been disregarded, re-establishing them when they have been violated, and implementing them when their exercise has encountered unjustified obstacles. This is what the principle of equal and rapid access to justice means; namely, the real possibility of access to justice through the means that domestic law provides to all persons, in order to reach a just settlement of a dispute; in other words, formal and genuine access to justice. [...]This access is facilitated by due process, which the Inter-American Court of Human Rights has examined fully in the exercise of its advisory and contentious competence. Strictly speaking, due process

[14] Mikaela Heikkilä, International Criminal Tribunals and Victims of Crime: A Study of the Status of Victims before International Criminal Tribunals and of Factors affecting this Status (Institute for Human Rights, Abo Akademi University, Turku, 2004).

> is the means to ensure the effective exercise of human rights that is consistent with the most advanced concept of such rights: a method or factor to ensure the effectiveness of law as a whole and of subjective rights in specific cases. Due process – a dynamic concept guided and developed under a guarantee model that serves individual and social interests and rights, and also the supreme interest of justice – is a guiding principle for the proper resolution of legal actions and a fundamental right of all persons. It is applied to settle disputes of any nature – including labour disputes – and to the claims and complaints submitted to any authority: judicial or administrative.[15]

The fact is that without providing guarantees for the rights of individuals under the procedures of an appropriate court led by an impartial judge, rights lose their legal validity and cannot be trusted under the machinery of criminal justice. That is why the administration of justice and the framework of criminal legislations also need to ensure the objective enforcement of the rights of all parties without privileging any one party over another. The principle of equal and speedy access to justice is also considered fundamental under the principles of international human rights law. Reference to these rights is not limited to any particular person, but is the basic requirement for the establishment of supreme equal justice.[16]

1.5. Preventing Witness Tampering

A judge is a chosen or elected magistrate who presides over court proceedings within the realm of national or international justice. As previously mentioned, judges are responsible for ruling on questions of

[15] Concurring Opinion of Judge Sergio García Ramírez in Relation to Advisory Opinion OC-18/03, *Juridical Condition and Rights of the Undocumented Migrants*. September 17, 2003. Series A No. 18, paras. 36 and 37. http://www.cidh.org/countryrep/accesodesc07eng/Accesodesciv.eng.htm#_ftn7.

[16] Examine Ondřej Svaček, 'The Human Rights Dimension of the ICC's Complementarity Regime', *Czech Yearbook of Public and Private International Law*, 2015, Vol. 6, pp. 273-288; Reisman W. Michael, 'Legal Responses to Genocide and Other Massive Violations of Human Rights', 59 Law and Contemporary Problems (1996).

criminal law using provisions applicable to the given crime. This implies the fact that the judge must ensure that the provisions referenced during the proceedings are relevant and applicable to the case. The judge is the one who litigates between parties and makes decisions on legal criminal issues. It is therefore the duty of the judge to hear allegations and listen to the testimony of witnesses in all circumstances. The judge is even responsible for visiting the location of the crime, if necessary, in order to be more familiar with the case and reach a decision concerning the admissibility of the case. Moreover,

> along with all of the many legal decisions judges must make in the execution of their responsibilities, they must always be making decisions about allocation of court resources. Trusteeship implicates a broad array of institutional responsibilities – core commitments such as fidelity to legal (especially constitutional) authority, impartiality, independence, accountability, and practical wisdom – to which judges must be committed. They must have good judgement about these matters of resources just as they do in their application of the law. Such good judgement and practical wisdom is, for many if not all judges, and whether they mention it or not, likely a matter of conscience at some level.[17]

Judges are responsible for questioning witnesses and evaluating whether their statements are true or false, since witnesses may be tampered with or be biased. In particular, it has been seen that many offenders and victims pay witnesses to help their case and convince the court and jury of their side of the story. This is particularly harmful when the case relates to murder and can lead to long prison sentences. Although it is the duty of the judge to determine the guilt or innocence of criminal defendants and make decisions about appropriate sentences if the defendants are found guilty, the judge must ensure that they carry out these duties fairly. Furthermore, it is also their duty to ensure that a case has been presented accurately and was not tainted by false witness testimony. This function of the judge is

---

[17] Sarah M. R. Craven, *In Good Conscience: Expressions of Judicial Conscience in Federal Appellate Opinions,* (Akron Law Publication, 2012), pp.1-67, at 8.

especially imperative when one realises that a considerable number of other legal clerks work under the supervision of the judge. All this implies the fact that a judge ought to be fully aware of their duties and of the potential consequences of miscarriages of justice.

1.6. Judges Interpreting Criminal Legislation

In the past, all features of the law were the privilege of legislators, which is why judges were not allowed to interpret the law. However, this constraint was altered by the Napoleonic Codes, and the interpretation of the law then fell to the judges.[18] This is not to say that judges in France were or are permitted to formulate laws or rules, but that following the adoption of the Napoleonic codes, they have been permitted to deduce, reason, and interpret the law depending on the circumstances of the given case. However, we must emphasise that the Napoleonic Code was not the first legal code adopted in Europe.

Before the Napoleonic Code, there were other codes or legal mechanisms adopted under the civil legal systems of other countries. That said, the advantage of the Napoleonic Code was the considerable number of new rules drafted within it, which set it apart from other codes due to its ability to provide new sanctions for the implementation of the law by judges. Since then, judges have tended to interpret and highlight the literal meaning of codes. The Napoleonic Code was also one of the indispensable factors in the progress of civil law and its acknowledgment by a number of European states during and after the Napoleonic Wars. The Code rapidly spread outside of Europe, and prompted legal reforms in many countries

---

[18] Lorenz Kristen, Les Quarante Codes des Francais Composés des Charte de 1830, Code Civil (Berlin: Deutschland, 1845); Stock Photo - justice, laws, France, Code Civil des Francais (Code Napoleon), title, 1st edition, Paris, 1804, Napoleonic Code, law, book, 19t; Napoleonic Code (France, 1804), available https://www.britannica.com/topic/ Napoleonic-Code, 24 January 2017.

in Africa, South America, Asia, and the Middle East, among them the Persian Civil Code.[19]

The development of law in the Civil Code has been in the hands of many private and public entities which present different arguments, while the interpretations by judges are the most effective in ultimately bringing cases to the desks of legislators. A Civil Code can be modified by a parliament and allows for the creation of new laws. This is also true in the Islamic system, with the difference that the Islamic system is based on *Shariah* Law or Islamic Law.[20] However, *Shariah* is a very flexible law and adapts to the changing times. This is one of the virtues of Islamic law, which has unfortunately been ignored in practice by the Islamic states and their judges. The reason behind this is that most people interpreting the law are religious authorities or judges who have monopolies on the law.[21]

In addition, deciding whether or not Islamic law has a good nature is completely irrelevant based on the fact that religious norms, rules, provisions, and explanations can still be seen within the majority of European laws. The difference is that European laws are no longer called Christian laws, although their origins are Christian in nature. The problem with judgements made within Islamic systems is that judges rely on traditional interpretations of laws that Europeans no longer accept. Furthermore, the title of "Islamic law" has been preserved over the centuries even as the law has changed. For instance, judges in Iran have been using a combination of Islamic law and French law. Prior to the unlawful imposition of Islamic rules by the Islamic regime, the judges under the last king of Iran used a criminal code which was based largely on Islamic law. One of the most problematic laws enforced by these judges

---

[19] However, the Code has many problems of its own. It increased the authority of men over their family members. The rights of women were decreased, along with those of illegitimate children. See also the History of the Napoleonic Code, available online at https://www.thoughtco.com/the-napoleonic-code-code-napoleon-1221918.

[20] Farhad Malekian, 'The Homogeneity of International Criminal Court with Islamic Jurisprudence,' 9 (4) *International Criminal Law Review* (2009), pp.595-621; Farhad Malekian, *Principles of Islamic International Criminal Law: A Comparative Search* (Netherlands: Brill & Nijhoff, 2011); Malekian, *Corpus Juris of Islamic International Criminal Justice*, note 3.

[21] *Id.*

was Code 179 which permitted a man to kill his wife if he found her having sexual relations with another man (committing adultery). This law can trace its roots to the Book of Exodus, codified for the Israelites at the biblical Mount Sinai. The monopolisation of law by religious rules is found even in communist nations such as in China. *Although it seems that religious theories have no place in any legal system, the ideas of* equality between citizens and the equal distribution of resources -- which are central to communist ideology, are have their roots in religious principles.

1.7. Principles of Criminal Justice

Both national and international criminal laws are based on certain principles which are necessary corollaries to their legal characters.[22] Judges of all courts are obliged to not violate the fundamental principles of criminal justice which are integral to criminal justice. Moreover, the system of criminal justice cannot function without principles and cannot be authentic without the respect of certain principles that are vital for its existence and for common respect. The function of these principles becomes more obvious when the principle of integrity of justice, the impartiality of judges, and the independence of judgements are in focus. A judge of a national, regional, or international criminal court should fully respect the following consolidated principles of criminal justice:

a) Prohibition of *ex post facto* law (retroactive law);
b) *De lege ferenda* (the law for the future);

---

[22] Kevin Boyle, *Arc of Justice: A Saga of Race, Civil Rights, and Murder in the Jazz Age* (2002); B. E. Harcourt, *Beccaria's on crimes and Punishments: A Mirror on the History of the Foundations of Modern Criminal Law* (2013); Matthew Lippman., *Contemporary Criminal Law: Concepts, Cases, and Controversies* (5th ed., 2021); Richard G. Singer., *Examples & Explanations for Criminal Law* (7th ed., 2018); Farhad Malekian, *The Monopolization of International Criminal Law in the United Nations, A Jurisprudential Approach* (Almqvist Wiksell International, 1st ed., 1993), (2nd ed., 1995); Farhad Malekian, *The Mirage of International Criminal Law: Kant's Metaphysics of Mens Rea* (Cambridge Scholars Publishing, 2018); Malekian, *Conscience of Prosecutors in International Criminal Law, the Heart of the Matter*, note 3.

c) *De lege lata* (the law in force);
d) *Nullum crimen sine lege* (a conduct cannot be treated as criminal unless a rule of law has already declared it to be criminal, and as such, punishable);
e) *Nulla poena sine lege* (no punishment without law);
f) Principle of the inviolability of the rights of individuals;
g) The principle of the burden of proof, implying that there must be enough evidence to prove guilt;
h) The principle of the right to remain silent;
i) The respect of the principle of *ni bis in idem* i.e., double jeopardy, which implies that a person should not be charged twice for the same conduct;
j) *Nullum crimen nulla poena sine stricta* (prohibition of inhumane sanctions);
k) *Nullum crimen nulla poena sine lege scripta* (careful application of punishment in violation of unwritten law);
l) Conformity (opportunity to follow the law);
m) Humanise (punishment should be made more humane if other forms of penalties are available);
n) Equivalence (similar conduct should have similar punishment);
o) The application of the principle of proportionality;[23]
p) The requirement of the principle of *habeas corpus.*

1.8. Common Roles of Judges

A judge is commonly known as a person who has been chosen to conduct court proceedings according to the legislation of a country. Judges decide about a variety of cases that come before the courts. These include family cases, civil suits, and criminal cases. One of the chief duties of the judges is that they must maintain their impartiality at all times, concerning

[23] Farhad Malekian, 'Comparative Substantive International Criminal Justice', in Ronald Slye (ed.), *The Nuremberg Principles in Non-western Societies: A Reflection on their Universality, Legitimacy and Application (*2017), pp.10-44.

all matters. It is also an established duty of judges to understand that they are obliged to interpret the relevant law in order to understand its content the best they can. Thus, they must also keep their objectivity towards both sides of a case and try to provide a balance between the law, the offender, and the victim. Since lawyers represent the voices of the victims or the accused during trial, judges are required to respect their voice and listen to them carefully. If the suspect cannot afford to hire a lawyer, judges are usually responsible for assigning a lawyer to represent them. Additionally, judges also set the bail for the accused and sign search and arrest warrants.

Even if a case is submitted by the prosecutor of the court to the judge, the latter is responsible for ensuring that there is sufficient evidence of a crime. With this we mean that evidence must be objective and not based on personal thoughts or outside information and must not be influenced by cultural differences or unreliable information such as the fading memories of witnesses, cultural understandings of certain behaviours, or financial circumstances. A judicial criminal evaluation of evidence is therefore a rather sensitive task which requires the judge to be experienced and follow the rules. However, concerning certain visible criminal cases, requiring evidence may just be a procedural matter and not an actual condition for the proof of brutal international crimes such as those committed in Srebrenica and Palestine.

Thus, the judge must make a decision concerning the accused and their actions prior to examining the case. If the accused has an attorney, and bail has been set, the accused is then able to enter a plea of guilty or a plea of not guilty. Here, the most significant question for a judge is to determine whether or not the plea expressed by the accused has been made voluntarily and not under a *force majeure* situation in order to cover for someone else. This is particularly important in the case of corrupt states where truth is rare, this includes states such as Hungary, Romania, Spain, Russia, China, North Korea, Iran, Saudi Arabia, Egypt, and Nicaragua.[24]

---

[24] For further examination see Malekian, *Trading Virginity of International Criminal Justice*, note 1; Farhad Malekian, *Allegations by Political Laundering* (Cambridge Scholars Publishing, 2019). Examine *also* Farhad Malekian, *Orchestrating Diversity in International Criminal Justice* (New York: Nova Science Publishers, 2021); Farhad Malekian, *Gravity of Wisdom in International Criminal Law* (New York: Nova Science Publishers, 2021);

1.9. Primary Roles of a Judge

It is important to question what the real role of a judge is in criminal justice proceedings. Some of the vital roles of the judge of a criminal case include the following:

1. The judge must maintain their complete objectivity concerning the given case;
2. The judge has to decide whether the accused is guilty or innocent;
3. The judge has to determine the length of the sentence given to the accused after they have been found guilty of the commission of the given crime;
4. The judge is obliged to listen to all evidence without passing any kind of judgement until all evidence has been presented properly and objectively. Thus, the judge must ensure that they receive a complete picture of the events surrounding the given case;
5. If there is a jury, the judge has to follow their decision regarding the guilt of the accused;
6. The judge's duty is to conduct court proceedings and to not allow their emotions to influence their judgements. Thus, they must be careful not to allow their personal opinions and biased reactions affect a case;
7. The role of the judge is not only to remain objective, but also to properly interpret the relevant criminal law, its significance, and the consequences of the given law on the parties involved in the case;
8. The judges of a given criminal case must also be of high moral character and as such, are not permitted to use unprofessional language during or following criminal procedures. Additionally, judges should remain level-headed and not allow anger to influence the proceedings;

Malekian., *International Criminal Law, the Law of Somebodiness, the Law of Nobodiness*, note 7.

9. Judges must also show compassion towards all involved in the case and respect all parties equally;
10. If the defendant is unable to afford a lawyer, the judge must appoint one for them.

1.10. Duties of Judges Governing the Rights of the Accused

As required by the moral and ethical pillars of justice, we must not cause harm to any individual. The judicial conscience of judges plays a particular role in the context of criminal jurisdiction, which is especially significant in international criminal justice when it comes to the final decision concerning the accused.[25] The fact is that the accused may be harmed through violations of *actus reus* committed by a judge, and when this occurs, the judge must face the appropriate legal consequences.[26]

Additionally, we are all aware of the fact that the terms "judicial conscience," "ethical conscience," and "principles of moral" are abstract concepts which are not found within legislative writings. Additionally, written codes of judicial ethics remain intangible and only serve to guide judges in the right direction. It is therefore logically somewhat impossible to precisely define "ethical conduct," since it is hard to demonstrate the understanding and virtue of all individuals.

One of the most important ethical duties of prosecutors and judges is to respect the rights of the accused and to not violate them in any way. The criminal law of states is directed against the integrity of individual members of a society, and it is the duty of a judge to not violate this integrity. The provisions of the administration of criminal justice must tackle the following principles seriously and should not ignore these

---

[25] Consult also P.M. Bekker, 'The undefended accused/defendant: a brief overview of the development of the American, American Indian and South African Positions' *XXIV CILSA* (1991), pp.151-188.

[26] *Id.*

principles under any circumstances.[27] A selection of the most important rights of people accused of national, regional, or international crimes are, inter alia:[28]

i. The right of the accused to be informed of the charges against them;
ii. The right of the accused to remain silent;
iii. Respect for the rights of the accused during the pre-indictment stages of the trial;
iv. Accused persons shall not be held with convicted persons and shall receive treatment appropriate to their status;
v. Accused persons should not be discriminated against based on their sex;
vi. The treatment of accused persons should not depend on their former social positions;
vii. Accused persons should not be deprived of sleep or rest;
viii. Acceptable living conditions must be made available to accused persons;
ix. Under necessary supervision, accused persons shall be allowed to have contact with their family and friends at regular intervals, both through correspondence and in person. Furthermore, accused persons have the right to read books and newspapers;
x. Accused persons should not be kept in places harmful to their health;
xi. The health of accused persons should be respected at all times;
xii. Based on an official certificate from a legitimate doctor, an accused person has the legal right to medical treatment;

---

[27] Consult L. M. Baum, 'Pursuing Justice in a Climate of Moral Outrage: An Evaluation of the Rights of the Accused in the Rome Statute of the International Criminal Court,' 19 *Wisconsin International Law Journal* (2001), 197; Bekker, 'The undefended accused/defendant: a brief overview of the development of the American, American Indian and South African Position', note 25.

[28] Adopted from Farhad Malekian, 'Emasculating the Philosophy of International Criminal Justice in the Iraqi Special Tribunal,' Vol. 38: 3, *Cornell International Law Journal* (2005). Available online at: http://scholarship.law.cornell.edu/cilj/vol38/iss3/2.

xiii. The right to food should not be denied;

xiv. Force feeding detainees (nutrient enema) constitutes a serious criminal violation of international human rights law;

xv. All those who are interacting with the accused during criminal proceedings should remain impartial regarding the political, juridical, economic, social, cultural, religious, and theoretical beliefs of the accused;

xvi. The rights of the accused should not be disregarded during the proceedings due to certain judicial expediencies;

xvii. An accused person has the legal right to be immediately informed of the charges against them and the grounds for such charges, in a language that they understand;

xviii. The accused person has a legal right to adequate facilities and time to prepare their defence;

xix. The accused person has a legal right to assistance from legal counsel;

xx. The accused person has a legal right to abstain from testifying during the proceedings;

xxi. The accused person has a legal right to a fair trial and a public hearing held within a reasonable period of time;

xxii. The accused person has a right to public hearings when brought before a criminal court. This right is granted by international norms governing the protection of human rights and is based on the theory that if a tribunal wants to ensure fairness, it must hold open and public hearings, including by publicly announcing all judgements;

xxiii. An accused person is presumed innocent until proven guilty;

xxiv. The accused person has the right to be present when the trial begins;

xxv. No political officials should overlook the rights of the accused during the proceedings of the tribunal/court;

xxvi. The accused person has a legal right to defend themselves in person or with any other judicial assistance, based on which alternative they wish;

xxvii. The accused person should have access to a free interpreter if they do not fully understand the language of the court;

xxviii. The accused person has the right to examine witnesses. In certain extraordinary circumstances, the witnesses may be examined under oath prior to court hearings upon authorisation by the court or judges of the court;

xxix. The accused should not be convicted for an act or omission that was not a crime at the time it was committed/omitted according to the provisions of national criminal law, regional criminal law, and international criminal law;

xxx. Confessions obtained through coercion do not have any legal or juridical validity in the proceedings of a criminal court;

xxxi. The threat or use of degrading and humiliating treatment against accused persons or their families for the purpose of extracting evidence should not be admissible in fair and just proceedings of national, regional, or international criminal courts;

xxxii. The accused person has a right to appeal;

xxxiii. Capital punishment is prohibited. This principle has been established in the provisions of most human rights instruments.[29]

1.11. JUDGES RESPECTING *HABEAS CORPUS*

There is a principle in law which exists to protect victims called *habeas corpus.*[30] *Habeas corpus* is essentially the essence of ancient writ relating to temporary restraining orders. A court may assume control over the body of a detainee or convict given that they will release them if no legal justification for further detainment can be established. The principle of

---

[29] Malekian, *id.*, at 712-3. Malekian, *Trading Virginity of International Criminal Justice*, note 1, pp.175-176.

[30] May Lary, 'Habeas Corpus as *Jus cogens* in International Law' *4 (3) Criminal Law and Philosophy (2010), 249–265.*

habeas corpus is also supported under both civil law and common law systems. The intention of both systems is the protection of the personal freedom of accused persons. Within both systems, *habeas corpus* safeguards the release from any form of illegitimate custody, whether imposed by highest authority of a high court or by the lowest authorities of the lower courts. Thus, the legal position in both legal systems is contrary to imprisonment. The notion of *habeas corpus* re-establishes personal liberty for anyone who has been unlawfully accused of a crime.

The function of *habeas corpus* is to provide a guarantee to the accused and their family that the accused will be released from any arbitrary detainment which violates the spirit of human rights law. *Habeas corpus* maintains the right of an individual or group to petition authorities to prevent an unlawful verdict against a convicted person. Judges and prosecutors must protect the spirit of legal principles and allow for an acquittal on the grounds of error of fact, procedure, or law. The judge of a court should take measures to protect this right of *habeas corpus* whenever necessary in order to ensure that ethical conscience is not violated.

The concept of *habeas corpus* is a recourse in law which demands justification for a person's imprisonment. One should be aware of the fact that the use of *habeas corpus* does not create a right against the unlawful arrest of the detainee. However, *habeas corpus* emphasises the right to be released from detention or custody after arrest, accusation, or the levying of allegations.[31] *Habeas corpus* gives the accused the right to claim certain rights while in the custody of legal authorities after a decision has been made to temporarily imprison them – which is a restriction of their freedom. Thus, the accused or suspected person must follow the law according to the conditions of the criminal law which prevails in the relevant country. Obviously, any intentional failure to apply *habeas corpus* is itself subject to further proceedings regarding the violation of state or public criminal law.[32]

---

[31] *Id.*

[32] "Habeas corpus, an ancient common-law writ, issued by a court or judge directing one who holds another in custody to produce the person before the court for some specified purpose. Although there have been and are many varieties of the writ, the most important is that used to correct violations of personal liberty by directing judicial inquiry into the legality of a

The function of the principle of *habeas corpus* is to provide a guarantee the accused and their relatives and facilitates the release of the accused from arbitrary criminal detainment, which violates the values of international human rights law. *Habeas corpus* establishes the right to petition authorities to prevent an unlawful verdict against the convicted person. In addition, judges and prosecutors are responsible for protecting the spirit of the principle and allowing for the acquittal of the accused on the grounds of errors of fact, procedure, or law. Thus, compliance with *habeas corpus* is one of the main ethical and judicial duties of a judge.

Under other legal systems such as Islamic criminal law, the right to *habeas corpus* is very significant, and judges of Islamic states are compelled to respect this right. However, many judges do not respect this right, and a large number of prisoners remain unjustly in prison and tortured or raped, regardless of their gender. It has been argued that Islamic law contains principles of *habeas corpus* and constitutionalism which are distinct from Western principles, although this has not been thoroughly investigated. The articulation of legal rights in orthodox Islam is not only congruent with many internationally recognised norms, but is also distinct in so far as it relies primarily on the legal sources of Islam for its enforceability and credibility.[33] This means that the leading authorities in Islamic states who violate *habeas corpus* are not only violating the system of international human rights law, but also the spirit of Islamic law and its criminal provisions.[34] However, there are also a number of other courts in

---

detention. The habeas corpus remedy is recognized in the countries of the Anglo-American legal system but is generally not found in civil-law countries, although some of the latter have adopted comparable procedures." Britannica, available online at https://www.britannica.com/topic/habeas-corpus.

[33] *Hasnet Lais, Islamic Law and Human Rights: An analysis of the right to fair trial and due process* (Research Gate, 2012), p. 1. Available online at http://www.newcivilisation.com/home/ideas-philosophy/islamic-law-and-human-rights-an-analysis-of-theright-to-fair-trial-and-due-process-pt-1/.

[34] Mashood A. Baderin, 'Effective Legal Representation in '*Shariah*' Courts as a Means of Addressing Human Rights Concerns in the Islamic Criminal Justice System of Muslim States.' 11 *Yearbook of Islamic and Middle Eastern Law* (2006), pp.135-167; A. Mashood Baderin, *International Human Rights and Islamic Law* (New York, NY: Oxford University Press, 2005); A. Mashood Baderin, *International Law and Islamic Law* (Ashgate, 2008); A Mashood Baderin, 'A Comparative Analysis of the Right to a Fair Trial and due Process under International Human Rights Law and Saudi Arabian Domestic Law', 10 (3) *The International Journal of Human Rights* (2006); M. Cherif Bassiouni, 'Protection of

the world which do not respect the restriction of personal freedom even after the accused has been proven innocent.[35] This has mostly been seen in countries in which the imprisonment of political dissenters is common and where there is a lack of independent judicial conscience, including in places such as Russia, North Korea, and China.[36]

Diplomats under Islamic Law', 74 *American Journal of International Law* (1980), pp.609-655; M. Cherif Bassiouni, 'Islam: Concept, Law and Word *Habeas Corpus'*, 2 *Rutgers Camden Law Journal* (1970); M. Cherif Bassiouni, *Studies in Early Hadith Literature* (Indianapolis, 1978); M. Cherif Bassiouni, 'Sources of Islamic Law and the Protection of Human Rights' in Bassiouni, the *Islamic Criminal Justice System* (1982); M. Cherif Bassiouni, *The Shariah and Islamic Criminal Justice in the Time of War and Peace* (Cambridge University Press, Cambridge, 2014); Mashood A. Baderin, 'Islamic Socio-Legal Norms and International Criminal Justice in Context: Advancing an 'Object and Purpose'cum 'Maqāṣid' Approach' in T. Gray, *Islam and International Criminal Law and Justice* (Torkel Opsahl Academic EPublisher, 2018).

[35] See Malekian, *Trading Virginity of International Criminal Justice*, note 1.

[36] *Id.*

Chapter 2

ETHICAL STANDARDS IN THE INTERNATIONAL CRIMINAL COURT

2.1. CONSCIOUS CAPACITY OF JUDGES

The duties of judges are very important, particularly with reference to the fact that they are responsible for serving justice and finding the truth. Although we all understand that judges are human beings, this should not allow judges to interfere with the rights of the accused and victims. Judges have views and obligations that are significant to them, both in their personal and official capacities. Judges often perform their duties based on these important commitments, both professional and personal. Therefore, in the decision-making process, it is the objectivity of the judge which establishes how just a judgement is.[37]

Sometimes as a matter of conscience, judges express their concerns about cases and the law in general in writing with the hope that changes can be made in the future. Thus, judges may make different statements depending on the state of their conscience and their experiences. Judges

[37] Elena Cima, 'Ethical Conduct in International Criminal Courts: Whose Ethics?', *American Journal of International Law*(2019), pp.296-301. Available online at https://www.researchgate.net/publication/335848353_Ethical_Conduct_in_International_Criminal_Courts_Whose_Ethics.

may even explicitly speak out against certain expressions of conscience in order to prevent other judges from acting inappropriately. In some cases, the judge may question the modesty and morality of an opposing opinion in a case.[38]

We must not put aside the fact that there are two ways of expressing conscience. One method concerns making conscientious commitments to reach an appropriate decision, while the second deals with what judges essentially express about their own conscience in the given case, i.e., their own experiences and opinions. The first method of expressing conscience relates to the conclusion of a case based on legal provisions and the limit of the law, while the second is based on the experience of the judge and their personal requirements for conscience. Although both methods are present during a case, the second evaluates normative questions concerning whether the law has taken sufficient action or has been practical and useful in the given case. The opinion of the judge may therefore concern the level of right or wrong in the larger context of the judicial role.[39]

We must also remember that all judicial decisions are generally considered as "opinions," and these opinions may be seen as good or bad depending on the context. They may also be drawn upon in future cases to aide in the interpretation of the law. Thus, the judicial decision of the judge is solely an opinion and includes the deduction, interpretation, understanding, or explanation of the judge, and in certain given cases, the

---

[38] Consult also Alasdair MacIntyre, *After Virtue: A Study in Moral Theory* (Notre Dame: University of Notre Dame Press, 1982).

[39] According to one view "Troubling or not, judges' emotional reactions are inevitable. Judges are not computers. By design, the justice system is a human process, and, like jurors, judges are influenced by their emotions to some degree, even when we would prefer that they were not, and however sincerely they may try to prevent it.263 This is simply reality. If we criticize judges for this "shortcoming"—which, of course, entails advantages as well as disadvantages—then we might as well criticize successful species such as alligators for their inability to fly. The problem is not that judges cannot do something that they are supposed to do; rather, the problem is that we ought never to have expected them to be able to do it in the first place.264 Our unrealistic expectations set them up for failure and set us up for disillusionment. The more constructive approach is to acknowledge the reality that judges are influenced by affective responses to litigants, and to the extent that we are uncomfortable with that fact, to take steps to ameliorate it." Andrew J. Wistrich, Jeffrey J. Rachlinski & Chris Guthrie, 'Heart Versus Head: Do Judges Follow the Law or Follow Their Feelings?', 93 *Texas Law Review* (2015), pp.855-923, at 912.

opinion of the jury. Certainly, following judicial opinions is not obligatory in the system of criminal justice, however these opinions help us to gauge the conscious capacity of judges. In other words, judicial conscience expresses the limits of its legitimacy in the sphere of criminal justice including the ethical or moral understating of the case.[40] Although judicial conscience has its own criteria, it cannot simply be separated from any other ethical or moral commitment, including upholding the principle of non-discrimination.[41]

2.2. Good Conscience of Judges

The judges of courts are supposed to work and function with good conscience.[42] This is precisely the situation of the prosecutors of the court. The judges of the courts are under obligation to follow the ethical standards of justice and to not neglect or omit ethical considerations in their decisions. But what the ethical standards are, and what criteria are necessary to meet these standards, differs between countries and is very broad in nature. This denotes the fact that the judges of any criminal court have certain recognised responsibilities and duties according to the legislations of the courts, and certain ethical and moral obligations which compel them to remain unbiased in their thoughts, decisions, conducts, and behaviour.[43]

---

[40] Consult Rosalyn Higgins, 'Ethics and International Law', 23 *Leiden Journal of International Law* (2010), pp.283-287.

[41] *Id.*

[42] Consult Malekian, *Conscience of Lawyers in International Criminal Law, the Borden of Doppelgängers*, note 8, Malekian, *Orchestrating Diversity in International Criminal Justice*, note 24; Malekian, *Gravity of Wisdom in International Criminal Law*, note 24.

[43] "The intention behind all these rules and regulations is to prevent any harm to any party including the victims, as well as the accused, witnesses, or even the relatives of relevant parties. All this reflects the clear ethical standard behind the prosecution and the prosecutor. Here, the ethical standard refers to the duties and responsibilities of the prosecutor which are fundamental for the proper investigation of a criminal case and protection of victims. Therefore, due to the gravity of certain international crimes such as war crimes, all parties have the legal and moral right to access accurate information and to follow the case in the most logical manner. As a result, the prosecutor of a national or an international criminal

A judge who has carried out criminal conducts cannot remain a judge or an ethical authority. In short, judges present their views about the principles of institutional conscience which are connected to their legal duties and statements of their own personal understanding of conscience, which in turn relates to their ethical and moral duties. This implies to the individual values and beliefs of the judge, who is the messenger of their conscience, and compels judges to have, and carry out good thoughts, actions, and deeds.

Criminal cases are brought before a court after a decision has been made by the office of the prosecutor, and it is then that the real work of judges begins. Judges therefore occupy a very sensitive position in the criminal justice system, particularly when it comes to decisions governing sentencing and punishment. Therefore, judges play a dynamic role in the criminal justice system. Any decision taken by a judge can impact the procedures of justice and the future development of the administration of justice. This is particularly evident when the accused is sentenced to imprisonment, since imprisonment impacts the social development of the accused and their family. Thus, all cases should be thoroughly investigated and all suspects should be vetted for the sake of justice and all parties involved.

It is also important, and even necessary, for judges to be of good conscience when serving in international criminal courts, particularly in the ICC, since the ICC serves the entire international community. Whilst we do not reject that there a large number of codes of ethics governing the good conscience of the judges of the ICC, the reality is that the good consciences of the ICC judges vary based on their personal backgrounds, which may directly or indirectly affect their judicial conscience as well. The ICC is in fact an institution for the implementation of human rights norms.[44] In 2003, the United Nations Secretary General asserted that the

---

court must maintain a good conscience throughout the proceedings." Malekian, *Conscience of Prosecutors in International Criminal Law, The Heart of the Matter*, note 3, p.144.

[44] "If the ICC is not a human rights body, then what is it? The ICC is the final stage of a human right body, and thus cannot escape from its basic function by asserting that it is a criminal body. The ICC's duty is to see if the complementarity principle is really being respected, and if it is not in cases relating to core international crimes, they it must reopen cases and

ICC judges embody "our collective conscience"–which may be true to a certain degree, depending on how we interpret collective conscience. However, it may be true that the judges of the Court possess a collective conscience which is used to implement criminal justice and uncover the truth.[45]

2.3. What Is Judicial Conscience?

We must emphasise that judicial independence reflects the institutional or administrative relationships between the executive and legislative branches of the government of a state.[46] What constitutes the exact function of a judge is one of the most significant questions of justice. For some writers and experts, the duties of judges only apply to the interests of the law or what is written in the law. This means that judges are only the tools of the machinery of criminal justice and are used in the implementation of its provisions both nationally and internationally. However, "if a judge cannot find a precedent, or simply cannot in good conscience apply a law, that judge can always resign-in fact, that may be the only alternative."[47]

The judicial conscience present in all methods of criminal justice is there only for show, and not to prevent the influence of the experience and beliefs of the judges on proceedings. We should not forget the fact that judges are human, and human beings are capable of feeling sympathy for others. Thus, judges are compelled by the system of justice to do what is

---

bring the offenders under the jurisdiction of the ICC. The implementation of the system of international criminal justice is not based on criminal provisions alone, but more specifically on human rights law. In other words, the ICC is not only a criminal body, but also a human rights body which represents the victims. If this were not the case, the ICC could not function as human rights body or as a proper criminal body because if the former is missing, the latter cannot function properly. In other words, criminal bodies are connected to the provisions of international human rights law and their significant and vital functions in the body of criminal justice." Farhad Malekian, Orchestrating Diversity in International Criminal Justice (New York: Nova Publishers, 2021), p.226.

45 Examine also Gene E. Franchini, 'Conscience, Judging, and Conscientious Judging', 2 *The Journal of Appellate Practice and Process* (2000), p.25.

46 Gene E. Franchini, 'Conscience, Judging, and Conscientious Judging', 2 *The Journal of Appellate Practice and Process* (2000), pp.19-25.

47 *Id.*, p.23.

right and uphold the principles of impartiality and proportionality. Rawls says:

> Justice is the first virtue of social institutions, as truth is of systems of thought. A theory however elegant and economical must be rejected or revised if it is untrue; likewise laws and institutions no matter how efficient and well-arranged must be reformed or abolished if they are unjust. Each person possesses an inviolability founded on justice that even the welfare of society as a whole cannot override. For this reason justice denies that the loss of freedom for some is made right by a greater good shared by others. It does not allow that the sacrifices imposed on a few are outweighed by the larger sum of advantages enjoyed by many. Therefore in a just society the liberties of equal citizenship are taken as settled; the rights secured by justice are not subject to political bargaining or to the calculus of social interests. The only thing that permits us to acquiesce in an erroneous theory is the lack of a better one; analogously, an injustice is tolerable only when it is necessary to avoid an even greater injustice. Being first virtues of human activities, truth and justice are uncompromising.[48]

Some may believe that judicial conscience refers to the satisfaction of the norms of the law, and therefore a judge does not need to perform justice, but rather must enforce the strict role of the law concerning the given case. This has become routine for a considerable number of judges across the globe, as they act in accordance with what the law says, and not with how it should be interpreted. This can particularly be seen in the practice of certain Islamic regimes which apply the law without adjusting it to reflect the times. For example, judges apply the death penalty rigidly, without considering that the practice is prohibited according to other Islamic rules and provisions. This means that strict rules of Islamic law are

---

[48] John Rawls, *A Theory of Justice* (2ed., 1999), pp.3-4. In furtherance of this statement, Rawls believes that the "question of equal liberty of conscience is settled. It is one of the fixed points of our considered judgments of justice. But precisely because of this fact it illustrates the nature of the argument for the principle of equal liberty. The reasoning in this case can be generalized to apply to other freedoms, although not always with the same force." *Id.*, p.181.

mitigated and lead to forgiveness, which in turn leads to a reduction of punishment and the abolition of certain penalties.

In other words, if a legal system permits the application of capital punishment, the judge of such a system must be very cautious in the application of such law, since application of capital punishment constitutes a serious violation of both natural and moral law. Moreover, such punishment is against the principles of international human rights law and cannot be recognised as valid law under any circumstances. That being said, the purpose of the bench of justice is not solely to levy punishment, but also to work to reduce criminality and violations.[49] As a result, judges who apply capital punishment not only violate the systems of international human rights law and universal natural law, but also commit a crime themselves as a result of enforcing biased criminal legislation.[50]

2.4. Limit of the Conscience of Judges

Although judicial decisions may follow the provisions of a given legal legislation, they may still be re-evaluated by judges based on their ethical and moral capacity and knowledge. This is particularly significant in the case of countries with legislations which do not comply with international human rights standards. While we do not deny the fact that the personal conscience of a judge should not have any effect on their decisions, judges still must follow certain general ethical standards of criminal justice and should not violate certain consolidated rules of law and morality.

Mention may be made here to state legislation which allows for the application of capital punishment, the prohibition of the freedom of personal decision, and which discriminates between men and women on the basis of sex. Furthermore, there are certain legislations which permit the application of harsh penalties because of the restriction and prohibition

---

[49] Makane M. Mbengue, *Challenges of Judges in International Criminal Courts and Tribunals, in Challenges and Recusals of Judges and Arbitrators in International Courts and Tribunals* (Chiara Giorgetti ed., 2015).

[50] *Id.*

of the political freedoms of individuals. In other words, the legal norms here are contrary to moral norms and as a result, create tension between the sphere of legality and the concept of morality. There is however a tentative doubt about what the conscience of judge is able to do here against the judicial conscience and the provisions of the given legislation. In this case, the judge is put in the difficult position of having to choose between either upholding their conscience or the relevant legislation.

However, there is no clear outline for how judges should apply their ethical conscience in situations where the offender may receive serious punishment that could violate the basic principles of criminal justice. There is a similar lack of ethical provisions within the law and practice of many states. This is particularly critical when a judge is aware of the fact that an offender has been subjected to torture before or during the procedures of criminal justice. Thus, judges may have different personal attitudes towards the case and the accused.[51]

That is the reason why there are cases in which judges may agree about the basic facts of the case concerning the line between right and wrong, but differ in their consciences. That is why we may find that different judges provide different justifications for their decisions and explanations for cases. This means that judges may present their arguments and opinions quite differently, even if they reach the same legal conclusion about a case. This implies the fact that their approaches and explanations vary from one another. Thus, it is possible that even when judges apply the law as it is, their personal and ethical understanding as well as their consciences could lead to different facets of the case being emphasised or to disagreement concerning certain matters, such as believing that the condemned should have received a lighter punishment than required by law.

---

[51] Consult the Palestinian case in the ICC https://www.icc-cpi.int/RelatedRecords/CR2021_01167.PDF What is really the definition of a state for the judge of the ICC?.

2.5. ETHICAL NORMS FOR JUDGES

Speaking about the ethical norms of the office of the judges is very intensive and requires a great deal of analysis.[52] When we speak about the ethical norms in the house of judges, we are pointing to the very high standards which all judges should follow while executing their duties. The ethical standards of judges thus shed light on the principles of reason and judgement and speak to why criminal jurisdiction should be healthy and not violate the high standards of criminal justice. All ethical duties are also connected to the relevant circumstances and satisfy the necessities of judicial freedom in order to not be connected with any matter except the truth.

However, what we recognise as the ethical duties of judges concerning criminal justice may still not be the complete picture, based on the fact that the ethical standards of the judge may vary on a case-by-case basis. Therefore, our clarification cannot preclude reasonable disagreements about the application of ethical standards in the house of judges or in the court. Overall, many statements or principles of ethical reasoning are mostly advisory in nature since it is the judge alone who has the ability to make correct judgements as a result of their experience and to avoid violating the rights of any party involved in a given case.

Generally, the goals of ethical standards for the judges are to assist them in the execution of their professional duties and also make it clear to the public that there is a big difference between ordinary social work and criminal justice which is based on judges remaining impartial and trustworthy. In other words, the duties of judges should not be regarded as a code of ethics or morality alone, but as a safeguard for the interests of the population and diversity.[53] The theory is that the ethical and moral considerations in the work of judges do not relate to what is permitted or not, but rather to what is in the best interest of all parties and the general

---

[52] Kimberley Brownlee, 'Responsibilities of Criminal Justice Officials', *Journal of Applied Philosophy* (2010), pp.1-17.

[53] See H. Jefferson Powell., *Constitutional Conscience: The Moral Dimension of Judicial Decision* (University of Chicago Press, 2008).

public. Thus, the judge is not restricted in their pursuit of the truth, and justice is preserved.

2.6. The Borders of Good Conscience

Judges often use the term "good conscience" in a variety of situations and with reference to different interpretations and legal, moral, ethical, and personal conclusions. It is problematic and difficult to reach a specific consensus about the meaning of "conscience," and the situation becomes even more difficult when it comes to the term "unconscionable." In general, one may say that the definition of both terms depends on the personal understanding of the relevant judge as well as their background, emotions, will, economic status, their moral and ethical awareness, and their personal relationships. However, some factors are more important than others when it comes to the evaluation of good conscience.

The terms "good conscience" and "unconscionable" may thus refer to the moral standard of the understanding of the judge. This implies the moral sense of what is right and wrong. Since a judge is a lawyer and the representative of the state in the most sensitive position of the given society, they should not only have an accurate explanation for their good conscience as well as their unconscionable reactions, more importantly, they must follow the moral rules that are required for the implementation of criminal justice. Thus, a judge must be honest. However, the honesty of a judge may be subject to debate and is difficult to ascertain, particularly when comparing judges in different nations because the requirements of honesty may differ across the globe. As correctly stated:

> Ethics plays a crucial role in international adjudication, in particular in the context of international criminal proceedings where the liberty of the accused is at stake. Criminal courts have been trying to create an "international judicial culture" based on shared ethical standards. In doing so, however, they are constantly faced with an obstacle inherent in the very idea of ethics: the impossibility of defining what constitutes

> "ethical conduct" divorced from one's culture, tradition, legal system, or professional background. This contribution intends to explore the complexity of trying to define the contours of ethical standards in international criminal proceedings, in particular in the absence of precise written rules, by focusing on the Furundžija case. Even when rules are codified, however, they often remain open to divergent interpretations depending on one's cultural, social, and legal background. Ultimately, it is not simply a matter of codifying ethical rules but, more importantly, of agreeing on "whose ethics" these rules should reflect.[54]

This situation implies that there is a lack of a definite definition and differentiation between the terms 'morality', 'ethics', 'conscience,' and 'justice', as all must be present in the processes of criminal justice in order to ensure the best results. The problem becomes more serious when one realises that there are different types of legislations all over the world which are based on different cultural attitudes. All this means that the terms "good conscience" and "unconscionable" must be defined differently. However, the philosophy of must not differ when it comes to the recognition of certain criminal conducts, since certain crimes, such as murder, rape, and torture prompt the same moral understanding.

2.7. *Modus Operandi* of the Duties of Judges

The difficulty with the consideration of the duties of judges is that there is not one set of standards defining judicial conscience and drawing a line between various appropriate conducts or misconducts. Although the criminal systems of some states provide lists to differentiate between good and bad behaviour, such a list can never be comprehensive as long as the case under consideration is not measured accurately and objectively. That is why every person has the right to be heard by an independent judiciary;

---

[54] Cima, 'Ethical Conduct in International Criminal Courts: Whose Ethics?', note 37, pp. 296-301.

however, to what extent the judiciary decision is respected and accepted by political authorities is an important question.

A judge must be, and be understood to be, free to make their decisions without interference from others. Honesty and independence are two of the leading principles of the office of the judge. This means that there should not be any external political, legal, or financial pressure or influence exerted on the judge under any circumstances, and the judge must ensure that this remains the case. Nothing should be able to restrict or limit the judicial objectivity of the judge or to use the notion of *modus operandi* in order to uncover the crime. A precedent set by earlier laws or decisions that provides guidance is normally permitted. Thus, earlier evidence of another case in which the offender was involved, may be admissible to prove their guilt. The limitation and restriction of any person or authority would deny the very significant function of criminal jurisdiction and reduce its ethical, legal, and moral value.

Moreover, a judge can fully understand that the rights of appropriate judgement and equal decision based on the impartial administration of criminal justice are essential for a stable criminal jurisdiction. Fair and independent judges understand that any personal influence on the mechanism of justice invalidates the principle of truth and creates chaos in the legal discipline of criminal justice. That is why judges have the duty to uphold judicial independence at all times and not give privilege to any matter other than the judicial conscience.

Clearly, it should be the constitutionally guaranteed right of every citizen to submit their disputes to a trustworthy administration of justice and for their cases to be heard and decided upon by impartial judges. The fact is that the ethical and professional duties of judges are fundamental and necessary for the administration of justice and contribute to the trustworthiness of the judge. The duty of the judge is not to satisfy one particular party, but to arrive at the correct conclusion while upholding the principles of objectivity, neutrality, and impartiality, and to preserve the independence of criminal procedures.

There are also certain duties on the part of criminal justice administration to guarantee that judges are not bribed in any way by any party involved in a criminal case. However, this is one of the most difficult tasks in the administration of criminal justice based on the fact that controlling the judges and the parties to a case leads to interference in the proceedings and makes the case more public than it was to begin with. Thus, this is a problematic situation and the question still remains at the end, whether or not the administration themselves could have been bribed by someone involved in the case, even by the judge.[55] This difficulty has been seen in nations such as Russia, Italy, and China, to just name a few examples. Of course, if bribery is involved in criminal proceedings, then the ethical and moral principles of the court are violated.

For example, it is very difficult to control the administration of justice in Romania and Hungary, which are both members of the European Union.[56] This problem exists in many countries around the world, particularly when lawyers are involved. Thus, lawyers and parties to criminal cases may be involved in unfair and immoral businesses and as a result, the weaker party which lacks financial strength may be found guilty even when they are innocent. Furthermore, the situation is more harmful when the judge or the prosecutor of the case sides with one of the parties involved in committing serious crimes whether at the national or international level. That is why the principle of *modus operandi* and the privileges of the administration of prosecution should not be restricted in any way.

---

[55] Siri Gloppen, Courts, *Corruption and Judicial Independence*, available on line at https://www.cmi.no/publications/file/5091-courts-corruption-and-judicial-independence.pdf.

[56] Romania criminal justice reform proposal weakens fight against corruption and serious crime, available online at https://www.coe.int/en/web/portal/-/proposed-reform-of-criminal-justice-legislation-in-romania-weakens-the-fight-against-corruption-and-other-serious-crimes-according-to-venice-commissio; Reuters Staff, Romanian president approves corruption investigation against former PM (13 January 2021), available online at https://www.reuters.com/article/us-romania-corruption-idUSKBN29I1S7.

2.8. Substance of the Objectivity of Judges

The principle of objectivity or impartiality implies that a judge does not actively support a specific party involved in a case. This means that the objectivity of the judge must be substantial and not fake. This includes both national and international ones. Particularly, this is evident when we try individuals accused of committing grave international crimes such as genocide, war crimes, crimes against humanity, and the crime of aggression.[57] The judge's impartiality is therefore a cornerstone of justice, and of criminal justice in particular, which ensures the quality of their judgments. Objectivity requires judges to not interfere in cases or guide them in any particular direction for any reason. A judge must maintain their objectivity regarding all matters and this must be guaranteed to ensure the maintenance of a pure jurisdiction. This means that there are certain conditions for objectivity. The objective conditions and guarantees include principles such as the security of tenure, security of remuneration, and immunity from civil liability for judicial acts. Therefore, judicial independence is dependent upon unbiased conditions and guarantees fairness in the exercise of judicial functions.

The seeds for the impartiality of judges include the following:

- A judge should not interfere in the administration of criminal justice;
- A judge should not accept any payment for their duties from any parties involved in the case;
- A judge should not privilege one party over another;
- A judge should resist sympathising with any of the parties to the case;
- A judge should not meet any party outside of court proceedings;

---

[57] For instance, "The preliminary examination process is conducted on the basis of the facts and information available, and in the context of the overarching principles of independence, impartiality and objectivity." OTP, *Policy Paper on Preliminary Examinations*, 1 November 2013, para.25, available online at https://www.icc-cpi.int/iccdocs/otp/OTP-Policy_Paper_Preliminary_Examinations_2013-ENG.pdf.

- A judge should not accept any invitation by any of the parties;
- A judge should reject any type of gift;
- The moral feelings of a judge should be the same towards both the victims and the suspects;
- A judge must report false evidence;
- Moral conscience should be the guiding principle for a judge;
- Ethical consideration should be a part of the knowledge of a judge;
- It is the duty of a judge to respect the law;
- A judge should not be influenced by political parties;
- A judge should not report progress to political parties;
- It is imperative that a judge maintain distance from any political authority who shows interest in the case at hand;
- A judge should not preside over a case involving a relative;
- A judge should not accept a case in which friends are involved;
- A judge should not show preference for any cultural, religious, social, or ethnic group;
- A judge should not apply new law to the case if it would not serve the interests of all parties equally;
- Punishment should not be a judge's main intention when seeking justice;
- If a new law would lead to the mitigation of punishment, a judge should apply it retroactively;
- A judge should never make a decision based on a desire for revenge;
- A judge is required to respect all parties equally;
- A judge should not release information to public before proceedings are over;
- A judge must provide clear justification for their decisions;
- A judge's written statements should demonstrate a balance between the law and moral ethics;
- Gender equality should be respected by the judge;
- A judge should not invite any of the parties involved in a case to their home or any other location;

- Justice and judgements should not be intentionally diluted by the judge;
- As much as possible, a judge should promote peace and transparency between the parties of the case;
- A judge should uphold good behaviour in the courtroom and be polite towards all parties.
- A judge should not use abusive language;
- A judge should not get angry;
- Serving justice should be the sole intention of a judge;
- A judge should only pursue the truth.

2.9. Dynamic Role of the Judge

Judges play a dynamic role throughout a trial.[58] They should have sufficient control over the case in accordance with the applicable law and practices of their country or under international law.[59] Although there may be many differences between the duties of judges in national and international criminal jurisdictions, the ethical and legal considerations still recognise that judges of all courts share the responsibility of maintaining their impartiality and not omitting any important evidence. This is based on the fact that evidence which appears to be irrelevant at the beginning of a case may become relevant later on and impact the final decision of the judge. As the case progresses, judges should make note of the evidence and decide on legal issues, for example, whether evidence is admissible. Thus, the judge has dynamic rules under their control and is the only real voice of the relevant rules.

More significant is that in the procedures of a case, the judge must ensure that the subject of the case remains central in all discussions about the case, especially when it relates to cases of murder or rape. Additionally,

---

[58] Vladimir Tochilovsky, 'Objectivity of the ICC Preliminary Examinations', in Morten Bergsmo and Carsten Stahn (editors), *Quality Control in Preliminary Examination*, Vol. 2 (Torkel Opsahl Academic EPublisher, Bruss, 2018).

[59] *Id.*

within international criminal jurisdictions, judges must not forget the fact that the courts were established to decide about crimes, for example, genocide or apartheid, which are identified based on the intention of the offender and the systematic nature of the crime. At this stage, the judges of international criminal courts may be more cautious than those of national courts who deal with cases of murder, but not of genocide.[60] The judge is therefore responsible for highlighting the strengths and weaknesses of all arguments and evidence that are presented during a trial.

2.10. CONFESSION WITHOUT FORCE

Judges are responsible for evaluating cases very carefully and determining whether there is sufficient evidence to reasonably believe that a crime was carried out as described. In addition, judges are responsible for appointing lawyers for those who are unable to afford to hire one themselves because without a lawyer, it is difficult for anyone to prove their innocence and ensure that the judge has reviewed all relevant evidence. Following this legal process, the criminal investigation and examination of the case begin and the integrity of the accused must from then on be protected up through when the final ruling is made. This means that the accused maintains their right to a fair trial from the beginning through the end of proceedings.[61] Article 6 of the European Convention for the Protection of Human Rights and Fundamental Freedoms (1950) refers

---

[60] On a profound examination of the notion of apartheid consult L. Rubin, Apartheid in Practice (1971); Bernhard Graefrath, 'Convention Against the Crime of Apartheid', vol. XI *German Foreign Policy* (1972), pp. 395-402; J.K. Feimpong & S. Azadon Tiewel, 'Can Apartheid Successfully Defy the International Legal System?' 5 *The Black Law Journal* (1977), pp. 287-311; Garry Seltzer, 'The Rule of the South Africa Criminal Code in Implementing Apartheid', 8 *Georgia Journal of International and Comparative Law* (1978), pp. 176-194; F.V. GraciaAmador, 'The Crime of Apartheid: Responsibility and Reparations', *Review of Contemporary Law* (1981), pp. 31-38; Paris Declaration, *International Conference on Sanctions Against South Africa (And Special Declaration on Namibia)* (the United Nations Center Against Apartheid, 27 May 1981); Enuga S. Reddy, *Apartheid: The United Nations and the International Community* (1986); Enuga S. Reddy, 'India and the Struggle Against Apartheid', 26 *Indian Journal of International Law* (1986), pp.551-567; Farhad Malekian, vol. I *International Criminal Law* (Almqvist Wiksell International, 1991), pp. 324-375.

[61] Malekian, *Judgments of Love in Criminal Justice,* note 1, p.301.

to the right to a fair trial and emphasises this right. Thus, these rights have international validity and should be respected by all criminal courts, even if their state is not party to the relevant convention. These rights are thus an integral part of the international customary rights of the accused:

> In the determination of his civil rights and obligations or of any criminal charge against him, everyone is entitled to a fair and public hearing within a reasonable time by an independent and impartial tribunal established by law. Judgement shall be pronounced publicly but the press and public may be excluded from all or part of the trial in the interests of morals, public order or national security in a democratic society, where the interests of juveniles or the protection of the private life of the parties so require, or to the extent strictly necessary in the opinion of the court in special circumstances where publicity would prejudice the interests of justice. 2. Everyone charged with a criminal offence shall be presumed innocent until proved guilty according to law. 3. Everyone charged with a criminal offence has the following minimum rights: (a) to be informed promptly, in a language which he understands and in detail, of the nature and cause of the accusation against him; (b) to have adequate time and facilities for the preparation of his defence; (c) to defend himself in person or through legal assistance of his own choosing or, if he has not sufficient means to pay for legal assistance, to be given it free when the interests of justice so require; (d) to examine or have examined witnesses against him and to obtain the attendance and examination of witnesses on his behalf under the same conditions as witnesses against him; (e) to have the free assistance of an interpreter if he cannot understand or speak the language used in court.[62]

However, the judge must guarantee that if the accused pleads guilty to a crime, that they did so of their own free will and not while under duress. The role of a judge during a hearing depends on whether or not prosecution is conducted in accordance with the rules, and if a jury is required by the relevant national law. However, the presence of a jury depends on the severity of the relevant crime. In certain countries such as the United States

---

[62] *The* European *Convention for the Protection of Human Rights* and Fundamental Freedoms (1950) came into force (1960).

and the United Kingdom, a jury is required to be present during proceedings concerning serious first-degree crimes.

As a general rule of national and international criminal justice, no confession made by force can be valid and judges should not base their judgements on such confessions. Without hesitation, judges who accept forced confessions violate the sources of the system of criminal law and the general and particular codes of ethics. Thus, any forced confession is inadmissible in court, including confessions resulting from torture or threat.[63]

[63] Under national criminal law "empirical researchers have documented and analysed how and why contemporary methods of psychological interrogation can, and sometimes do, lead innocent individuals to confess falsely to serious crimes. The consequences of these false confessions are disastrous for innocent individuals who are wrongfully convicted and incarcerated. As a result, empirical researchers have also suggested ways to minimize both the number of false confessions that police elicit and the number of false confessions that, once elicited, lead to wrongful convictions." Richard A. Leo., 'False Confessions: Causes, Consequences, and Implications' 37 (3) Journal of the American Academy of Psychiatry and the Law (2009), pp.332-343, also available online at http://jaapl.org/content/37/3/332.

Chapter 3

Evaluation of Justice by Judges

3.1. The Validity of the Oaths of Judges

Judicial oaths require that judges put their feelings towards the litigants aside.[64] However, to what extent this oath is respected again depends on many factors concerning the judge themselves and how they evaluate judicial conscience and its independence.[65] While the obligations of a lay judge differ from those of a professional judge who should take an oath before accepting their duties, the lay judge must still take a judicial oath. This oath generally requires the confirmation of conscience and honour in combination with some brief training. The basic reason for taking the oath is for the lay judge to promise that they will adjudicate as justly as possible, and not entertain views which are irrelevant or inappropriate. The lay judge also agrees to not disclose or disseminate information revealed during trial. Such information should not become public knowledge, including information discussed during private deliberations of the court. For instance, a Swedish lay judge provides the assurance that they will apply Swedish legal rules in compliance with the adjudication process.

---

[64] Examine *Thousands of U.S. Judges who Broke Laws or Oaths Remained on the Bench*. Visited online at https://www.reuters.com/investigates/special-report/usa-judges-misconduct/.

[65] *Id.*

With this introductory paragraph we wish to indicate that oaths are not only required for suspects, victims, and witnesses, but also for those who are involved with the principal mechanism of criminal justice, i.e., prosecutors, judges, lay judges etc. However, the oaths of judges are more important than those of other individuals because the parties involved in a criminal case may lie under oath in order to shift blame to others. The oaths made by judges should not be fake statements and should be made with the intention of fulfilling the conditions which are required for carrying out their duties. The oaths of judges must be authentic, honest, ethical, and ensure the independence of the judiciary.

A number of countries in different parts of the world require that judges take oaths, however, the content of these oaths may differ across countries, and in some cases may even violate the fundamental principles of the independence of juridical mechanism and reduce the value of the impartiality of judges, the independence of criminal jurisdiction and above all, violate the basic principles of international human rights law. For instance, an oath made by a judge under an authoritarian tyrannical regime cannot be considered a pure oath, but rather must be seen as a violation of natural law and a way to help powerful politicians who have monopolised the criminal jurisdiction. There have been a number of examples of regimes under which judges confirm through their oath that they will support the leaders of the regime and swear to never undermine their religious, political, economic, military, or social power. This situation clearly indicates the dependency of the judicial conscience and the restriction of the freedom of criminal justice. For instance, judges in Iran must make the following oath: "In the name of God, the most merciful and most compassionate

> I, as a judge, in the presence of the Holy Qur'an and before Iranian nation, swear to omnipotent God to follow the Prophet of Islam and the sacred Imams, peace be upon them, and seeking help of the spirits of the martyrs of Islam, guard justice and righteous, and undertake upon my human dignity to be diligent in seeking the truth and justice, administer Islamic justice to demand from oppressor and restore it to its owner and with sustained effort in Judicial position fulfil my obligation to Islamic

> republic with strengthening the foundations of the Islamic republic and supporting The Leader.[66]

The loaded term in the above quote is "Leader," which positions a political authority as being above all laws, even the law of God. This means that the leader understands the Quran better than most and that the Quran is essentially his property. Taking oaths in the name of God is common in many nations of the world. Thus, the word 'god' is used as a synonym for strength, confidence, trust, faith, and reliability. Countries which require an oath in the name of God include the United States, Finland, Germany, the United Kingdom, and South Africa. However, one of the serious criticisms of the use of the phrase "god" may be that a number judges are not religious and do not believe in any particular god, faith, or leader. Despite this, they are still forced to take an oath in the name of God, even though they would still able to be honest and have integrity without uttering that phrase. In the Swedish oath of a judge or lay judge there is no reference to God, however the oath is still strong in its own way. It reads:

> I, (name), promise and affirm on my honour and conscience that I will and shall impartially, as to the rich as well as to the poor, administer justice in all matters to the best of my ability and conscience, and judge according to the law of the Realm of Sweden; that I will never manipulate the law or further injustice for kinship, relation by marriage, friendship, envy, ill-will, or fear, nor for bribes or gifts, or any other cause in whatever guise it may appear; nor will I declare guilty one who is innocent, or innocent one who is guilty. Neither before nor after the pronouncement of the judgement of the court shall I disclose to the litigants or to other persons the in camera deliberations of the court. All this, as a honest and righteous judge, I will and shall faithfully observe.[67]

However, the Finish judges express:

---

[66] Emphasis added.
[67] RB 4:11 (Swedish basic law).

> I, (name), do promise and swear by God and His Holy Gospels that to the best of my understanding and conscience I wish to and shall in all judgements render justice to poor and rich alike and render judgement in accordance with the laws and lawful rules of God and country: I shall never, under any pretext, pervert the law nor promote injustice because of kinship, relationship, friendship, envy, hatred or fear, or for the sake of gifts or presents or other reasons, nor shall I find an innocent person guilty or a guilty person innocent. Furthermore, I shall not, before pronouncing a judgement or thereafter, reveal to the parties or to anyone else anything about the deliberations that the Court has held behind closed doors. All of this I wish to and shall fulfil faithfully, honestly and as an earnest judge, without deceit and intrigue, so help me God, in body and mind.[68]

An oath is even taken by the case of judges of the ICC, although there is no particular norm which clearly expresses why an oath is taken or the intention behind it. However, although it seems that taking an oath is part of the procedures for initiating a judge into the Court, there is no paragraph or sub-section within the Statute of the ICC which clarifies the reason why judges take an oath. Thus, oath-taking is based on traditional procedures within national jurisdictions and is as an integral part of the customary law of courts and helps the public to trust the courts and judges.

3.2. Professional Value of Oaths

Oath-taking has a greater social/psychological impact than a legal one. In other words, the honesty of the oath depends on moral or ethical capacity of the judge as well as how the judge plans to interpret their oath. The oath of judges of the ICC is as follows: "I solemnly undertake that I will perform my duties and exercise my powers as a judge of the International Criminal Court honourably, faithfully, impartially and conscientiously and that I

[68] Code of judicial procedure (4/1734).

will respect the confidentiality of investigations and prosecutions and the secrecy of deliberations."[69]

The content of this statement is broad but is ultimately dependent on the understanding of the judges of the ICC and their abilities. Thus, it is a main and immutable pillar of justice that judges must work ethically in order to continue to serve on the bench. That means that the assumption is that the independence and impartiality of judges are acknowledged as essential prerequisites of the rule of law in the system of international criminal justice. Thus, through their oaths, judges ensure the protection of judicial conscience and their wilful respect of the provisions of international human rights law. The system of international criminal justice requires a fair trial and, as a corollary, the supremacy of ethical conscience in the conducts of judges and their decisions represents potentially the most important pillar of the Court concerning holding offenders accountable.[70]

The vital fact is that with the oaths of the judges of the Court, we are emphasising that judicial conscience is a constantly present *leitmotif* of the Court. Despite this, the situation concerning the judicial conscience is often unstable because there is not one common understanding concerning which behaviour, which decision, which question of the judge, or which voice of the judges indicates the final judgement. Thus, all questions relating to matters of honesty, impartiality, and diligence remain matters of choice, although a judge of international criminal justice should realise that certain international crimes, such as those committed in Palestine, are

---

[69] Int'l Criminal Court, Rules of Procedure and Evidence, UN Doc. IT/32, Rule 5.

[70] We should keep in mind that the "obvious requirement is that judicial officers hear and decide cases with reasonable efficiency, and not unwillingly extend the length of trials. They should achieve an acceptable rate of disposal of cases compatible with maintaining high guidelines of justice and fairness. They should not by their own tardiness exacerbate court delays. Neither should they unnecessarily postpone the handing down of reserved judgments. *Similarly, it goes without saying, judicial officers should adequately perform the administrative functions associated with their role. They should maintain accurate court records, and resist any temptation to edit or 'doctor' transcripts to their own advantage.*" David Wood, *Judicial Ethics: A Discussion Paper, Australian Institute of Judicial Administration* (1996), p.16. Emphasise mine. Quoted in Stephen Colbran, 'Diligent as a Criterion for Judicial Performance Evaluation', 11 (1) *Griffith Law Review* (2002), pp.198-222. The fact is that when it comes to the question of accountability under the ICC supervisor, the big criminals are always found innocent and never guilty.

so clear that any decision denying their occurrence is illogical and in violation of the judge's oath.[71]

Another complication of taking oaths is that although judges take an oath, they are still human beings, and they may thus understand the words or terms of oath differently, which may create serious questions regarding the oath's professional value in the eyes of the conscience of judicial independence. As a result, although an oath is meant to be taken as it is written, spoken, and heard, the person taking the oath may interpret it differently. It is therefore significant that the sincerity and purity of the judge not only stems from their oath, but also from their moral capacity and personal integrity which allows them to value the true meaning of the oath.

> The united value of human essence should serve as the guideline for the system of justice such that true justice can take shape in the mirror of justice. Here, no God or religious rules, serve as the honest representatives of humanity, rather judges do. That is why agreements on international human rights law respect all individuals through a rights-based mechanism, not an oath-based one. However, the question of whether or not the principles of international human rights law are respected in reality is a continuing dilemma for criminal justice. Qualification of law does not imply qualification in practice.

3.3. Juridical Principles without the Power of Enforceability

There are a number of sources in the system of judicial jurisdiction that encourage the maintenance of judicial ethics. One of these significant developments can be seen with the provisions of the Bangalore Principles of Judicial Conduct which were adopted by the Judicial Group on Strengthening Judicial Integrity and revised at the Round Table Meeting

[71] Farhad Malekian, 'Judging International Criminal Justice in the Occupied Territories,' 12 *International Criminal Law Review* (2012), pp.627-869.

of Chief Justices held at the Peace Palace.[72] The intention behind the Principles was to create a professional standard of ethics which addressed issues facing criminal justice in order to take a significant step towards increasing the basic values of the social community and creating guidelines for judges. According to these principles, judges are recognised as being accountable for the proper enforcement of justice and the maintenance of impartiality.

However, the major weakness of the Bangalore Principles is similar to that of other ethical codes–: the enforcement measures for these principles are weak, and therefore impossible to enforce. Despite this, a fair number of European countries and other states view the Bangalore Principles as the most authoritative and modern approach to judicial ethics. Similarly, one may also mention here the commitments made by the International Association of Judicial Independence and World Peace in the Bologna Milano Global Code of Judicial Ethics, which was approved at the International Conference of Judicial independence in 2015. The Code's intention is to provide appropriate judicial guidance to the judges of the world and to prepare a judiciary framework for regulating judicial conduct.

The Judiciary Report 2009-2010 issued by the European Network of Councils also puts emphasis on the notion of judicial ethics. According to this report, the affirmation of the principles of professional conduct concerning the impartiality of judges and their significant function may highlight the strength of public confidence in the judiciary and promote an enhanced understanding of the major role played judges in the given society. It therefore promotes judicial ethics with the purpose of empowering trust in the jurisdiction and value of the work of judges. Again, the intention here is to create full trust in the system of justice and in judges in order to collectively respect and honour the judicial office as a public forum. According to the European Court of Human Rights and Article 21of the European Convention on Human Rights, the objective is

---

[72] The Hague, November 25-26 (2002).

to cultivate more transparency regarding the existing obligations and thereby increase public confidence in the court.[73]

As we have previously mentioned, the principles within the Code of Judicial Ethics of the International Criminal Court serve as guidelines on the essential ethical standards as imperative requirements for judges in the performance of their judicial duties. The principles are essentially advisory in nature, and they seek to assist judges with ethical and professional issues. This means that the judges of the Court should demonstrate greater professional ethical standards in criminal justice than is required by the Code. The intention is not only to support judicial independence, but also to increase its effectiveness and natural strength of enforceability.

3.4. Equality before the Judge

One of the essential principles of criminal justice is that judges should treat all individuals equally and not give priority to individuals of a certain sex, nationality, religion, culture, language, ethnicity, etc.[74] In fact, the equality of individuals before the eyes of justice is considered as one of the most essential requirements of justice across the globe. Thus, judges are required to respect this principle, including at the international level.[75]

---

[73] For European Human Rights consult Ed Bates, *The Evolution of the European Convention on Human Rights: From Its Inception to the Creation of a Permanent Court of Human Rights* (Oxford University Press, 2010); Marton Varju, *European Union Human Rights Law: The Dynamics of Interpretation and Context* (Edward Elgar Pub, 2014); Mark W. Janis, Richard S. Kay, Anthony W. Bradley, European Human Rights Law: Text and Materials (Oxford University Press, 2008); William A. Schabas, *The European Convention on Human Rights: A Commentary* (Oxford University Press, 2015).

[74] Consult Guide on Article 6 of the European Convention on Human Rights (31 August 2021), available online at https://www.echr.coe.int/documents/guide_art_6_criminal_eng.pdf; Concerning the practice of the US courts see 'Judges and Discrimination Assessing the Theory and Practice of Criminal Sentencing' (2003), available online at https://www.ojp.gov/pdffiles1/nij/grants/204024.pdf.

[75] The principle of equality deals with one of the essential principles of criminal justice. The principle is also stated in Article 21(1) of the Statute of the ICTY: "All persons shall be equal before the International Tribunal." The Appeals Chamber of the ICTY has describes the above provision. According to it, "*the Prosecutor, in exercising her discretion under the Statute in the investigation and indictment of accused before the Tribunal, is subject to*

In order for the system of international criminal justice to respect different cultures, a large number of rules of national criminal justice were formulated in the Rome Statute. They highlight the legitimacy of different elements of criminal jurisdiction. When selecting judges, the states parties to the Statute have to take the judicial systems of different states into account. The principles to be followed include i) the representation of the principal legal systems of the world; ii) equitable geographical representation; and iii) a fair representation of female and male judges.

A judge is therefore legally and ethically responsible per the provisions of the system of international human rights law to take the principle of equality into consideration when discharging their duties. A judge of an international criminal court, for example, is not permitted to discriminate between individuals for irrelevant reasons or based on how they see the facts and how they respect the law. Justice should be carried out without the consideration of these factors. If a person abuses the jurisdiction of an international criminal court or a national criminal court, the judges of the court must maintain their neutrality and not treat them differently. This implies the fact that the judge must maintain their impartial attitudes towards parties and should not influence other judges' opinions in any way.

We should remember that fair trial rights represent the manifestation of a hybrid category of human rights, which some legal scholars have even characterised as imperative norms in national, regional, and international courts.[76] When we talk about the impartiality of judges, we mean that they are to be fair in their conducts and should not give priority to any one individual over another. Nor should they give priority to any one subject based on their political or personal interests. Thus, judges must have an equal and impartial understanding of all matters. This is particularly

---

the principle of equality before the law and to this requirement of non-discrimination." Zejnil Delalic (IT-96-21-A), Judgement, 20 February 2001, para.605.

[76] For instance consult Konstantinos D. Magliveras, 'The Special Court for Sierra Leone: A New Type of Regional Criminal Court for the International Community?' 17 *International Enforcement Law Reporter* (Feb. 2001); David M. Crane, 'The Special Court for Sierra Leone, in International Criminal Law', Vol. III (M. Cherif Bassiouni, ed. 2008) pp. 195-218; C. Sriram, 'Wrong-sizing International Justice? The Hybrid Tribunal in Sierra Leone', 29 (3) *Fordham International Law Journal* (2006), pp.472-506.

notable with international crimes which are deeply interwoven with political considerations. In national or international trials, fairness represents the respect of the *somebodiness* of all parties and not the privileging of one over the other. This not only encourages the maintenance of individual rights including the right to defence, but also refers to the maintenance of fair justice for the public's sake. While the right to a fair trial is not listed as a non-derogable right under article 4(2) of the *International Covenant on Civil and Political Rights*, the Human Rights Committee has historically treated the right to a fair trial as such. Even in circumstances when derogation from Article 14 is acceptable, the principles of legality and the rule of law necessitate that the essential requirement of an impartial trial be respected.

Moreover, the principle of good conduct and treatment of others by judges of courts requires the fair treatment of all parties without any prejudice, such that a judge maintains their impartiality and ensures a fair trial. Moreover, the insurance of a positive view of the proceedings by the general public concerning the judicial process is so significant and essential that the judge has to maintain their impartiality, the independence of the court, and fairness in the procedures of justice. As a result, the judge should strive to behave appropriately and to treat everyone equally. The principle of equality before the judges has to be respected by all courts. The principle of equality also creates trust in the system of criminal justice and prevents discrimination between the parties. Any violation of the principal results in the disrespect of the principles of international human right law and can be a large factor in the reduction of the value of the decisions of judges, and in certain cases may cause a case to lose its legal validity, thus requiring it to be reinvestigated by a court or judge who fully respects the equality of parties.[77]

---

[77] Malekian, 'Conscience of Prosecutors in International Criminal Law', The Heart of the Matter, note 3, pp.28, 45, 99, and 119. "The moral standards of law enforcement and criminal justice demand the gavel of morals. The same variations of attitudes towards all persons who are engaged in mechanism of criminal justice constitute an elementary and necessary requirement for a successful criminal justice if their soft judgments are not the leading principle of their ethics. They should all seek to uphold and respect human rights for all and to remain objective towards all parties involved i.e., victims, the accused, and witnesses.

3.5. PROCEEDINGS WITH JURIES

A jury is a group of lay people selected to hear a criminal case and then deliberate and vote on whether they believe the accused to be guilty or not guilty. Long ago the American trial lawyer Clarence Darrow expressed that: "Jurymen seldom convict a person they like, or acquit one that they dislike. The main work of a trial lawyer is to make a jury like his client, or, at least, to feel sympathy for him; facts regarding the crime are relatively unimportant."[78] Similarly, another United States Circuit Judge Jerome Frank stated even more clearly: "Mr. Prejudice and Miss Sympathy are the names of witnesses whose testimony is never recorded, but must nevertheless be reckoned with in trials by jury." As the American poet - Robert Frost correctly asserted, *"A jury consists of twelve persons chosen to decide who has the better lawyer."* These statements may not be entirely true, but they share strong messages about the nature of our trust in those who may easily falter.

Juries must function as the evaluators of fact, and thus examine all documents and evidence which are submitted to the court in order to come to the conclusion about whether or not the suspected person was capable of committing the crime they were accused of. However, it must be emphasised that the judge is also an evaluator, albeit with the difference that juries evaluate the guilt of the accused, while judges evaluate the law and therefore must ensure that the court proceedings comply with the law. Still, it is possible that in certain, less severe cases, that the judge serves both functions, and evaluates both fact and law. However, in this case, both the state and the defendant must agree in writing to not have a jury trial.

We must nonetheless emphasise that not all countries allow for trial by jury. In countries without trial by jury, judges may, with the assistance of secondary judges, make the decision about the guilt of the accused. The

---

This is the way in which we can eliminate cheating within the system of criminal justice and instead cultivate humanity with equality and love for all citizens." *Id.*, p.168.

[78] Quoted in Andrew J. Wistrich, Jeffrey J. Rachlinski & Chris Guthrie, 'Heart Versus Head: Do Judges Follow the Law or Follow Their Feelings?', 93 *Texas Law Review* (2015), pp.855-923, at 856.

presence of a jury during criminal proceedings is dependent upon the country's legislation. Thus, the presence of a jury is significant when it comes to cases involving serious criminal accusations. The task of the jury is simply to determine whether the defendant is guilty of the relevant crime or not. If a jury is present, the function of the judge is simply to guide the law and ensure that the proceedings comply with the applicable rules set by the law. In the common law system, judges, and sometimes juries, have a binding duty to hear all the evidence and legal arguments put forward by each side.

Therefore, judges and juries have to evaluate and examine every piece of evidence that is submitted and decide which party has put forward the most ethical or logical argument or proof. In a criminal case, it is typically a judge who decides on the sentence, regardless of whether there is a jury or not. For instance, in American criminal courts, the jury decides whether the defendant is guilty or innocent, while the judge decides on the sentence i.e., how many years a person who has been found guilty will be imprisoned. Normally, in the common law system, when a trial draws to a close and all the hearings have been held, the judge or the jury listen to the summary of the case by each party. The presence of a jury during proceedings creates the legal responsibility for the judge to present their own summary concerning the subject of the case to the jury. The judge should carry out the entire process of prosecution before submitting their own summary to the relevant court in which the case will be discussed for the delivery of the final verdict.

In countries which do not have juries or they are not required, the judge has two functions i.e., to try the fact and the law. In most countries of the world without juries, the judge makes the ultimate decision concerning the guilt of the accused. In minor criminal cases, there is normally no jury. Here, we are referring to countries which have jury systems. This procedure must however be agreed upon by both sides. In sum, when there is no jury, judges are responsible for determining the facts, interpreting the applicable law, applying the law to the evidence, and for making the final decision concerning culpability.

Judges are generally known for issuing sentences in criminal cases and fines in civil cases. As we will see later, judges have different duties regarding juvenile cases based on the fact that juveniles cannot be charged with crimes in the same way as adults due to their reduced accountability. Here, since the court investigating the criminal behaviour is not a criminal court, juveniles do not receive a jury trial. Nevertheless, in some countries, this may not be respected and juveniles may be prosecuted in criminal courts depending on how their age is calculated under the court's jurisdiction.

3.6. Lay Judges

The adquisitorial legal system represents a method of adjudication in which one or more lay judges assist the professional judge in order to arrive at the correct decision. It is a process of cooperation between a primary judge and several other secondary judges. The term "juror" refers to a lay judge, and is commonly used for a lay judge who is a member of a jury and therefore must work under oath to deliver a verdict in a case. Lay judges can also be called justices of the peace, as seen in England and Wales.

These lay judges are selected from the local community and may not have any legal knowledge concerning the legal decision-making process of the given courts. They may also be referred to as magistrates. It is important that lay judges are honourable individuals without criminal records. They are typically honest individuals who are trusted by the public to uphold morals and conduct themselves ethically in order to carry out their responsibility.

Lay judges may be elected by the government agency responsible for monitoring criminal courts. These judges may function as volunteers for a certain time or serve a term prescribed by law. For instance, to serve as a lay judge in the Swedish legal system is a task of honour. The intention behind having lay judges is to maintain public confidence in the administration of justice, and it is also a way for the general public to gain insight into the operation of the court system. Lay judges assist with different issues including the evaluation of evidence and issuing sentences.

In certain civil cases, when a lawyer selects the lay judge, they must exercise a substantial amount of caution in order to make sure that they choose the right person. Volunteer lay judges in criminal cases are called 'Schoeffen' in German or, if the person before the court is a young person (up to 17 years) or a juvenile (18 - 20 years) then they are known as 'Jugendschoeffen.'"

> What are called proposal lists are drawn up every 5 years by a local authority for lay judges in criminal cases and by the Youth Support Committee for youth lay judges, based on which a Lay Judge Selection Committee at the Local Court selects the lay judges for Juvenile and adult courts. Any person of German nationality, who on the day their duties are due to begin is at least 25 and not more than 69 years old, may be a volunteer lay judge. Specific criteria (being in a profession or job connected with the law, having a criminal conviction, being a declared bankrupt etc.) debar a person from serving as Magistrate. The person selected must accept the position.[79]

British lay judges are present in the lower courts. They may offer opinions on cases or make decisions on traffic violations, small civil claims, and other minor domestic matters. At least two lay judges must hear the summary of a minor offence in the lower magistrates' court in England. In the United Kingdom, there are certain conditions for the resignation and removal of lay justices. These are:

> (1) A lay justice may resign his office at any time.
> (2) The Lord Chancellor may [F1, with the concurrence of the Lord Chief Justice,] remove a lay justice from his office by an instrument on behalf and in the name of Her Majesty—

---

[79] "Lay judges sit in criminal cases in the courts of first instance i.e., in local (Amtsgericht) and Regional (Landgericht) courts and in appeal proceedings at the Regional court. In each event there are 2 lay judges sitting; in addition, depending on which court it is, there are 1, 2 or 3 professional judges." Available at http://www.schoeffen.de/ lay-judges-in-germany.html (19 June 2017).

(a) on the ground of incapacity or misbehaviour,
(b) on the ground of a persistent failure to meet such standards of competence as are prescribed by a direction given by the Lord Chancellor [F2 with the concurrence of the Lord Chief Justice], or
(c) if he is satisfied that the lay justice is declining or neglecting to take a proper part in the exercise of his functions as a justice of the peace.

In the United States, like in the United Kingdom, lay judges are present in the lower courts. In the former country "the debate over lay judges continues. Little has been done of late either to put this debate to rest or to address the true issues. Much heat has been generated by courts and commentators, but, unfortunately, little light."[80] In the Chinese legal system, lay judges are present in the people's courts and are known as assessors. Their function is to serve as adjudicators serious criminal cases. These assessors are elected or temporarily asked to assist a court.

The lay judges replace the jury system, which, in the common law system, is entrusted with providing the necessary balance between the machinery of the state which acts against the accused, and the rights of the accused, which have to be protected along with the interests of justice. The lay judge's main function is to keep the professional judge from acting in an arbitrary manner. Lay judges may also prevent justice from being immoral.

The lay judge must also take care not to let political influence interfere in the adjudication process. This can be very difficult at times, since political party integrity is very high and a lay judge may therefore, in one way or another, be influenced by politics or may even be a supporter of a certain political group. In some states, the number of lay judges depends on the seriousness of the case, the level of the court in the country, and the prescribed laws of the country. This means the duties of lay judges may

[80] Examine Allan Ashman and David L. Lee, 'Non-Lawyer Judges: The Long Road North' 53 (3) Chicago Kant Law Review (1977), pp.565-595, p.579.

vary from country-to-country, however, their judicial conscience must not.[81]

3.7. International Criminal Court without a Jury

In the system of international criminal courts, there are no juries, and cases are decided in accordance with the judge's decision. Similarly, in the system of international criminal justice, there are no juries, and the ICC does not take its final decision based on a jury's opinion. In other words, decisions in the ICC are taken by only its judges in its relevant chambers, which includes both the pre-trial and appeals chambers. The decisions of the chambers are final and cannot be modified, except by the appeals chamber.

One important principle of the judgements of the ICC is that all judges are obliged to be present for every stage of the trial. For this reason, the presidency may, on a case-by-case basis, depending on the availability of the judges, designate a new member for the Trial if one of the members is not able to attend one of the stages of the criminal trial. Hence, the Trial Chamber cannot carry out its work when one of its members is absent. The reason for this is simply that a decision of the Trial Chamber must be made by all judges, and the absence of one of the judges of the Court negatively impacts the value of the proceedings.

Some of the most important cases brought before the jurisdiction of the ICC include the cases of Thomas Lubanga Dyilo,[82] Germain Katanga,[83] Mathieu Ngudjolo Chui[84], and Bosco Ntaganda,[85] who were accused of committing crimes against humanity and war crimes including rape and

---

[81] This is a difficult job and they may politically be divided dues to a number of reasons.

[82] Thomas Lubanga Dyilo (ICC-01/04-01/06), *Warrant of Arrest*, 10 February 2006.

[83] Germain Katanaga (ICC-01/04-01/07), *Situation in the Democratic Republic of Congo*, 2 July 2007.

[84] *Id.*

[85] Bosco Ntaganda (01/04-02/06), *Situation in the Democratic Republic of the Congo*, 7 August 2006.

torture in the Democratic Republic of the Congo; Joseph Kony,[86] Vincent Otti,[87] Okot Odhiambo,[88] Dominic Ongwen[89], and Raska Lukwiya[90] who were accused of committing war crimes and crimes against humanity in Uganda; and Ahmad Muhammad Harun ("Ahmad Harun"),[91] Ali Muhammad Ali Abd-Al-Rahman ("Ali Kushayb"),[92] Omar Hassan Ahmad Al Bashri[93], and Bahar Idriss Abu Garda[94] who were accused of committing war crimes and crimes against humanity in Darfur, Sudan.

Certainly, all these cases demonstrate the significant function of the judges of the ICC in the identification of international crimes, international criminals, and in the application of appropriate punishment. The ICC is therefore responsible for implementing the principles of international human rights law in equal measure. This is only possible if the ICC maintains its independence concerning its judicial conscience and the impartiality of its judges.

3.8. *MENS REA* AND *ACTUS REUS* ON THE DESK OF JUDGES

One of the primary duties of judges relates to the identification of the principles of *mens rea* and *actus reus* in national or international criminal justice.[95] The sanctions of criminal law vary in the degree of severity of the

---

[86] Joseph Kony (ICC-02/04-01/05), Warrant of Arrest for Joseph Kony issued on 8 July 2005 as amended on 27 September 2005.

[87] Vincent Otti (ICC-02/04), Warrant of Arrest, 8 July 2005. He is accused of thirty three counts of crimes.

[88] Okot Odhiambo (ICC-02/04), Warrant of Arrest, 8 July 2005. He is accused of nineteen counts crimes.

[89] Dominic Ongwen (ICC-02/04), Warrant of Arrest, 8 July 2005. He is accused of thirty-three counts crimes.

[90] Raska Lukwiya (ICC-02/04), Warrant of Arrest, 8 July 2005. He is accused of nine counts crimes.

[91] Muhammad Harun (ICC-02/05-01/07) Warrant of Arrest, 27 April 2007.

[92] Ali Abd-Al-Rahman (ICC-02/05-01/07), Warrant of Arrest, 27 April 2007.

[93] Omar Hassan Ahmad Al Bashir (ICC-02/05-01/09), Warrant of Arrest, 4 March 2009.

[94] Bahar Idriss Abu Garda (Summons to Appear issued under seal by the ICC), 7 May 2009.

[95] Examine Johan D. Van der Vyver, 'The International Criminal Court and the Concept of *Mens Rea* in International Criminal Law,' 12 *U. Miami Int'l& Comp. L. Rev.* 57 (2005), pp.57-

mens rea, and as such, sanctions become stricter when the degree of *mens rea* is proven to be greater. These are examined by the judge of a court, and the judge not only has a legal duty, but also an ethical duty, to make a correct judgement concerning these two important principles of criminal justice. The concept of *mens rea* is accordingly a criterion which determines whether the accused receives a light, moderate, or heavy penalty – or even no punishment at all. An accused person can also be released from all allegations against them if it can be proven that they were not involved in either the *mens rea* or *actus reus* of the crime. This is because the judges of a case base their understanding of the degree of the criminal conduct on their evaluation of the guilty mind of the offender. For example, in the cases involving murder, the same criminal court may deliver different judgements and punishments in different cases depending on the *degree* of the *mens rea* of the accused. Consequently, it is always necessary to look at the language used by the judges concerning the mental state of the offender at the time of the commission of the crime.

A judge should be very careful in their consideration of *mens rea* or *actus reus*.[96] This is because they may unintentionally fabricate the concept of *actus reus,* or the physical element of a crime, and thereby criminalise all acts which are actually integral aspects of human rights laws.[97] For example, a number of Muslim states criminalise acts that are integral parts of substantive criminal law such as adultery or sexual relations between

---

149. Available online at: http://repository.law.miami.edu/umiclr/vol12/iss1/3. In the judgment of the International Criminal Tribunal for the Former Yugoslavia, it was stated that "Because the distinction in the judgement between references to the views of the ICRC and expression of the Trial Chamber's own understanding of the *mens rea* requirement is not always easy to identify, the precise scope of the relevant *mens rea* for the crime of outrages upon personal dignity is left somewhat open. It is apparent from the Appeals Chamber's judgement that it did not regard the mental element of the offence as involving any *specific intent* to humiliate, ridicule or degrade the Victims. It noted particularly that it did not interpret the ICRC Commentaries' statement that the term "outrages upon personal dignity" refers to acts "aimed at humiliating and ridiculing" the victim as suggesting a requirement of a *specific intent* to humiliate, ridicule or degrade, but as seeking "simply to describe the conduct which the provision seeks to prevent." *Kunarac, Kovac, & Vukovic*, (IT-96-23-T & IT-96-23/1-T), Judgment, 22 February 2001, Paras.509-511.

[96] Examine Mohamed Elewa Badar, *The Concept of Mens Rea in International Criminal Law* (Hart Publishing, 2013); Malekian, *Trading Virginity of International Criminal Justice*, note 1.

[97] *Id.*

people of the same sex, and therefore recognise acts as crimes, which are not considered as such under international human rights law. As a result, *actus reus* manifests where the physical state of mind is part of individuals rights. Additionally, the basic duty of the prosecution is to prove the existence of both elements of the crime to the satisfaction of the judge or jury beyond a reasonable doubt.

The judge must be aware of the fact that as a rule of criminal law (with certain exceptions), one cannot commit a crime without the presence of the state of mind. In other words, other types of crimes which are committed by someone sans *mens rea* or *actus reus* are not truly crimes, but they are still identified as such within the criminal law of all states. It is the duty of the judge to recognise this and analyse the given situation. This is because the corpus of criminal law is based on the existence of these two core principles of *mens rea* and *actus reus,* without which, other arguments would be necessary in order to reconcile their absence. The development of our criminal laws contains different theories concerning the proof of criminality, despite the consensus that the presence of *mens rea* is not a necessary prerequisite for the recognition of criminality. This is what the judge should consider while drawing on their own experiences in order to come to the appropriate conclusion.

The reasoning above has been greatly modified in the system of international criminal justice however, and international tribunals have been reluctant at times to accept the argument that there was no *mens rea* present in the commission of a crime. Regarding crimes such as genocide, crimes against humanity, rape, and torture, guilt arises from the commission of the conduct itself, and no further theoretical proof is required. This is what the judges of the international criminal tribunals are dealing with.[98] For instance, the crime of genocide is so obvious that *mens*

---

[98] For genocide, see for further analysis and references id, p.119. For example, on the non-ratification of the international Convention on Genocide, see J. Duffett, *Against the Crime of Silence* (New York, London, 1968). W. Michael Reisman, 'Legal Responses to Genocide and Other Massive Violations of Human Rights', 59 *Law and Contemporary Problems* (1996), p.75; William L. Hurlock, 'The International Court of Justice: Effectively Providing a Long Overdue Remedy for Ending State-Sponsored Genocide (Bosnia-Herzegovina v. Yugoslavia)', 12 *American University Journal of International Law and Policy* (1997), p.299; Beth van Schaack, 'The Crime of Political Genocide: Repairing the Genocide

rea and *actus reus* do not need to be proven. For a judge who deals with the questions of genocide in an international criminal court, it should be obvious that

> The objective of genocide as embodied in the requirement of special intent limits the kind of acts that would constitute genocide. However, the objective of genocide can also serve to bring into the confines of the actus reus a broad perception of killings, the causing of bodily or mental harm, inflicting conditions of life, preventing births, and transferring of children. The actus reus may indeed include acts not mentioned in the definition of genocide but which have been committed as part of the same pattern of conduct." Massive deportation (ethnic cleansing) may be construed as a first step in a process of elimination; destruction of places of worship as a means of annihilating the religious group associated with those religious objects; destruction of libraries intended to annihilate the culture of the target group; systematic rape of women intended to transmit a new ethnic identity to the child conceived by that atrocious act-such acts may all become part of the actus reus if committed with intent to destroy, in whole or in part, a national, ethnic, racial or religious group.'[99]

Similarly, when grave crimes are committed, the gravity of the conduct implies a guilty mind, even if its proof may not be straightforward from a procedural point of view. Examples of such crimes include murder, war crimes, trafficking, and aggression. The presumption is that it is free will

---

Convention's Blind Spot', 106 *Yale Law Journal* (1997), p.2259; John D. van der Vyver, 'Prosecution and Punishment of the Crime of Genocide', 25 *Fordham International Law Journal* (1999), p.286; Mary Robinson, 'Genocide, War Crimes, Crimes Against Humanity', 25 *Fordham International Law Journal* (1999), p.275; William A. Schabas, Genocide in International Law, the Crime of Crimes (2000); Matthew Lippman, 'Genocide', in *International Criminal Law*, Vol. I (M. Cherif Bassiouni, ed., 2008) pp.405-455. In particular, see the statements of Bertrand Russell and the Russell International War Tribunal held in Stockholm, Sweden, May 2-10, 1967 and Roskilde, Denmark from November 20 to December 1, 1967. For British commission of genocide in Persia consult Mohammad Gholi Majd, T*he Great Famine & Genocide in Iran: 1917-1919* (2nd ed., University Press of America, 2013); Mohammad Gholi Majd, *Victorian Holocaust Iran in the Great Famine of 1869-1873* (Hamilton Books, 2018).

[99] der Vyver, 'The International Criminal Court and the Concept of *Mens rea* in International Criminal Law,' note 95, p.92.

which affects the commission of crimes such as murder, and not *mens rea*. Here, the concept of *actus reus* relies not only on the physical element, but also on the *degree of severity* of the wrong which has been ordered, and it is the responsibility of the judges to understand this fact.[100] Thus, for the judge, it is criminal responsibility which is the most significant question of criminal law, not the questions of *mens rea* or *actus reus*, although both concepts can still prove useful in the final decision of the relevant judge.

For this reason, on the desk of the judges of international criminal tribunals, the position of *actus reus* in the system of international criminal justice is measured against the actual position of the elements of criminal law within both the common and civil law systems. In general, the constituent elements of *actus reus* are based on the physical element of the crime and also deal with the questions of guilt and fault, and the presence of intent and/or knowledge concerning the preparation of the crime. All these arguments serve to clearly identify *mens rea* and *actus reus* in order to identify the proper subject for the attribution of criminal responsibility, which is the responsibility of the judge.

Beyond all this, the judge must be aware of the fact that *mens rea* and *actus reus* are both integral parts of the same phenomenon, and that it sometimes it is difficult to identify them independently. The reason for this is simply that the notion of *actus reus* cannot be defined without the notion of *mens rea* and *vice versa* as they are not mutually exclusive.[101] One essential reason for this is that certain elements of crimes intersect with other elements at various points, and the separation thereof is thus problematic for judges.[102] *Mens rea* may have the equivalent elements to *actus reus,* and they may even arise concurrently. Both principles may often intersect with one another, and when the *mens rea* becomes the physical element of the crime it may create doubt in the mind of judges vis-à-vis the identification of criminally wrongful conduct. These are all the duties of judges and their practical experiences within national and

---

[100] See Malekian, *Trading Virginity of International Criminal Justice*, note 1, pp.23, 37, 52-53.
[101] Consult *Badar., The Concept of Mens Rea in International Criminal Law*, note 96.
[102] *Id.*

international systems. They must examine the situation with open eyes and with full respect for the frame of judicial conscience.[103]

3.9. Rights of Suspects

Even if we believe that the prosecutor and the judges of the ICC are fulfilling their legal, moral, and ethical responsibilities, there are still a number of provisions which call for the respect of the suspect, including treating them as innocent until proven otherwise– although the court can still restrict their freedom in the meantime. Nonetheless, suspects have the right to be present during their trial and judges are responsible for guaranteeing that this is possible. Moreover, suspects have the right to a public, fair, and objective trial before the ICC. A few further rights of suspects include:

1. Having access to a lawyer or defence counsel as per the wishes of the suspect;
2. A suspect has the right to present relevant evidence and call witnesses to support their case;
3. Suspects should be provided information in their native language;
4. A suspect should have sufficient time and support for the preparation of their defence;
5. Suspects should freely communicate their wishes concerning the presentation of evidence and have full access to their counsel;
6. Suspects should be tried in a timely manner, and this should be insured by the judges of the ICC;
7. Judges should not force the suspects to admit guilt in any matter;
8. Judges should in no way influence the suspect to plead guilty;
9. All judges should respect the choice of a suspect to remain silent;
10. The engagement of a suspect in other matters during the trial should not affect the decision of judges of the Court;

---

[103] *Id.*

11. Suspects have right to ask the Prosecution to disclose evidence to the defence which could prove the suspect's innocence;
12. The judge of the Court should disclose evidence which could potentially mitigate the guilt of the accused;
13. These rights apply to the evidence submitted during the trial as well as any evidence which emerges following the conclusion of the trial.

Chapter 4

Legal Validity of Judgements of the International Criminal Court

4.1. Unanimity of Decisions of Judges

The Statute of the International Criminal Court signed at The Hague encourages judges to reach unanimity in their decisions. However, if this is not possible, then the decision can be made by the majority of the judges. The decision of the Court must be made in writing and should contain the justifications for the findings and conclusions of the Trial Chamber. The judges of the Trial Chamber are also allowed to issue a decision. If unanimity cannot be reached between the judges, the Trial Chamber's decision should contain not only the views of the majority, but also the minority. Subsequently, the decision or a summary of the decision should be delivered in an open court.[104]

---

[104] Consult *The Significance of the ICC Appeals Chamber's Ruling in the Afghanistan Situation*, available online at http://opiniojuris.org/2020/03/10/the-significance-of-the-icc-appeals-chambers-ruling-in-the-afghanistan-situation/; see also Marco Longobardo, Factors Relevant for the Assessment of Sufficient Gravity in the ICC. *Proceedings and the Elements of International Crimes* (2016), available online at http://www.qil-qdi.org/factors-relevant-assessment-sufficient-gravity-icc-proceedings-elements-international-crimes/.

The provisions presented above require the presence certain imperative pillars of the proceedings of the Court. These are: a) the presence of the judges, b) the pure value of evidence, c) the value of each proceeding, d) the integrated value of the overall process, e) the limitation of a decision on the charges, f) the principle of unanimity, g) the reasons for the majority decision, h) the reasons for the minority decision(s), i) the principle of secret deliberation, and j) the deliverance of the decision in an open court. The respect of these pillars is obligatory and should not be ignored in the procedures of international and national criminal justice.

The principle of unanimity constitutes an important requirement within the mechanism of the jurisdiction for judges. This principle ensures that a single opinion is issued by the court. For that reason, the Statute encourages the judges to reach unanimity in their decisions, unless the decision is taken by a majority of the judges. As an accepted principle of jurisdiction and decision making, the deliberation of a trial has to remain secret. This principle also has to be respected by the Trial Chamber of the ICC. Additionally, all decisions of the Trial Chamber must be made in writing and include the justifications for the Trial Chamber's findings and conclusions. If a decision represents the majority opinion regarding the case, the minority opinion must also be presented in an open court which can be attended by anyone.

However, it is difficult to avoid political influence and reach a unanimous decision in a case since politics are inherent in the Rome Statute of the ICC. The court was not established to serve political authorities, however its legacy has demonstrated the opposite:

> The problem of the model which is offered by the Statute of the ICC may be that it may lead to controversy between the judges. It might have been better for the Court to adopt a method that relied on the majority decisions of the judges. This is because the problem will be more serious when several judges have the same nationality or different nationalities where they have social or political activities in common. This means that we may have two judges with different nationalities but who also share the nationality of a third state. Moreover, the first nationality (original) of X and Y may be E, but X may also have the nationality of S, where he has

social and political activities, and Y may also have obtained the nationality of S, but without social activities. How can we believe that those two judges are not simultaneously influenced by their own first nationality, while one speaks for the original and the other for the adopted nationality? Moreover, the transparency, integrity and independence of a judge is not guaranteed by rules or by their being a specific sex, but through a full understanding of humanity, of the ethical and philosophical reasons for the existence of the law and, not least, of justice as a norm of human nature and a reliable social phenomenon.[105]

Political decisions often endanger the security of international criminal justice and create serious problems for the judicial independence of criminal justice. Although ICC judges are strictly prohibited from interfering with their own political decisions, this is not really possible, and any judge who says that they have maintained their impartiality and were not influenced by politics is hard to believe, as was the case with the dissenting opinion in the Israel/Palestine case. The sole question that remains: if Israel had been occupied by the Palestinians instead, and Palestine had violated the relevant resolutions of the Security Council what would the position of Hungarians or the dissenting judge, Judge Péter Kovács, have been?[106]

As a principle of international criminal jurisdiction a judge must be able to remain politically, personally, and religiously neutral in the execution of their duties. A judge who is Muslim, Jewish, Christian or who belongs to any other faith should make judgements free from religious influence. This is because justice which is influenced by religion is not true justice, and it violates the integrity of the united human essence. Humanity

---

105 Farhad Malekian, *Jurisprudence of International Criminal Justice* (Introduction by Professor Benjamin B. Ferencz, the former Prosecutor of the Nuremberg Tribunal (Cambridge: Cambridge Scholars Publishing, 2014).

106 Malekian, 'Judging International Criminal Justice in the Occupied Territories', note 71, pp.627-869. We must here emphasise that Péter Kovács claims to be a specialist in minority protection, human rights, international humanitarian law, and comparative international jurisprudence. However, he failed to demonstrate his knowledge and understanding of the norms of international law through his decisions and failed to counteract bias. https://www.icc-cpi.int/CourtStructure/Pages/judge.aspx?name=Judge%20P%C3%A9ter%20Kov%C3%A1cs.

is not religion, although religion may speak about humanity. Humanity is the norm of the universal essence of man which lacks political, religious, cultural, economic, or social ties. A judge must have a considerable number of freedoms including freedom of the mind, freedom from politics, and freedom from hidden economic interests, and they cannot allow their personal life to interfere with their duties or to influence their judgements. Certainly, in both their professional and private lives, judges of national, regional, and international courts must bear in mind how their actions, conducts, and behaviour influence the reputation of the mechanisms of justice and how they can paralyse the independent judicial conscience. As the case of the Israeli crimes in Palestine in the ICC demonstrates, the Hungarian judge baptised his decision with the assistance of Israel government and its requirements.[107] The recent killings and destruction in May 2021 demonstrates this further.

4.2. Institutional Independence

One of the chief duties of judges is to maintain the institutional independence of the judiciary. This duty is not just a matter of ethical understanding, but is one of the obligatory duties of a judge. For this reason, judges are entitled to work towards this end, and should not cause harm to the integrity of judicial independence in any way, since this preserves the objectivity of the judge and the court. In other words, judicial independence is not a matter of choice, but rather a basic underpinning of

[107] In his very controversial and discriminating statement, he clarifies that "53.The Majority follows more or less the Prosecutor's approach as expressed in her primary position which seems to accept that the validity of the accession is at the heart of the present question and that any a posteriori assessment of statehood would equate to challenging the validity of such accession. As I previously mentioned, I do not think that the validity of the accession is at stake and I do not share the Majority's view that an assessment of the elements of statehood would equate to challenging the validity of the accession. Rather, I think that these two issues can be separated and be treated independently. 54. In my view, the central issue relates to the existence or non-existence of the 'territory' or more precisely, the 'territory of the State' as understood under contemporary international law." https://www.icc-cpi.int/RelatedRecords/CR2021_01167.PDF What is really the definition of a state for the judge of the ICC?

judicial objectivity. Judicial independence should also be considered as a basic right by every court in the world.

Objectivity of the judiciary denotes the indispensable collective and individual character of the court and should be respected in all times. Judicial independence also denotes the legal validity of the work of the court and its relation with other organs of the state. This means that judicial objectivity should not be considered as the subjectivity of the judge under the control of criminal jurisdiction. Thus, no legal entity is permitted to interfere in the procedures of a court. Judicial independence should not be misused by any judge against other entities or systems to impact their independence through fear mongering. This implies that the other branches of government should work and express their opinions without any hindrances. The reason for this is that judiciary independence should not be interpreted as the power of the judges or the court to force others to admit their personal views.

The scope of judicial independence also implies the ethical obligations of judges. Here, ethical obligation not only refers to the legal obligation of judges to maintain their objectivity regarding the given case, but also their moral duties. The judges' ethical obligations also compel judges to deal with legal issues appropriately. Judicial objectivity hinges upon both individual and institutional ethical connections. Therefore, the ethical independence of judges must be present at all times in order to preserve the institutional objectivity of the courts. Thus, all judges of international courts and tribunals must remain objective while deciding about the guilt of the accessed following a thorough examination of the evidence.

4.3. Creating Judicial Conscience in the ICJ

Professor Vespasian Pella, the father of international criminal and justice, was the first person to use the term 'judicial conscience' in reference to the system of international criminal law. For Pella, conscience is something that is desired as being indispensable for the corpus of justice. We may assume that the term 'judicial conscience' as used by Pella means

a) the applicability of universal moral principles, b) a court's approach to the judicial principle of legality in a manner consistent with the fundamental rights of common law and civil law systems, c) the principle of proportionality in the execution of all decisions, including in wartime, and d) the principle of due process of the law. In other words, judicial conscience means purity in law, purity in proceedings, purity in sanctions, and purity in judgements.[108]

Conscience is often linked to the eternal response of the law. We come across certain matters which deeply touch our conscience such as the choice between right and wrong. As a result, when certain matters relate to questions of law, legal principles, and judgements, which can in turn affect the conscience of judges, prosecutors, or legal personnel who are supposed to understand the real intention of the law, they become matters of 'judicial conscience.' In reality, no principle of any system should go against the element of judicial conscience. For that reason, judges frequently employ the term 'judicial conscience' (or similar terms) in their judgements in order to emphasise the roots of the term, which arise from 'common conscience.' In the procedures of international criminal justice, the ICC relies on its Statute, and the Statute in turn relies on the application and interpretation of core legal principles. All this also means that judicial conscience has to be respected.

4.4. Dissenting Written Statements

A dissenting opinion is written by a judge or judges who disagree with the conclusion reached by the majority of judges involved in a decision.

---

[108] Vespasian V. Pella, *Plan for World Criminal Code*, 17 *Revue Internationale de Droit Penal* (1946); V. Vespasian Pella, *La criminalité collective des états et le droit pénal de l'avenir*, Bucarest: Imprimerie de l'état, (1925) ; Vespasian V. Pella, *Fonctions Pacificatrices du Droit Pénal Supranational et Fin du Système Traditionnel des Traités de Paix*, 1 *Le Droit Internationale Public* (1947). Consult *also* Vespesian V. Pella, 'Towards an International Criminal Court', 44 *American Journal of International Law* (1950); Mircea Duțu, Vespasian V. Pella (1897-1952): *Founder of International Criminal law, Promoter of the Unification of the Criminal Law, Architect of the International Criminal Justice* (Universul Juridic, Bucharest, 2012).

Dissents may differ depending on the dissenting judge's view, and on the way in which the majority opinion was formulated. A dissent may also entirely reject the majority opinion. Additionally, several dissenting views may be written for a single case. The dissenting judge normally distances themselves from the majority decision and offers a partially or totally new conclusion for the case. Thus, dissenting views are permitted in certain legal systems and reflect the fact that a judge or judges disagree with the majority decision of a case. Significantly, in very serious cases, the dissenting opinion is written and submitted to the Court and documented alongside the original judgement or decision.

The main difference between the dissenting and majority opinions is that dissenting opinions are not binding.[109] The dissent is there to demonstrate that some judges did not agree with the majority decision. Although dissenting opinions are not legally powerful and cannot create case law, they still have potential, and deliver a strong message about the case. Nevertheless, dissenting opinions can lead to certain criticisms of the law and may affect the future recodification of the relevant law in certain situations. They can also open debates among the public, and may even be referred to as a form of persuasive authority when certain arguments arise in the procedures of criminal courts. For example, in the past, a dissenting opinion about the application of capital punishment would have been considered pointless, but now this opinion represents the heart of judicial conscience and of judgements.

Judges are responsible for undertaking the ethical consideration of their legal obligations, particularly when they are aware of the fact that the interests of conflicting parties may overlap, and thus impact the proper application of the administration of justice and the proof of judicial conscience. This is indeed a real dilemma when it comes to the analysis of criminal justice and what should constitute the real application of judicial conscience. In the face of rhetorical improbability, different views may be

---

[109] This is the same concerning the decisions of the International Court of Justice and International Criminal Court. Consult Sardar MA, Waqar Khan Arif, 'Judicial precedent and its authority under international law', 3 (6) *International Journal of Law* (2017), pp.75-81, at 75. Available online at file:///C:/Users/admin/AppData/Local/Temp/3-6-25-878.pdf.

presented, and according to certain judges, a dissent view of a judge may be evaluated as a matter of individual judicial opinion or individual judicial conscience.

Thus, the content of judicial consent can be seen from another perspective and not as a value of the given judgement. According to some judges, this means that the existence of a dissenting opinion cannot reduce the value of a judgment. However, certain dissenting opinions may play a large role in the future development of the law, and may also highlight the flaws in the administration of justice. Consequently, there may not be any particular effort for the understanding of judicial conscience of the judge; nevertheless, a dissent may be an appropriate signal for the future positive development and modification of the legal discipline.

Judges may write a dissent based on their belief that the case was wrongly interpreted, their belief that the majority misinterpreted the law, their belief that the punishment was either too harsh or too light, or based on a misunderstanding of *de lege lata.* The unfortunate fact is that a considerable number of legislations in the world do not put any weight on dissent arguments, and do not even record them. This means that a number of arguments for or against the law are ignored. In these cases, only fellow judges are able to evaluate the dissenting opinions. However, the European Convention on Human Rights clearly supports dissents and declares that "if a judgement does not represent, in whole or in part, the unanimous opinion of the judges, any judge shall be entitled to deliver a separate opinion."[110] However, it must also be said that it is possible that a dissenting opinion of a judge was written in accordance with their religious or political views, which in turn endangers the system of international criminal justice.

[110] Article 4, 2.

4.5. Embarrassment of Conscience

Judges may have different objections to the outcome and implementation of their judgements. Additionally, judges may further express an embarrassment of conscience concerning their inability to follow the provisions of the established law. They may refuse to accept the judgement by issuing a dissent. Although this can occur under the criminal procedures of any state, it is more difficult for judges in authoritarian or corrupt regimes who fear the loss of their position. Thus, the presentation of both personal and institutional embarrassments of conscience may be based on several hidden facts.[111] This is mostly notable in countries with dictatorial or tyrannical regimes and which enforce the law based on power politics and not on pure judgements, particularly when it concerns politically motivated criminal violations against the authorities in power.[112]

A protest by a judge may therefore lead to their permanent resignation from office, and can even result in them being punished. However, if this occurs, then this shows that the judiciary is not functioning properly. Here, the judge may sacrifice their own position for the sake of justice if they realise that a certain punishment is too harsh and harmful to the administration of justice and the conscience of humanity. This situation also implies the fact that ethical consideration may be stronger than juridical consideration in certain circumstances. Thus, the judge may later speak about the shortcomings of legislation and call for the modification of the law, if they are permitted to do so.

A dissenting opinion may not be appreciated by all judges or the machinery of criminal justice as whole. It may also be criticised by political authorities and be regarded as the division of the legislation of the country and represent a loss of trust in the machinery of criminal jurisdiction. Although all these arguments are more or less acceptable in

---

[111] On the notion of conscience consult also Paul Ramsey, War and the Christian Conscience (Durham, N.C., The Duke University Press, 1961); and R. B. Potter, War and Moral Discourse (Richmond, Va., John Knox Press, 1969).

[112] Clark Ramsey, *War Crimes – A Report on United States War Crimes against Iraq* (Maisonneuve Press, 1992).

the social and legal development of the law, the fact is that the machinery of criminal justice cannot lose its freedom of expression and independence, as then we could not speak of judicial independence. More significantly, international human rights law permits debate and disagreement, and if this is hindered by the courts, then the courts cannot maintain their independence. This means the moral attitudes can disappear.[113]

4.6. Reasonings behind Judgements

Judges should ensure that cases are tried in accordance with the rules of the relevant jurisdiction and that they are based on the truth. This is particularly significant in the case of serious criminal cases such as those dealing with murder, genocide, crimes against humanity, war crimes, aggression, rape, and torture. A court may have one or more judges. The high judge is the chief and decision maker and their decision should be taken in consultation with other judges of the court. The judges of a court are obliged to follow the rules of the court and the rules concerning which evidence is permissible in court. The function of the rules is to ensure that court proceedings run in accordance with the legislation. Rules assist in protecting the rights of all individuals who are involved in cases heard by the court. The intention is simply to promote fairness for all parties as well as equality before the law. The duty of the judge is to help ensure that all these rules are applied correctly and objectively. This means a fair opportunity should be granted to all parties presenting their case by the judge. The judges are obliged to remain objective and provide a suitable

---

[113] "When I say that moral attitudes are part of our humanity, I mean those attitudes that appeal to sound principles of right and justice in their explanation. The reasonableness of the underlying ethical conception is a necessary condition; and so the appropriateness of moral sentiments to our nature is determined by the principles that would be consented to in the original position.20 These principles regulate moral education and the expression of moral approval and disapproval, just as they govern the design of institutions. Yet even if the sense of justice is the normal outgrowth of natural human attitudes within a well-ordered society, it is still true that our present moral feelings are liable to be unreasonable and capricious. However, one of the virtues of a well-ordered society is that, since arbitrary authority has disappeared, its members suffer much less from the burdens of oppressive conscience." Rawls, *A Theory of Justice*, note 48, Pp.428-429.

environment for all parties to present their facts or evidence in. This is particularly significant when a national court deals with international crimes.[114] For instance, one of the serious problems with the judges of the Rwanda tribunal was their juridical dependency. Consequently, the question of how to deliver justice for survivors was curiously given little attention during the procedures of the International Criminal Tribunal for Rwanda.[115]

> From 1997 to May 2002, 7,211 people accused of genocide were judged. This is an impressive achievement, especially in comparison to the ICTR's results. The Rwandan judicial system did so with the essential support of NGOs like Citizens' Network (RCN) and Lawyers Without Borders (ASF). It is important to underscore that no inmate is currently incarcerated without a charging file. This alone is a significant achievement by the prosecutor's offices.
> As for judicial independence, a majority of lawyers and magistrates estimated that judges are not independent from the executive power. This lack of independence has several sources: financial dependence on the executive branch, modest compensation that could lead to conflicts of interest, and a low level of training for a large number of judges, which weakens the judiciary overall. However, the self-censorship by judges themselves was noted as a strongly determinative factor of dependence. Magistrates must have the courage to exercise their judicial independence and denounce interference in their decision making by the Supreme Court and the National Commission on Human Rights (NCHR), even though they do not feel sufficiently protected by the Supreme Court.[116]

Any decision taken by a judge must be authentic, based on legitimate evidence, and should have independent nature. Additionally, the decisions

---

[114] For instance, consult Natasha Price, Kate Grady and Rachel Ibreck, On justice after sexual violence: Problems in Practice at the International Criminal Tribunal for Rwanda, Conference: Political Studies Association (2010), https://www.researchgate.net/publication/267306846_Problems_in_Practice_at_the_International_Criminal_Tribunal_for_Rwanda.

[115] *Id.*

[116] Assessment of the Judicial Sector in Rwanda, https://pdf.usa*Id*.gov/pdf_docs/PNACR573.pdf.

of judges must be justified through a written or oral statement, depending upon the gravity of the given crime and the way in which the judge presents their final decision. The reasons of the judges may thus be given in the court when they issue their decision on the case. The written reasons are given when the decision is delivered and then the judge makes their final decision at a later time in order to close the case.

In the case that a jury is present during a trial, the judge should comply with their decision about the case. A judge must ensure that the rules are being followed in this case and cannot ignore the rules of procedures based on the fact that juries make their decisions based upon evidence and reason. The jury agrees about which evidence is relevant and legitimate, and makes their decision about the case in compliance with the directions given by the judge. Therefore, the judge is responsible for giving clear instructions concerning relevant laws, and it is with these instructions in mind that the jury hears the case and arrives at their decision.

In the system of international criminal justice, judges of courts or tribunals should also clearly state the justifications for their judgements. Similarly, the judges of the ICC are responsible for basing their judgements in reason and justifying why they reached the conclusion that they did. The essential function of justification is particularly imperative in the case of international crimes which have a broader aspect of recognition and relate to the criminalisation of certain criminal conducts. The margin of genocide, for example, cannot be proven without logical reasoning concerning why the judges of the ICC believe that the circumstances and evidence presented in the case imply the commission of crimes such as crimes against humanity, war crimes, and genocide.

4.7. Development of Practical Moral Conscience

While there may be some disagreement about the meanings of the principles of "ethics" and "morality," both initially had the same value and fulfilled the same function in the system of criminal justice, and judges have often used the terms interchangeably.[117] Although the principal logic behind these principles may be similar, the notion of morality is based on the personal moral capacity to distinguish between good and bad, while ethics relate to compliance with certain rules of criminal law which distinguish between good and bad, and right and wrong. This means that both notions evaluate our actions, decisions, and judgements.

The definition of 'wrong' is similar under both principles; however the definitions may differ when a judge of the international criminal court reaches a conclusion which is ethical, yet seen as wrong by other judges. This means that their personal moral opinions and codified ethical understandings and conclusions converge in the final stage of interpretation. However, there are situations in which no ethical code of conduct exists in the evaluation of criminal justice at the time of the commission of international crimes. In this case, the judges of an international criminal court may evaluate an ethical code retroactively or base their judgement on their personal moral opinions. This was done after the Second World War when the judges of the International Criminal Tribunal in Nuremberg referred to consolidated moral attitudes of the civilisation of mankind and emphasised that the criminal conducts of the German government were in violation of the principle of morality, and therefore could not be tolerated by human civilisation.[118]

The conclusion of judges of the Nuremberg Tribunal led to German criminals being prosecuted for their crimes. Thus, the standard of humanity took priority to the lack of an appropriate code of ethics in international criminal justice. This means that although we have two different sources for the implementation of good or bad, in certain cases which lack a code of ethics, the personal moral codes of civilisation can function in its place. A further example of this was the case of the 60,000 Muslim Bosnian

---

[117] Consult also MacIntyre, *After Virtue: A Study in Moral Theory*, note 38.

[118] See Ronald Slye, *The Nuremberg Principles in Non-western Societies: A Reflection on their Universality, Legitimacy and Application* (International Nuremberg Principles Academy, 2017); George Augustus Finch, 'The Nuremberg Trial and International Law,' 41 *American Journal of International Law* (1947). Malekian, 'Comparative Substantive International Criminal Justice', note 23, pp.10-44.

women who were raped during the Yugoslav Wars, as it was unclear whether or not these rapes could be considered war crimes. However, the judges of the ICTY decided that they had to be considered as such.

4.8. Morality of Sleeping during Procedures

One of the serious issues plaguing criminal justice arises when one finds out that certain judges or some jury members fell asleep during court procedures, which naturally affects the outcome of the trial and the integrity of the proceedings.[119] Judges may fall asleep during trials for a number of reasons including sleep deprivation, warm court rooms, boredom or lack of interest, or because they have already made their mind up about the case. For instance, in a Japanese criminal court which I was visiting, there were four judges present– two were napping and one was sleeping during the proceedings. This phenomenon is not exclusive to Japan and can be observed in many other courts. Thus, the question becomes how can a decision have integrity if the judges were not fully present for the duration of the trial because they fell asleep?

The functions of criminal courts, criminal justice, and criminal judges, bear a particular demanding duty to serve as guarantors of accurate justice and appropriate outcomes. This demanding duty of judges becomes more important if a judge falls asleep during the trial.[120] In a complaint made by the condemned, a court decided that judges falling asleep has no bearing on a case. Thus, a judge falling asleep did not lead to a mistrial in this case "Because the evidence in this case was overwhelming and the parties did not call upon the trial judge to make any evidentiary rulings at a time when the judge was asleep, the judge falling asleep was harmless error."[121] However, this motivation of the court has been rejected in other earlier

---

119 Matthew Hector, *Justice Never Sleeps – but what if a Judge Does?* https,://www.isba.org/ibj/2018/01/lawpulse/justiceneversleeps-whatifjudgedoes; Rhandi Childress, *Convicted by a Sleeping Jury: Harmless Error or a Challenge to the Integrity of our Criminal Justice System*, 44 J. Marshall L. Rev. 751 (2011).

120 Spree-killer Nicholas Sheley, *People v. Sheley,* 2017 IL App (3d) 140659.

121 *Id.*, paras.16 and 21.

cases including one in which a dissenting Justice O'Brien argued that "falling asleep in the instant case was tantamount to the judge physically leaving the bench in *Vargas*."[122]

For the dissent, sleeping or napping during the trial is equivalent to a judge leaving the courtroom in *People v. Vargas*.[123] O'Brien therefore argued that falling asleep indicates that the relevant judge is "unable to supervise the courtroom, rule on objections as they arise during the course of the proceedings, and deter any objectionable conduct to the detriment of the defendant," and that "the judge falling asleep could have given the jurors the impression that the trial was unimportant or that they did not need to pay close attention to the testimony of the witness."[124]

According to one author, in order to solve the problem of judges falling asleep in court, we must establish certain rules within the judiciary. Thus, the trial judge should instruct the jury that they must stay awake and attentive throughout the duration of the trial. Judges should also emphasise the importance of being completely conscious and aware of everything during the trial. Another recommendation is that it should be clearly emphasised that sleeping in the jury box is expressly prohibited. The final element of the instruction should present an affirmative action regarding how the jurors can react in order to remedy this problem during trial. This includes allowing the option for jurors to ask for a break if multiple jury members feel drowsy. In that case, one may inform the judge if a juror feels like they might fall asleep. Jurors can also make an effort to keep fellow jurors attentive if they witness someone is tired or dozing off.[125] Moreover,

> With new pre-trial jury instructions implemented that create a duty for jurors to remain awake and attentive, naturally, courts should have a similar duty. Consistent with what some courts have already held, trial courts should have an affirmative duty to conduct a hearing after being

---

122 *Id.*, para.35.

123 174 Ill.2d 355 (1996).

124 *Id.*, paras.35-36.

125 Rhandi Childress, Convicted by a Sleeping Jury: Harmless Error or a Challenge to the Integrity of our Criminal Justice System, 44 *J. Marshall L. Rev.* 751 (2011), p.768.

> reliably informed that a juror is sleeping. The purpose of this hearing is to determine the extent of a sleeping juror's inattentiveness, including what portions of trial were missed. This hearing also serves as added protection from reversal on appeal. If the court finds that a juror was asleep during a substantial portion of trial, that particular juror should be replaced with an alternate. If, on the other hand, the court finds that the juror was not asleep during a substantial portion of trial, then the trial can proceed with the hearing on the issue in the record. Of course, creating this new duty curbs the amount of trial court discretion in handling sleeping jurors, but it does not eliminate it. The judge still has discretion regarding the findings made from the hearing.[126]

The examples provided above are just a selection from many examples around the world, and the issue of judges falling asleep is especially common when judges have other jobs and are unable to be fully rested for trial. This has occasionally been seen in United States. As has been stated, "A judge cannot be actively present on the bench when he is asleep."[127] Similarly, in Australia "the judge in *Cesan and Mas Rivadavia's case* fell asleep for significant periods during the proceedings, which caused concern to both of the defendants and their criminal lawyers."[128] In the United Kingdom a female judge slept while hearing a case about children: "While concluding that this amounted to conduct which had the potential to undermine public confidence in the judiciary, the Lord Chancellor and the Lord Chief Justice took into consideration that the judge fell asleep only momentarily and has expressed remorse."[129]

In Sweden, in a criminal case in the Court of Appeals "the judges fell asleep during the negotiations according to both lawyers and prosecutors,"

---

[126] *Id.*, p.769.

[127] Steve Schmadeke, Judges sleeping through evidence not cause for new trial, Illinois appeals court says (2017), https://www.chicagotribune.com/news/breaking/ct-met-judges-can-sleep-during-trial-20171105-story.html; see also Viveca Novak, The Case of the Sleeping Justice (2008), https://www.factcheck.org/2008/11/the-case-of-the-sleeping-justice/.

[128] Ugur Nedim, *Judges that Fall Asleep During Trials* (2015), https://nswcourts.com.au/articles/judges-that-fall-asleep-during-trials/.

[129] James Mills, SNORE COURT Judge, 68, disciplined for FALLING ASLEEP while hearing a case in the High Court: Lawyers complained after a judge dozed off while hearing important details of a High Court case (2019), https://www.thesun.co.uk/news/8387146/judge-68-disciplined-for-falling-asleep-while-hearing-a-case-in-the-high-court/.

which meant that the case had to be retried.[130] In the *Blagoveshchensk* case in Russia a video demonstrated that "le procès pendant lequel le juge s'était endormi avait abouti à la condamnation de l'accusé à cinq ans de camp." (During the trial the judge fell asleep, which resulted in the accused being sentenced to five years in a work camp).[131]

A judge falling asleep during a trial therefore prompts serious discussions about the validity of court decisions. This is particularly significant if the lawyer of the condemned complains. There may be some alternatives for the submission of complaints, but the question remains the same about the ethical, legal, or moral validity of a decision made by a judge who was not fully present during the trial. Sleeping or napping during a trial can lead to an atmosphere of prejudice due to the absence of ethical discipline and may even harm the value of the administration of criminal justice.

4.9. Violation of the Code of Morality by Judges

All these considerations described in the aforementioned sections depend on the freedom of a judge to express their opinions freely and without fear of repercussions. For example in an Islamic court, a judge may understand that the punishment of someone for possessing a bottle of wine is certainly not logical and cannot be based on good moral conscience. The judge may believe that punishment for this "crime" violates international human rights law and yet still issue the punishment in order to not be criticised by Islamic authorities. Furthermore, in certain cases, a judge may lose their position based on the order of a high mullah (priest), who is also the chief of the administration of criminal justice in a city. This means that a judge may obey the rules and respect the role of criminal justice, while

---

130 Domare sov - rättegång görs om, https://www.gp.se/nyheter/sverige/domare-sov-r%C3%A4tteg%C3%A5ng-g%C3%B6rs-om-1.692879.

131 Le juge dort en audience: la vidéo qui scandalise la Russie (2013), https://www.sudouest.fr/2013/01/31/le-juge-dort-en-audience-la-video-qui-scandalise-la-russie-952423-4803.php?nic.

at the same time violating their own proper conscience. Such judges differentiate between good and bad in accordance with the provisions of the law, and not in accordance with the conscience of humanity and the moral and ethical rules of criminal justice.

Thus, judges in certain regions may only follow the order of the criminal justice of the big political parties or religious authorities, which means they may uphold laws which should have been abandoned centuries ago. However, it is hard to express why judges who have accepted moral and ethical legal principles do this. No reliable patterns exist in analysing their moral and legal accountability before the system of ethical morality which has been established by different codes of ethics. The judgements of any judge from a region which follow the order of religious authorities, certainly violate the system of international criminal justice and the Code of Judicial Ethics. The worst thing that judges can do is to cover up criminal activity and hide the truth from the public. These expressions of conscience give the wrong impression of the legislation of such countries, and of judges dealing with victims, offenders, and witnesses of national or international crimes in order to deliver judgments.[132]

---

[132] Examine following sources A. Cassese, *The Human Dimension of International Law. Selected Papers* (2008); Farhad Malekian, *International Criminal Law, the Law of Somebodiness, the Law of Nobodiness* (New York, Nova Publishers, 2021); Farhad Malekian, *Judgments of Love in Criminal Justice*, note 1; Malekian, *Documents on the Principles of International Human Rights* (2007); Farhad Malekian, 'Armenian Genocide and the Questions of Responsibility of the Turkish Government,'*House of Commons Conference on the Armenian Genocide, Armenian Solidarity, British-Armenian All-Party Parliamentary Group, No Security Publication* (2007), pp.31-9; Andrew Clapham, 'the Role of the Individual in International Law', 21 (1) *The European Journal of International Law* (2010), pp.25-30; Farhad Malekian, *Prohibition Governing Child Soldiers Constituting an Integral Part of Jus cogens and Obligatio Erga Omnes*, XVII *World Congress of the International Association of Youth and Family Judges and Magistrates*, Belfast, Northern Ireland, 27 August – 2 September (2006); Farhad Malekian, 'Emasculating the Philosophy of International Criminal Justice in the Iraqi Special Tribunal,' *Cornell International Law Journal*, 58/5 (2005), pp.675-725; Farhad Malekian, 'The Child as an Autonomous Subject of Justice' in Farhad Malekian, Kerstin Nordlöf, *Sovereignty of Children in Law* (Cambridge: Cambridge Scholars Publishing, 2012), pp. 2-55; Farhad Malekian, 'The Laws Governing Crimes against Women Constituting *Obligatio Erga Omnes*' in David Wingeate Pike, Crimes Against Women (New York: Nova Science Publishers, 2011);Tilmann Altwicker, 'Transnationalizing Rights: International Human Rights Law in Cross-Border Contexts', 29 (2) *European Journal of International Law* (2018), pp.581–606.

Our dissent does not try to paint a picture of authoritarian regimes, but rather explain how judges from certain regions violate the system of traditional ethics, even within their own legal regions. Thus, we are discussing the result of a criminal administration when it is ignored even by its own judges and the actions of the court are not based on traditional moral support. Whatever one may glean from that effort, the consequence is that trust in the system of criminal justice disappears, which is dangerous. For example, in countries such as Iran, Saudi Arabia, Egypt, China, Romania, and Russia, judges are respected, not based on the quality of their decisions, but due to their national positions and ability to take action against defendants including corruption. The code of morality for the mechanism of criminal justice is almost unknown. Simultaneously, the code of morality has a broad definition:

> We may have different interpretations of the principles of human rights law, and we may argue about the boundaries of their imperative position in the system of criminal laws. We may also emphasise that a legal duty constitutes an obligation, but a moral duty does not. For these reasons, we may never accept our responsibilities concerning violations of criminal provisions of human rights law. This means when we deliver guns to certain groups or states or trade in such weapons and, as a result, genocide, crimes against humanity, and war crimes are committed, we may not be accepting our responsibility. We may say that we did so but not with the aim of killing or destroying. We may present various reasons because we want to prove that our conduct was justified, unjustified, reasonable, unreasonable, right, or wrong. All this means that we are aligning ourselves to a code of morality that permits us to perform certain acts, the consequences of which may be killings in other nations.[133]

Although the code of morality and ethical conscience should hold a great value and demand respect in the administration of criminal justice, they are often violated by judges of certain regimes, particularly those based on Islamic regulations. For example in Saudi Arabia, prisoners are treated worse than animals. The Saudi Arabian government even produces

---

[133] Malekian, *Judgments of Love in Criminal Justice*, note 1, p.68.

false evidence through the Specialised Criminal Court (SCC) which is a political tool used to silence critical voices. The SCC was established in 2008 to condemn the terrorist acts against the Saudi Arabian government. A number of prisoners have been executed under the Court orders, with no right to appeal or to have lawyers. There are therefore a large number of political prisoners in Saudi Arabia who have not committed crimes, but rather promoted the establishment of the system of international human rights law and thus frightened the Saudi Arabian government. This has led to the detention of opposition members under the guise of counterterrorism. Similarly, a large number of Iranian prisoners are treated worse than animals under the authority of the Islamic Republic of Iran. This is seen particularly with the instances of torture, rape, and murder reported in *Evin Prison*. These political prisoners are the victims of international crimes—and the judges of the nation are aware of that fact. A notorious case brought to the recognition of Swedish authorities in Stockholm, is a criminal case concerning the brutal of conducts of Hamid Noury who is accused of committing serious violations of international human rights law and international criminal law. He helped to carry out acts of torture, capital punishment, and execution, while also serving as a prosecutor and assistant to a judge.

Chapter 5

Judges Performing the International Legal Personality of the ICC

5.1. Judicial Ethics of Judges in the ICC

Although the standard of judicial ethics for all judges of the world should be the same, there are unfortunately always some differences in the ethical considerations between states. This is especially significant in the case of the code of judicial ethics of the judges of the International Criminal Court. This is based on the fact that the ICC has its own international legal personality, and is therefore a model for the development of the judicial ethics of criminal jurisdiction for judges and other individuals involved in the administration of criminal justice. It is on this account that the public believes that the judges of the ICC are strongly motivated individuals who act in accordance with the Code of Judicial Ethics of the ICC (Code).[134]

Accordingly, the Code emphasises some of the most significant facts regarding the character, duties, and responsibilities of the judges. Due to

---

[134] For the Code see appendix.

the provisions in its preamble, the judges of the ICC, with due regard for Article 45 of the Rome Statute and rule 5 (1) (a) of the Rules of Procedure and Evidence, recall the principles concerning judicial independence, proper conduct, impartiality, and the insurance of the legitimacy and effectiveness of the international judicial process. They should respect the standards offset by the United Nations Basic Principles on the Independence of the Judiciary and any other international and national rules. The Code clearly states in its Article 11 that the principles presented in it "shall serve as guidelines on the essential ethical standards required of judges in the performance of their duties. They are advisory in nature and have the object of assisting judges with respect to ethical and professional issues with which they are confronted." Thereby clarifying that the principles embodied in the Code should not "in any way to limit or restrict the judicial independence of the judges." Therefore, with due regard to the responsibility of the judges of the ICC, the principles outlined in the following sections have been emphasised as being fundamentally significant for the function of the Court.

5.2. Judicial Independence of ICC

The judicial independence of the ICC is critical to the system of justice and is regulated in Article 3 of the Code of Judicial Ethics of the ICC.[135] This means that judges shall preserve the independence of their office in all times and shall not violate this independence. Judges are obliged to conduct themselves according to the principle of independence, and accordingly carry out their duties. Moreover, the judges of the ICC are required to not engage in any activity which may interfere with their

---

[135] "The elements of independence and objectivity institutionalize the quality of criminal justice in national or international aspect. Seeking responsibility of the prosecutor for the quality of criminal justice is solely an aspiration and cannot truly be achieved if the criminal justice of a country is plagued by the interference from authorities. Quality is not measured upon the statutes of national or international criminal courts but by how and how long they have preserved their objectivity and independence in political issues. Justice should not be imprisoned with injustice, although it often is." Malekian, *Conscience of Prosecutors in International Criminal Law, The Heart of the Matter*, note 3, p.29.

judicial functions, or insert themselves into situations which may affect confidence in the independence of their function. The nature of judicial independence and its maintenance is essential since the Court cannot function without it, and its judgements can be criticised if the independence of the Court is violated by the judges.

The question is more significant when one considers the difference between the judicial independence of the ICC and other international entities, taking into consideration that the ICC has its own international legal personality. This means the ICC is independent from other international entities or organisations and can make its own independent decisions and also sign international treaties with any state or the United Nations. The judicial independence of judges implies that they must be free to exercise their judicial powers without interference from litigants, any other state, or even the United Nations itself.[136]

Additionally, due to the principle of judicial independence, judges shall not engage in any activity which is likely to interfere with their judicial functions or which could decrease trust and confidence in their independence regarding all matters, including their decisions. Judicial independence of the Court is particularly important when one considers that any irrational conduct by any of the judges of the Court may affect the legal and social positions of all other judges, and thus lead to mistrust in the court and the guarantee for the objectivity of the judges disappearing.

5.3. Impartiality of Judges of the ICC

The principle of impartiality, as mentioned elsewhere, contains the most significant message to the pure jurisdiction of a criminal court and should be considered the main pillar of criminal justice, and particularly of the system of international criminal justice. This principle has also been taken under serious consideration by the Code of Judicial Ethics of the

---

[136] Ruth Mackenzie & Philippe Sands, 'International Courts and Tribunals and the Independence of the International Judge', 44 *Harv. Int'l L. J.* (2003), pp.271. 275.

ICC.[137] The ICC situates this principle as the most imperative for the Court and its purity. According to the provisions of Article 4 of the Code, the impartiality of the judges in the administration of criminal justice is guaranteed. Accordingly, "judicial independence is critical for the rule law."[138]

Judges of the ICC shall remain impartial in their judgements, activities, conducts, and decisions. They should ensure impartiality in the discharge of their judicial functions. This principle of the Code constitutes one of the most significant duties of the judges of the ICC, which judges must respect under all circumstances. Based on the principle of impartiality, the Code requires judges to avoid any conflicts of interest and any situations which could result in financial, political, cultural, ethical, or social interference in a case.

The intention of the Code is to emphasise that the impartiality of the judges of the ICC is a pillar that should not be violated under any circumstances. Impartiality in fact the central principle of the ICC, and the judges should not only respect this principle, but should view the principle as part of judicial conscience and the high the value of the rules of the Statute of the ICC and its Court. Since the judges of the Court are the most vital elements in the existence of the Court and in its decisions, the principle should be regarded as an integral part of the substantive rules of the administration of international criminal justice. The principle of impartiality may also be asserted as constituting the core of appropriate judgements.

Although international criminal courts and tribunals have codified a number of guidelines and principles regarding the ethical, moral, and judicial conscience of judges, the question is still metaphorical when it comes to emphasising what is good or bad, and what is right or wrong. Some of these international legal bodies, including the ICC, have, as we will see, supplemented certain codified legal documents in order to specify the obligations inherent in the exercise of the functions of the judges of the

---

[137] Theodor Meron, 'Judicial Independence and Impartiality in International Criminal Tribunals'. 99 (2) *American Journal of International Law* (2005), pp.359-369.

[138] *Id.*, p,359.

court. Furthermore, the ICC has adopted a range of rules and principles which must be implemented in the procedures of Court in order to ensure the impartiality of the judges.[139] As we will see, judges of the ICC should follow the Rules of Procedure and Evidence and the binding character of the Code of Judicial Ethics. Additionally, the Court has established comprehensive ethical standards for the defence counsel. These are comparable to those developments made by the International Criminal Tribunal for the former Yugoslavia (ICTY and the International Criminal Tribunal for Rwanda. The crimes which were investigated by the Rwanda Tribunal were some of the most savage crimes ever committed by one group against another. It is correctly asserted that:

> The Rwandan genocide stands alone for the way its organizers aimed to mobilize mass participation in murder. Far from hiding their objective, they advertised their goal of exterminating the Tutsi citizens of Rwanda in song and chant, through the press and over the radio. They exhorted Hutu to join the killing campaign, insisting that it "concerned everyone." They carried out the worst massacres in broad daylight and in many communities they left the dead in full view. By focusing fear and hatred on the Tutsi, the organizers hoped to forge solidarity among Hutu. But beyond that, they also aimed at creating collective responsibility for the genocide. People were encouraged to kill together, just as soldiers in a firing squad are ordered to discharge their weapons simultaneously so

---

[139] It is rightly stated that "The ICTR and ICTY were perceived to be political courts from their inception and may not have been in a position to acknowledge nationality-based challenges to the impartiality of their judges. However, international criminal justice has advanced such that recourse to the ICC is no longer considered especially controversial.288 The ICC and future ICTs, unlike the ad hoc tribunals, can acknowledge that judges are not always impervious to the interests of their states. The ICC and future ICTs should not place judges in the position of having to represent the international community in cases involving crimes allegedly committed by or against their fellow nationals. Judges should also consider recusing themselves in other cases that substantially implicate the interests of their states. A belief in international criminal justice is not incompatible with the recognition that judges' national allegiances do not entirely dissipate once they assume the robes of office." Milan Markovic, 'International Criminal Trials and the Disqualification of Judges on International Criminal Trials and the Disqualification of Judges on the Basis of Nationality the Basis of Nationality', 13 (1) *Washington University Global Studies Law Review* (2014), pp.1-48. Available online at https://openscholarship.wustl.edu/cgi/viewcontent.cgi?article=1472&context=law_globals tudies

that no one should bear individual or total responsibility for the execution. "No one person killed any one person," said one of the participants.

The leaders of the genocide, experienced at wielding power, knew how to use the state machinery and their network of personal contacts to mobilize large numbers of people. They expected to succeed and had planned carefully for the operation. With their quick, ruthless murders of political opponents that began on April 6, they intimidated the remaining dissidents. Then, strengthened by their apparent acceptance as a legitimate government by the international community, they pushed ahead with a speed and ease that may have exceeded their own expectations. By two weeks into the campaign, they had slain hundreds of thousands of Tutsi and squashed any significant open dissent. But ultimately they failed in their goal of total mobilization for extermination. Hundreds of thousands of Hutu who lacked the courage or resources to openly oppose them resisted passively, most by withdrawing from political and community life, a few by working within the system to restrain its excesses.

Among those who did carry out genocide, actors participated in many ways: from the national leaders who aimed to extirpate the Tutsi down to the level of ordinary people who showed no taste for violence but wanted only to enrich themselves through pillage. As the roles varied, so did the motivations of the actors, some moved by virulent hatred, others by real fear, by ambition, by greed, by a desire to escape injury at the hands of those who demanded they participate, or by the wish to avoid fines for nonparticipation that they could not hope to pay. Whatever the role, whatever the motivation, participants must accept responsibility and be appropriately punished. Outside Rwanda, most international leaders found mass slaughter of Tutsi tolerable provided it furthered or at least did not impinge on narrowly defined national interests. Many of their subordinates would not risk loss of favour and future advancement by arguing a moral position contrary to the course advocated by the powerful. A small number of foreigners did fight passionately to stop the slaughter, some in humanitarian and human rights organizations, some in governments and the U.N. An even smaller number struggled to save lives courageously within Rwanda.

> Accurate accounts of the genocide must establish in all their complexity the roles of the leaders, the followers, and the dissidents within Rwanda as well as the parts played by various international actors. This is essential both for assessing fairly the behaviour of individuals and for creating strategies for the future. We must find ways to increase the numbers and effectiveness of resisters against such crimes, whether within or outside the society at risk. We must understand how local and international protest can resonate back and forth to create the swell of outrage that will prevent or halt future genocides.[140]

Nonetheless, the issue of genocide and crimes against humanity are not still understood correctly by all judges of international criminal courts.[141] It is more problematic when one looks at the genocides which are being committed in the Middle East, although they are not treated as such. As a result, the perpetrators of these crimes go without punishment. This problem has still not been solved due to different cultural understandings of ethical conscience, moral capability, and judicial independence. For instance, a judge from Hungary, Romania, or Spain is more accustomed and familiar with having external interference in justice proceedings than judges from other states in Europe. We are also fully aware of the fact that in most sensitive political situations, within almost all European states, independence of the judiciary may be briefly suspended. This was seen with the case of Julian Assange in Stockholm and London, for instance. That is why the rules of the Code of Judicial Ethics remain open to various

---

[140] *Human Rights Watch, Justice and Responsibility* (1999). https://www.hrw.org/reports/1999/rwanda/Geno15-8-05.htm.

[141] Generally consult Malekian, *Jurisprudence of International Criminal Justice*, note 105. Malekian, 'The Homogeneity of International Criminal Court with Islamic Jurisprudence,' note 20, pp.595-621; Malekian, *Principles of Islamic International Criminal Law: A Comparative Search*, note 20; Farhad Malekian, *'Islamic Law Justice Systems' in* Jay S. Albanese, *The Encyclopaedia of Criminology and Criminal Justice*(United States: Wiley-Blackwell (5 volumes, 2013), vol. III, pp.1220-1225; Farhad Malekian, 'The Canon of Love against the Use of Force in Islamic and Public International Law: Part II: The Anatomy of Love Against Violations,' 15 *International Criminal Law Review*, 2015), pp. 861-895; Farhad Malekian, 'The Canon of Love against the Use of Force in Islamic and Public International Law: Part I: The Chamber of Love within Legal Discipline,' 15 *International Criminal Law Review*, 2015), pp. 591-628; Malekian, 'Comparative Substantive International Criminal Justice,' note 23, pp. 10-44.

interpretations based on social, cultural, legal, and political views. According to one opinion:

> The disagreement over the proper characterization of the Prosecution's conduct in Furundžija illustrates the difficulties in creating a corpus of ethical standards that is genuinely shared by more than one hundred states and a wide variety of cultures and legal traditions. The absence of clear and precise standards risks creating a profound feeling of uncertainty around what is expected of each individual who participates in the proceedings. Codifying clear rules and thresholds, on the other hand, seems to reduce these risks, but only to a certain extent: the terms used in the various Codes are often vague and open to divergent interpretations, and because they are interpreted and applied by Tribunals on an ad hoc basis, they do not entirely eliminate unpredictability.[142]

Furthermore, certain international courts demand the impartiality of their judges, procedures, and judgements. They therefore require sincerity alongside impartiality. A clear example of this is the ICTY Appeals Chamber, which, in one of its judgements in the Furundžija case, placed their faith into the European Court of Human Rights and its jurisprudence. The Chamber's requirement of impartiality demands that a tribunal is "not only genuinely impartial, but also appears to be impartial," and that to assess the "appearance of impartiality," a tribunal should see whether the situation would require a reasonable and informed observer to step in due to questioning bias.[143] This way of approaching the question of impartiality and its legal scope appears to have set a framework for the impartiality of judges in international criminal proceedings. It has also been followed by other national and international courts and tribunals.

---

[142] Cima, 'Ethical Conduct in International Criminal Courts: Whose Ethics?', note 37, p.300.

[143] Prosecutor v. Anto Furundžija, Case No. IT-95-17/1-A, Appeal Judgment, paras. 182, 189 (Int'l Crim. Trib. for the Former Yugoslavia, July 21, 2000).

5.4. Integrity of Judges in the ICC

Significantly, the principle of integrity constitutes a key principle in a number of international agreements, including the ethical guidelines for judges from other countries. The term "integrity" constitutes a comprehensive concept that embodies several different characteristics of judicial ethics. The term implies, among other things, that judges should remain independent and reject every form of external influence. Judges must consequently be independent in their adjudication. They should have the courage to dissent to any painful or uncomfortable decisions. The judges of any court must certainly avoid acting unwisely and unethically, as this could harm the integrity and independence of the court. The fact is that "integrity" is invaluable to all jurisdictions, especially when we talk about the independence of criminal jurisdictions. Thus, any actions carried out by judges must conform with independence, impartiality, and equal treatment, as well as with good conduct and the proper treatment of others.

One of the vital questions relating to the administration of criminal justice, particularly in the ICC, relates to the integrity of judges of the ICC. This is specifically dealt with in Article 5 of the Code. The relevant article emphasises the importance of the nature of the integrity of a judge in a criminal case and its significant role in the outcome of a judgment. Accordingly, judges shall conduct themselves with probity and integrity in accordance with the provisions of their office, thereby increasing public confidence in the judiciary system and the administration of criminal justice by the ICC.[144] That is also one of the reasons why the provisions of Article 6 of the Code encourage and demand that the judges of the ICC

---

[144] However, "When the ICC intervenes in ongoing armed conflicts between different states or groups, in which foreign political powers are involved, it becomes very difficult for the court to maintain its ethical moral standard, and its policy of prosecution and punishment may thereby be weakened. Two clear examples of this are the Syrian and Yemeni Wars, in which many political parties and militarily strong states are involved; therefore, the ICC should not be 'surprised to find itself ending up in political struggles.'" Malekian, *Conscience of Prosecutors in International Criminal Law, The Heart of the Matter*, note 3, p.131. See also O'Connell, '*Jus cogens*: International Law's Higher Ethical Norms' in Childress, DE III (ed.), *The Role of Ethics in International Law* (2012).

respect the confidentiality of consultations which relate to their judicial functions and the secrecy of deliberations. Therefore, the principle of confidentiality constitutes one of the main pillars of the system of criminal justice, ensures an appropriate preparation of judgements, and preserves the impartiality of the procedures of justice.

The Code particularly emphasises that the judges of the ICC shall not directly or indirectly accept, receive, take, admit, consent, or agree to take any kind of gift, advantage, privilege, or reward in connection with delivering a certain outcome. Such behaviour or conduct may reasonably be perceived as being intended to influence the fulfilment and performance of their judicial functions. The provisions of Article 5 (2) attempt to prevent any form of money laundering or corruption in the administration of criminal justice by the ICC. Such actions are common among judges across the globe, which is why the Code seeks to prevent such behaviour. However, the conducts of the former prosecutor of the ICC proved the contrary.[145]

5.5. Pillar of Diligence of the Judges of ICC

The Code has also taken the principle of judicial conscience into account and developed it under the pillar of diligence in its Article 7. Accordingly, the judges of the ICC are required to act diligently in the performance and exercise of their given duties under the Statute of the ICC, and shall devote their professional activities to the fulfilment of these duties. This implies that the judges of the ICC should take any necessary and reasonable steps to uphold and enhance their knowledge, their skills, and personal qualities required by the judicial office of the ICC. In particular, judges are required to perform all judicial duties properly, accurately, appropriately, and expeditiously. The Code requires that the judges of the ICC deliver their decisions and any other rulings without delay in order to keep the procedures running as efficiently as possible.

---

[145] See *infra*.

The requirement for the diligence of the judges of the ICC has intended to shape good judges who find it important to maintain their knowledge, ability, and capacity of understanding criminal justice, and who know to limit their conclusions to their limited criminal legal knowledge. The principle of diligence therefore encourages the judges of the ICC to fully carry out their judicial duties with talent, cleverness, proficiency, and skill. They should give full attention to all matters and react competently and promptly. All this means that the judges of the ICC are responsible for devoting themselves to their judicial obligations and duties towards establishing the truth. Judicial diligence is an imperative measure of judicial performance and can be measured by a judge's attentiveness to oral argument, speedy disposition towards pending matters, preparation of qualified cases, and their willingness to work diligently and with rational punctuality in writing judgements. This means that one can achieve a satisfactory case-completion-rate compatible with upholding the lofty guidelines of justice, objectivity, and equality.

There is no difference between male and female judges when it comes to their diligence. The gender of a judge should not make a difference in their competence because both male and female judges are both able to satisfactorily perform their duties. A judge should be evaluated on their skills as a director of criminal justice. Additionally, judges should devote ample time to all pending matters, no matter who is involved in the case. They should also diligently discharge all their criminal administrative duties. This also implies the fact that a judge should be evaluated on their precision concerning the prompt disposition of pending matters under consideration or examination. They should therefore perform their duties according to the rules of the code of ethics and the given rules of the court.

In other words, the reasonable efficiency of the judges of the ICC is important for the creation and establishment of correct procedures and judgements. Judges should avoid extending the length of trials of the Court by all means. They should close a satisfactory proportion of cases while upholding high guidelines of justice and equality with full objectivity. Judges should prevent any unnecessary delay of criminal justice and should try to be flexible in gathering the necessary evidence for a case.

Correspondingly, judges of the ICC should sufficiently carry out the directorial functions of the Court in their imperative role. They should also continue to preserve the truthful records of cases and not hide or destroy any relevant evidence.[146]

It is also relevant to mention here that the respect of the principle of diligence can also be seen in the discussions of regional courts. For example, The Inter-American Court, in its exceptional judgement relating to the *Bulacio* case, qualified the rights of victims to swift justice and highlighted that justice should always be served within a reasonable timeframe.[147] The Inter-American Court stated:

> This manner of exercising the means that the law makes available to the defence counsel has been tolerated and allowed by the intervening judiciary bodies, forgetting that their function is not exhausted by enabling due process that guarantees defence at a trial, but that they must also ensure, within a reasonable time, the right of the victim or his or her next of kin to learn the truth about what happened and for those responsible to be punished...the right to effective judicial protection therefore requires that the judges direct the process in such a way that undue delays and hindrances do not lead to impunity, thus frustrating adequate and due protection of human rights.[148]

5.6. Behaviours of the ICC Judges

Behaviour of judges, the manner in which they talk, their wisdom of understanding, and their ability to speak with intention are some of the most significant ways that judges uphold the rules of ethics and ensure that they have the case under their control. These are some of the basic standards for the judges of any court and they ensure that the procedures

[146] New ICC Judges Must Ensure the Meaningful Participation of Victims in Criminal Proceedings, available online at https://www.fidh.org/IMG/pdf/iccjudges759ang_final.pdf.

[147] Bulacio Case, Judgement of September 18, 2003, Inter-Am. Ct. H.R., (Ser. C) No. 100 (2003), paras. 114 and 115. Available at http://www1.umn.edu/humanrts/iachr/C/100-ing.html (Accessed April 29, 2015).

[148] *Id.*

of criminal justice are not carried out under duress, and that all parties are treated with respect and are not degraded by the judges or the administration of criminal justice. Moreover, the use of inappropriate language or impolite, discourteous, rude, offensive, or aggressive behaviour goes against the integrity of the judges and the administration of the legal discipline, and may thus lead to retaliation.

Particular attention is given to the conduct of the judges of the ICC during court proceedings. This is covered in Article 8 of the Code. This article helps orient the judges in conducting judicial proceedings to keep and maintain order. As such, judges should act in accordance with commonly accepted decorum. Judges should also remain patient and courteous towards all parties to a case, as well as towards the members of the public. They should also require all participants at hearings to act the same. The judges of the ICC should exercise vigilance in controlling their manner of questioning witnesses or victims.[149] They must carry out any investigations and interrogations in accordance with the established rules.[150] They should also give special attention to the right of participants to be treated equally and to be protected by the law. It goes without saying that judges of the ICC shall avoid carrying out any conduct or make any comments which are racist, sexist, or otherwise degrading to the parties involved in the case in general. The judges should also ensure, to the best of their ability, that any person participating in the proceedings of the case refrains from making such irrational comments or carrying out such conducts.

5.7. Freedom of Expression of ICC Judges

The judges of the ICC are also restricted in most matters in order to protect their independent judgements, however they do still have the

---

[149] Examine *also* Elisabeth Baumgartner, 'Aspects of Victim Participation in the Proceedings of the International Criminal Court', 90 (870) *International Review of the Red Cross* (2008), pp.409-440. Available online at https://www.corteidh.or.cr/tablas/R21692.pdf.

[150] *Id.*

freedom of expression when it comes to certain matters. Freedom of expression constitutes an integral part of international human rights law, and as such the Code of Judicial Ethics of the ICC has also taken the social positions of the judges of the Court into consideration concerning their public expression and association in order not to restrict their private activities. Accordingly, the Code recognises the freedom of judges in certain social matters – under the condition that these freedoms not interfere with their duties relating to the ICC. Therefore, the ICC allows judges to exercise their freedom of expression and association; however they must conduct themselves in a manner that is compatible with the rules of their office.

Freedom of expression should not affect the judicial independence of the administration of criminal justice nor the impartiality of the judges of the ICC. While the freedom of expression and association for judges has been recognised, it has yet to be codified in a particular framework. Thus, although judges are free to participate in public debate on matters relating to legal or criminal subjects, they should still be very cautious with their statements and should not comment on pending cases. Judges should therefore avoid expressing views which may undermine the standing and integrity of the Court.

That is also the reason why Article 11 of the Code emphasises that nothing in the content of the Code is intended to restrict the judicial independence of the judges in any way. Article 11 deals with observance of the Code and consists of two sub-sections. The first sub-section reads: "1. The principles embodied in this Code shall serve as guidelines on the essential ethical standards required of judges in the performance of their duties. They are advisory in nature and have the object of assisting judges with respect to ethical and professional issues with which they are confronted." The second sub-section declares: "2. Nothing in this Code is intended in any way to limit or restrict the judicial independence of the judges."

5.8. External Judicial Activities of Judges

Generally speaking, judges should not be involved in any other juridical activities which could jeopardise the independence of the administration of criminal justice. It is particularly essential that judges limit their judicial involvement in matters or cases which could jeopardise their juridical conscience. The main intention of this principle is that the machinery of criminal justice must be pure concerning its judgements. However, certain legal provisions of criminal justice permit judges to carry out judicial activities, conducts, or actions which are not contrary to the rules of administration of criminal justice.

This is also clearly stated in the provisions of the Code of Judicial Ethics of the ICC which provides an outline for judges of the International Criminal Court. Article 10 of the Code of the ICC relates to these external judicial activities of judges. It clearly states that the judges of the ICC should not engage in any extra-judicial activity unless it is compatible with their present judicial function. This implies the fact that judges are not permitted to involve themselves in, or consent to, conducts or actions which are incompatible with their judicial requirements or their judicial conscience.

This requirement seeks to emphasise that any matter which reasonably appears to impact the administration of the ICC or its independence and the impartiality of relevant judges, cannot be valid and may be considered against the ethical norms of conducts. The intention of the ICC is clearly to create a safe and reliable atmosphere for the criminal jurisdiction as well as to prevent any other interference in the procedures of the case which may influence the outcome of the case and the lives of the parties involved. In other words, the external judicial activities of judges must be chosen with extreme caution and care in order to ensure the impartiality of criminal justice and the judges of the Court.[151]

---

[151] Consult Robert Cryer, *Prosecuting International Crimes, Selectivity and the International Criminal Law Regime* (Cambridge University Press, Cambridge, 2005).

5.9. Restrictions on the Political Functions of Judges

In order to ensure that the administration of criminal justice and the decisions of the judges of the ICC are not influenced by politics, the judges of the court are not permitted to participate in any political activities, carry out any conducts, or take on any positions which could jeopardise the independence of the court in order to preserve the integrity of the final decision. This principle is also one of the noteworthy principles that has been entered into the Code under the provisions of Article 10. The intention of the principle is to preserve the impartiality of the Court and the quality of the judgement in order to provide security for the parties involved in international crimes.

The impartiality of a judge in political matters, and their abstention from involving themselves in politics, should be respected at all, although it is quite doubtful that it is. The problem with the fact that judges of the ICC "shall not exercise any political function," is that it is nearly impossible to define what a political function is exactly, and where the boundaries are. There are obviously various understandings and explanations of the term "political function," which may only be a two-word phrase, but it hides within itself great questions of political motivation and is dependent on how people define political functions for themselves. As a matter of fact, some political functions, are invisible and difficult to discern. Moreover, the system of the ICC and its Courts are dependent on political motivation and support in order to continue to carry out their duties.

Many cases which are going to be submitted to the Court jurisdiction are first examined from a political standpoint. Thus, the ICC prosecutor must be engaged in political discussions in order to bring a case to the court. In other words, the office of the prosecutor of the ICC cannot achieve its mandate without carrying out "political functions." Although we fully respect and understand the philosophy behind this significant principle, one cannot deny the fact that the principle has several different interpretations. However, we believe that the ICC judges interpret the principle with good faith and good moral conscience as well as love for pure humanity in order to preserve the independence of the ICC. All these principles are still an integral part of *obligatio erga*.[152]

5.10. Clarity of the Language of Judges

The language which is used in a court and the writings which come out of it are very vital for the administration of criminal justice, particularly when the judges of a court are aware of the fact that most parties to a case are not familiar with legal terms, phrases, and vocabulary. This is particularly significant when the parties to a case lack formal education and thus may struggle to understand the legal motivations of the judges. Thus, judges of criminal courts must speak, motivate, formulate, and write their decisions in very clear language, which is accessible to all parties and does not impact the integrity of the case.

A distinction must also be made between oral and written language. Although the intentions behind both are the same and lead to the same outcome, a judge must be very cautious and ensure that their verbal language does not confuse the victims or offenders and result in any unwanted consequences. The clarity or ambiguity of language used by the judge could even encourage or discourage the parties. It is on this account that the formulation and motivation of judges have a decisive impact on

---

[152] "I am completely certain in one sense, however, that in order to exist, international justice cannot be isolated from the pure sense of universal morality of rights. These rights are not legislated by governments and international organisations, but by the perpetual protection of the rights of man stemming from our shared values as inalienable classical rights independent from manmade laws. These rights ascend to the echelon of jus cogens and therefore encompass the character of *obligatio erga* omnes, which is inderogable. Thus, the terms "jus cogens," "peremptory," and "erga omnes" all represent the modern version of the universal rights of man, love for justice, love of civilisation, and love for the health of our natural environment which are unchangeable. *My purpose here is not to convince international lawyers or the judges of the national and international courts that there is a powerful norm in law which is called love, but I definitely fear, and I am concerned about the truth that law which does not build its basic raison d'eˆtre on love for human beings cannot survive properly.*" Malekian, *Classical Morality in International Peremptory Criminal Law*, note 11, p.9.

the parties and their individual understanding and respect of the Court and the administration of criminal justice as a whole. Scrutiny of the multiplicity of terms employed by judges nonetheless reveals some broad categories of meaning when they refer, for example, to 'the law in force' which can be interpreted differently by different individuals. In other words, the term "law in force" may be clear for lawyers, but may not be fully understood by offenders.[153] The term is very broad and can refer to the entire legislation, only part of the legislation, or even a very limited part of the legislation, depending on who you ask.

However, we understand that sometimes it is a problem of the core definition of a term or a distinction between two terms, such as wrong and right, bad and good, and more obviously, a personal understanding of the judges, victims, or accused persons. Generally, the proper role of the court requires that when a judge speaks with the accused, witnesses and victims, they are able to understand what the judge is saying and the questions that they pose. Thus, the judge should ensure that their intention is not lost in legal jargon. Although the latter is important for the court, the function of the former is much stronger than the later, based on the fact that the whole institution of the court is established to give clear message to the parties.

All actions of the judge must therefore rest on their experience and their ability to present themselves such that their words or writings are not misunderstood by any party. This clarity of the language of the court constitutes therefore the value of judicial conscience and is fundamentally essential for the public. Additionally, we should emphasise that parties to a case have the right to understand the language of the judges of the court and even receive an interpreter if necessary. However, this right may be rejected in certain situations. For instance, this right was not accepted by the European Human Right Committee in the following case:

> The applicant complains that he was not given the free assistance of an interpreter for contacts with his defence counsel who did not speak the applicant's own language ... Article 6 (3)(e) in fact only applies to the

---

[153] This can also refer to *de lege lata* and not *de lege ferenda*. See *also* Tom R. Tyler, 'Understanding the Force of Law', 51 *Tulsa Law Review* (2016), pp.507-519.

> relations between the accused and the judge ... In the circumstances of the present case, the Com-mission cannot exclude that the preparation of the defence was made more difficult as a result of misunderstandings between the applicant and his counsel. Nevertheless the applicant must be taken to be responsible for that situation. It was indeed for him either to appoint another lawyer with a good knowledge of French or to call for an interpreter he would have remunerated. If he had not sufficient means to pay for a defence counsel and/or an interpreter, he could still have applied for free legal aid. The Commission notes in this respect that, according to Austrian practice, specific linguistic requirements are taken into account by the designation of a court appointed defence counsel. Furthermore free legal aid may be extended to include the service of an interpreter ...2.... one cannot derive from [Article 6 (3)] ... a general right for the accused to have the court files translated. The Commission recalls that the rights secured under Article 6 (3) are those of the defence in general and not those of the accused considered separately ... It should thus be pointed out that part of the file was drafted in German so that the applicant's lawyer could understand it while many documents were in French and could be read by the applicant himself. Again the applicant must assume personal responsibility for any remaining linguistic difficulty, for the very reasons set out above...[154]

The clarity of the language of the judges of criminal courts is also essential in international criminal courts. For example, when the ICC judges refer to the phrase *de lege lata*, this must be completely clear with reference to the text and the law in force, to which the ICC judges refer to. This is particularly evident when they refer to the commission of serious international crimes such as crimes against humanity and genocide. Particularly with reference to fact that legal language is itself subject to further interpretation and analysis because its complicated phrases should not be misunderstood by any party. The legal terminology or the *de lege lata* should not be made more complicated by judges, and should not create

[154] X v. Austria, 6185/73, 29 May 1975, DR 2, 68.

more confusion in the understanding of the framework of the given crimes.[155]

[155] "A simple explanation of the principle of *de lege lata* is that it should represent the total sum of norms and rules that have been nominated by all the people of our international legal and political community. They should represent those norms of international behaviour that nations have acknowledged as their values. Here we seek the recognition of an appropriate initial status quo in order to ensure that the principles of justice are based on the fundamental elements of criminal law. In order for the role of international criminal justice to be fulfilled correctly, it should be united with the juridical values of the principle of *de lege lata*. The implementation of the principle of equality may scarcely fulfil its function, if the fundamental intentions of the principle dismiss the reasons for the existence of the law." Malekian, *Jurisprudence of International Criminal Justice*, note 105, p.13.

Chapter 6

QUALIFICATION OF JUDGES WITHIN DIFFERENT CRIMINAL JURISDICTIONS

6.1. JUDGES OF VARIOUS CRIMINAL JURISDICTIONS

There are not many differences between the judges of the various criminal jurisdictions in the world. They have all the same responsibilities and duties from a judicial conscience or moral point of view. This implies their required qualifications.[156] It means that their impartiality should form the basis of their duties, and should be respected at all times. The methods or theories of criminal jurisdiction under which judges of criminal courts function in civil law and common law systems have the same intention regarding criminal justice—to encourage the appropriate implementation of the system of justice in which the truth, and only the truth, should dominate the procedures of justice and the outcome of the case. This can only be achieved by preserving the full impartiality of judges and prosecutors. The most common forms of criminal jurisdiction are based on

---

[156] "One of the most important parts of the machinery of justice of the permanent International Criminal Court is its judiciary system governing the qualifications, nomination and election of judges for the implementation of the provisions of the Statute." Malekian, *Jurisprudence of International Criminal Justice*, note 105, p.114. See also Malekian, *Corpus Juris of Islamic International Criminal Justice*, note 3, p.260.

civil law (inquisitorial, adversarial), common law, or on a mixed jurisdiction which is also called an *adquisitorial* system.

6.2. Conscience of Inquisitorial Judges

Civil law is statute-based law, which has been adopted by the legislature and is enforced by the courts. The civil law system is based on the assumption that the laws applied to citizens are drafted and adopted by citizens through their representatives or their legislative organs. The civil law system originates from Roman law and is also known as the civil code or continental law. The civil law system is probably the oldest domestic systems of law in the world. It can even trace its origins back to the Code of Hammurabi, under which the judges had the duty to perform justice with due regard for the provisions of the Codes.[157] The civil law system is the most common form of jurisdiction across the globe with specific regulations which are meant to be followed by judges. Civil law is drafted, discussed, and legislated by a parliament or representatives of government. The civil law system should not be confused with the common law system. Under the civil law system, the freedoms of the judges of the court are limited. The judges are mostly there to identify which regulations apply to a given case. The origins of this restriction of freedom can be traced back to the Napoleonic courts where judges were not permitted to interpret statutes and laws.

The main responsibility of judges is to direct the law to the best of their ability, and to not create new laws. Codified laws have a very significant function for the continuation and implementation of the law and in serving the needs of the relevant society. Therefore, the judges are obliged to follow the given legislation. Thus, there must be a harmonious connection between the relevant laws, and the legal philosophy of all laws. Conflicts of law should be avoided, although this is difficult in practice, and judges of civil courts normally come to different conclusions. This is why the

---

[157] Examine Malekian, *Judgments of Love in Criminal Justice*, note 1, p.256.

legislative may occasionally modify and realign the main intentions of laws. The role of the legislature becomes tenuous if they apply different laws to different populations.

The limit of the legal conscience of civil or inquisitorial judges is mostly dependent upon the legislation and to what extent it permits judges to interpret the applicable law and regulations. While the judges of the civil courts are restricted in their personal interpretation of the law, there is still the possibility for the judge to deduct the best possible solution from the provisions of the law in order to use them in the given case. Thus, the freedom of judge is not really as restricted as it seems and the intention of the legislator is to treat all suspected persons equally. As one of well-known American judges explained, "…if I had the right to choose, I would prefer to be prosecuted in civil law systems than our own common law method."[158]

Under the civil law system, all rules are written, and judges are required to follow the written law. Thus, the judge is not free to choose their own method of application or rules. The intention of the civil law system is to offer all citizens equal application of the principles of law and rules which are based on substantive law. Its aim is also to limit the authority of the judge and to create a reliable system of rules, which is accepted by the public. The civil law system is a forum of substantive laws that are the result of legislative decisions. Essentially, in the civil law system, the court is not bound by precedent. Whilst it is a fact that a judge has the duty to find and apply the relevant law in each case, earlier judgements may influence the new decision. It is sometimes impossible to

---

[158] In addition, "Perceptibly, the normative conflict between the two legal disciplines enhances the likelihood of a feud in public international law, and the presentation of legal evidence becomes compulsory for the parties. Similarly, the judges of an international court have to decide which norm takes precedence over another norm. The state has a legal right to direct its sovereign interests. At the same time, it must not violate the legal interests of the international legal and political community as a whole. For example, the application of capital punishment constitutes an individual irrational interest on the part of the state, e.g., in China, Iran, Saudi Arabia, and Afghanistan. There is not any hesitation that the abolition of capital punishment constitutes an integral part of peremptory international criminal law." Malekian, *Classical Morality in International Peremptory Criminal Law*, note 11, pp.94-95.

not overlook the decisions of other courts in a similar case, even though the court does not refer to precedent.

The active role of a judge in an inquisitorial system may differ to that of a judge in an adversarial system where judge has to maintain their impartiality. The consequence is that in the inquisitorial system, the court's job is to uncover the truth concerning the accusations by challenging evidence, questioning witnesses, and, if necessary, by directing an investigation and, ultimately, to sentence one of the parties in the conflict. Thus, in an inquisitorial system, the judge's duties start as soon as the court proceedings do, while the main duties of the judge in an adversarial or common law system are carried out at the end of the trial. The *inquisitorial* function of civil law systems requires judges to be active at all times, and not let cases go cold. They should remain impartial during proceedings. However, judges are responsible for identifying the facts of a case and uncovering the truth by examining evidence.

6.3. CONSCIENCE OF ADVERSARIAL JUDGES

In the common law system, the decisions of judges have an imperative task for the positive progress of the law or criminal law. The common law or adversarial system originated in England. Within this system, judges have the power to decide the meaning of laws if no prior explanation exists.[159] The judge is only person who is able to interpret the intention of the law. This means that abstract rules in the common law system are

---

[159] For instance, in the R. v. Tolsen case dealt with under the common law system, the concept of mens rea is clarified as: The guilty intent is not necessarily that of intending the very act or thing done and prohibited by common or statue law, but it must at least be the intention to do something wrong. That intention may belong to one or other two classes. It may be to do a thing wrong in itself and apart from positive law, or it may be to do a thing merely prohibited by statute or by common law, or both elements of intention may co-exist with respect to the same deed. There are many things prohibited by no statute –fornication or seduction, for instance – which nevertheless no one would hesitate to call wrong; and the intention to do an act wrong in this sense at least must a general rule exist before the act done can be considered a crime." (188 23 Q.B.D. 168, at 172. (the judgments of Wills J. quoted in Finbarr McAuley and J Pail McCutcheon, *Criminal Liability* (Round Hall Sweet and Maxwell, 2000), p.278.

drawn from previous cases. When an appellate court has already decided on the nature and character of the law, then that decision and precedent is binding for the future conducts of that appellate court.

In practice, this means that the decisions of the appellate court should be respected by all lower courts as long as the basic facts of a case remain largely unchanged. These decisions are binding and cannot be modified unless a higher court allows it. Thus, the decisions of the courts in a common law system are equivalent to laws and statutes. For that reason, the rules in a common law system derive from court decisions rather than from legislative rules. Subsequently, the decisions of an earlier court may be accepted by common law as precedent due to the conditions of case law. This implies that the case law is *stare decisis,* or represents the final argument of the precedent. The common law system as a whole implies the significant position of the judge within and outside of the law. "The doctrine of stare decisis means that 'past decisions must stand'. The idea that similar cases must be decided in similar ways may be the fundamental belief underlying common law systems."[160]

The judge's role in the common law system is to see and understand the law. Significantly, the role of the defendant is very substantial in most common law countries. This is because the criminal mechanism was established to hear the defendant and the victims, and the judge has to make this possible. Thus, the judge and the jury have particular roles in the development of the case and the ultimate decision. In cases where the defendant is unable to access the court system and requires legal representation, they can receive legal aid. In order for the adversarial system to operate reasonably and prevent justice from being violated, the judge may appoint a trial lawyer, at the taxpayers' expense, to defend the accused if they are unable to afford their own counsel.

One of the characteristics of common law systems is that courts are not only responsible for establishing clear evidence in a case, but they are

---

[160] Sardar MA, Waqar Khan Arif, 'Judicial precedent and its authority under international law' note 109, p.75. However, "the practices of international criminal court (ICC) and tribunals, such as, ICTR and ICTY, it argues that judicial decisions at International level are not binding." *Id.*, p.75.

also responsible for arguing all the applicable legal precedents laid down by previous courts in similar cases. The prosecution and defence lawyers not only use evidence relating to the case at hand, but they also refer to previous cases and reference them as precedent or justification for how certain cases should be handled and resolved. Similarly, judges and juries are also responsible for examining the facts relating to the present case and any other matters related to the arguments in previous cases. As a result of this process, judgements in common law cases may take much longer to reach than in civil law cases. The examination not only involves hearing the evidence and the witness testimony of the current case, but also of previous ones.

6.4. Conscience of Adquisitorial Judges

The mixed court or *adquisitorial* model represents another form of criminal procedure employed primarily in civil law countries. The adquisitorial court can also be seen in socialist and common law jurisdictions. Judges within adquisitorial or mixed-methods systems function similarly to judges of more traditional systems, however they seek to adapt new methods. The *adquisitorial* or mixed method of criminal jurisdiction is one of the methods of jurisdiction which has been officially recognised under the system of international criminal courts since the development of the Nuremberg Tribunal. We must emphasise that the adquisitorial system is a method of jurisdiction which embodies the fusion of two legal systems in order to achieve sustainable justice through the adoption of the best practices from both adversarial and inquisitorial methods of criminal procedure. There are a number of national courts and even international bodies such as the ICC that have started operating under the adquisitorial method. Ample examples of this fusion can be found in South African Laws and in the Rome Statute of the International Criminal Court. Antonio Cassese, the first President of the International Criminal Tribunal for the former Yugoslavia (ICTY) concluded that:

> International criminal procedure results from the gradual decanting of national criminal concepts and rules into the international receptacle. However, international criminal procedure does not originate from a uniform body of law. It substantially results from an amalgamation of two different legal systems, that obtaining in common-law countries and the system prevailing in countries of civil-law (although for historical reasons, there currently exists at the international level a clear imbalance in favour of the common-law approach). It is therefore only natural that international criminal proceedings do not uphold the philosophy behind one of the two national criminal systems to the exclusion of the other; nor do they result from the juxtaposition of elements of the two systems. Rather, they combine and fuse, in a fairly felicitous manner, the adversarial or accusatorial system (chiefly adopted in common-law countries) with a number of significant features of the inquisitorial approach (mostly taken in States of continental Europe and in other countries of civil-law tradition). This combination or amalgamation is unique and begets a legal logic that is qualitatively different from that of each of the two national criminal systems: the philosophy behind international trials is markedly at variance with that underpinning each of those national systems. Also the Statute and Rules of the International Tribunal, in outlining the criminal proceedings before the Trial and Appeals Chambers, do not refer to a specific national criminal approach, but originally take up the accusatorial (or adversarial) system and adapt it to international proceedings, while at the same time upholding some elements of the inquisitorial system.[161]

As we have mentioned previously, the judicial conscience of the adquisitorial system varies based on many factors. In general, the judges of an adquisitorial system have a great ethical responsibility to carry out their legal obligations objectively and with good moral conscience.[162] Therefore, judges should be very careful not to violate the independence of criminal jurisdiction, and not to lose their impartiality during the

---

161 Erdemovic (IT-96-22-A), Separate and Dissenting opinion of Judge Cassese, 7 October 1997, para.2.

162 MacIntyre, *After Virtue: A Study in Moral Theory*, note 38. Consult also Alasdair MacIntyre, *A Short History of Ethics: a History of Moral Philosophy from the Homeric Age to the Twentieth Century* (1965).

procedures of criminal justice. Judges in adquisitorial systems generally have greater responsibility for false outcomes of cases than judges in civil or common law systems. Essentially, their responsibilities are based on maintaining their honesty while investigating cases. Additionally, judges of the adquisitorial system deal more closely with international politics than judges of the civil or common law systems.

6.5. Powers of the Adversarial Judge

The adversarial system is entirely different from the system used by most European nations.[163] The role of judges in adversarial systems is, generally speaking, to ensure that proceedings are carried out in a fair and just manner as prescribed by custom and laws. Judges function as unbiased arbiters or as referees between the parties in the case. In the adversarial system, which is the predominant legal system in common law countries, the judge is legally permitted to interpret the constitution and statutes which have been passed by a parliament. This is regardless of the fact that the constitution in a common law system is the supreme law and that judges should not modify its core provisions. Comparatively,

> Adquisitorial is a concept that embodies the actuality of a fusion of two legal systems in order to achieve sustainable justice through the merging of best practices from the adversarial and inquisitorial methods of criminal procedure. There are some national courts and even international bodies such as the ICC that have started operating the adquisitorial method. Ample examples can be found in the South African Laws and in the Rome Statute of the International Criminal Court. It had been noted that the procedure used by ICC shows the characteristics of the Common Law System or Adversarial System and the Civil Law System or Inquisitorial System in a mixed mode.[164]

---

[163] Kafayat Motilewa Quadri, Hunud Abia Kadaouf, Mohammad Naqib Ishan Jan, Mohd. Iqbal AbdulWahab and Haniff Ahama, 'Adquisitorial: The Mixing of Two Legal Systems' 3 (1) *International Journal of Humanities and Management Sciences* (2015), pp.31-36.

[164] *Id.*, p.31.

Nonetheless, judges can interpret how the provisions of the constitution should apply in practice. This power of the judge is particularly evident in countries which have a more democratic approach to legislation. A court may conclude that the legislation drafted and adopted by a parliament is unfair because it violates other significant constitutional rights of citizens. A Supreme Court may also state this in its case law. In such cases, the parliament must potentially re-examine provisions which are deemed to be unconstitutional, which may in due course require an amendment or the repeal of a law in order to uphold the constitution. If parliament fails to take a court's decision into consideration, the application of the relevant statute will not be successful.

In comparison, in Scandinavian countries or civil law systems, the legislator has to take the consequences of previous law into serious consideration. For instance, the Swedish parliament acts, inter alia, in response to courts, judges, prosecutors, and those who asses/evaluate the provisions of a legal system. This hidden power of a judge in a common law system means that the legislation drafted by parliament does not have to clarify every possible situation that may arise during the application of the law. The legislation often mentions general principles and sets certain limits. For instance, it may set the maximum sentence an offender can face. The legislature leaves it up to the courts to determine exactly what the statutes and common law precedents really mean. As a result, judges are free to interpret the law more strictly or more freely.

However, with due regard to the procedures, the judge may issue their conclusive understanding of the corpus of the law. Although the provisions of criminal law bind a judge in an inquisitorial system of jurisdiction, in a common law system, the judge is bound by their thorough case-by-case understanding of hypothetical legislation. This theoretical or hypothetical norm broadly exists as legislation – not according to the norms of the civil law system, but rather according to the quantity and quality of existing case law. One advantage of common law systems may be that the judges are free to reduce accountability, which is not possible under civil law systems. Despite all this, civil law systems do incorporate some elements of common law systems, as judges also evaluate similar prior cases in order to make their decisions more constructive.

6.6. Qualifications of Islamic Judges

Under Islamic law, justice has to be investigated in a proper manner with full respect for the impartiality of the judge, who must be an upstanding and just person. The judge must observe certain rules, norms, and provisions and not violate the rules regarding the testimony of witnesses or evidence. With reference to the main mechanism of the law and major source "We have appointed you as a vicegerent in the earth; therefore judge between mankind with justice, and do not follow desires lest they should lead you astray from the way of God."[165] The respect of these rules is particularly important in the case of serious offences such as crimes against humanity, war crimes, and genocide. This means that a judge must, in addition to being qualified as a judge, also have sufficient knowledge of criminal justice. For that reason, there are certain imperative conditions for the qualification of judges in the administration of Islamic (criminal) justice.

Some of these requirements can be found within national criminal justice systems or within the body of international criminal justice in some form, and these requirements are essential for the application of fair and equal justice in all legal systems. The Islamic criminal jurisprudence established the following criteria for judges; however these principles are not always respected in practice and are often violated by some of the Islamic judges. The private interests of judges have become the most essential and fundamental guidelines for a large number of judges in the world.

A judge is supposed to have the following qualifications when sitting on the bench in Islamic courts:

---

[165] The Qur'an: 38:26. See also Ronald Slye, *The Nuremberg Principles in Non-western Societies: A Reflection on their Universality, Legitimacy and Application* (International Nuremberg Principles Academy, 2017).

i. A moral qualification. Both legal systems i.e., international criminal justice and Islamic criminal justice place considerable weight on the moral character of a judge. Accordingly, a judge must have a high moral standard and have an ethical reputation, an honourable record, a respectable personality, and be well-recognised. These qualifications do not necessarily mean that a slave or a poor person cannot be a judge, as these conditions do not preclude someone from being a judge, as a poor person could have a more honourable record than a rich judge.
ii. Islamic judges should not accept bribes or gifts.
iii. A judge should be wise.
iv. A judge should be intelligent.
v. A judge should have an understanding of Islam. This does not necessarily mean that a judge of the ICC must be a Muslim, however, they should respect all religions. The respect of different cultures constitutes one of the basic principles of the Universal Declaration of Human Rights.
vi. A judge must be impartial regarding the case. This means that they must not have any vested interest in the case and they must maintain their objectivity throughout the case.
vii. A judge must possess all the qualifications that are required of a judge in the relevant court.
viii. Islamic criminal justice insists on the relevant knowledge of a judge. They must have sufficient capacity to understand criminal law, proceedings, and judgements.
ix. According to the Statute of the ICC, a judge must be competent concerning international law, human rights law, humanitarian law, and have a professional legal capacity. These qualifications are also obviously an integral part of Islamic jurisprudence and the 1990 Islamic Universal Declaration of Human Rights.
x. Judges should not lend money.
xi. Judges should protect the public/international welfare.

xii. The opinion of judges must be authentic in the case of *Qiyas* or the analogical reasoning which also includes judgements (case law); as well as in the case of *Ijtihad*, or individual judgement; and also in the case of *Ijma*, which refers to consensus on certain matters.

xiii. It is good if a judge is a specialist in the protection of the rights of children, including abandoned children and orphans. This means that a judge should protect the rights of child victims of crimes during war or peacetime. A good knowledge concerning the provisions of the Convention on the Rights of the Child may not be necessary, but would be an advantage

xiv. Under Islamic jurisprudence, there is no appeals court in a modern sense. However, a defendant may appeal to the ruler after sentencing. If it can be proven that the punishment of the defendant was unlawful and the findings of the judge were not accurate, the judge could be subjected to the equivalent punishment and removed from their position. A false appeal by the defendant is also subject to punishment.

xv. A judge has to be courteous.

xvi. A judge has to have a culturally good moral background.

xvii. A judge must not be engaged in sexual misconduct.

xviii. The judge's position must have been obtained lawfully and not as the result of corruption.

xix. A sexist or discriminatory judge cannot be an accurate judge.

xx. A judge has to respect all religions without discrimination.

xxi. A judge must be a qualified and wise individual.

6.7. Comparative Judicial Independence of Judges

Ensuring independent juridical proceedings is one of the most essential parts of any criminal jurisdiction. This is because criminal jurisdictions are harmed by the lack of impartiality of judges, as well as by their lack of independence. There are a considerable number of jurisdictions in the world which are working and aiming to establish complete judicial independence. The intention is to ensure that judges of national or international courts are working in accordance with full and true judicial conscience, and are not influenced by politics or money in their decisions. It is supposed that "they share a common characteristic insofar as they all at least potentially play a central role in interpreting and applying international law. Judicial independence is recognised to be significant factor in maintain the credibility and legitimacy of international courts and tribunals."[166] However, maintaining this independence of criminal jurisdiction is very difficult and requires not only the full moral support of the judges of any court, but also the political guarantee that politicians will not interfere in the judicial system.[167]

For example, the 2006 Code of Judicial Ethics in Croatia emphasises that it was written in order to attain the maximum values of the constitutional order in the nation and to promote the respect of the rule of law, the principles of legality and humanity, as well as the ethics/conscience of juridical independence.[168] It was also the intention of the Code to emphasise the consciousness of personal and professional responsibility including efficiency in the processes of the judicial office. Judges in particular are responsible for upholding these requirements of the Code in order to ensure the appropriate consolidation of criminal justice.[169] Similar provisions can also be found in the 2004 Estonian Code of Ethics.[170] Judges of the relevant jurisdiction are aware of the fact that the impartiality, independence, and integrity of judges, along with the principles of fair trial and the practice of good conduct of judges, certain qualified requirements for judges, guarantee of an independent administration of jurisdiction, and the high moral and legal responsibility

---

166 Ruth Mackenzie & Philippe Sands, 'International Courts and Tribunals and the Independence of the International Judge', 44 *HARV. INT'L L. J.* (2003), p.271.

167 *Id.*, pp.271-3.

168 Consult the link: available online at https://www.venice.coe.int/files/un_social_media/cro.pdf.

169 *Id.*

170 Consult the link: available online at https://www.kohus.ee/en/judges/estonian-judgescode-ethics.

resting on judges, are some of the few significant rules of judicial conscience.[171]

Some Nordic countries also have certain codes, rules, and customs regarding judicial independence. This can be seen in the practice of Danish, Norwegian, Swedish, and Finish criminal procedures. Judges should ensure the respect of the Council of Europe's recommendations to maintain their independence, effectiveness, and responsibility concerning the judicial conscience. The principles of ethics in these countries promote significant conducts among judges which can create and increase public confidence in the works of courts and their judgements. Judges are thus responsible for conducting themselves in compliance with judicial ethics.

There are certain provisions in the Swedish Code of Judicial Procedure which create certain legal obligations for all judges, who should carry out their duties under ethical oath or the equivalent. The *oaths* of judges, victims, or witness are not binding within the judicial and legal systems. Moreover, the judges of a court and lay judges are not obliged to trust the expressed oath.[172] One of the intentions of the Code is to provide judges with guidelines for ensuring good judicial practices. Accordingly, a judge ought to act ethically and uphold due process in accordance with the law. It is the responsibility of the Swedish judges to guarantee their objectivity and independence. It is important to ensure that the general public has confidence in the judges, and that the judges and courts maintain their reliability, trustworthiness, credibility, and integrity for the sake of independence jurisdiction.

Similarly, the 2012 introduction of the Ethical Principles for Judges adopted by the Association of Finnish Judges strengthened the judicial independence among judges and the decisions of the courts. A further similar code is the Dutch Code of Conduct for judicial personnel which elaborates upon several significant vales of judicial independence such as autonomy, impartiality, expertise, professionalism, and integrity. Certain

---

171 *Id.*

172 Christian Diesen, Lay judges in Sweden: A short introduction, Dans Revue internationale de droit pénal 2001/1-2 (Vol. 72), pages 313 à 315, https://www.cairn.info/revue-internationale-de-droit-penal-2001-1-page-313.htm.

significant principles can also be founded in the NVvR Guide to Judicial Conduct of the Dutch Judges Association adopted in 2011.[173] The Guide provides practical guidance to judges regarding their actions and behaviour and aims to explain to society how judges deal with issues of integrity.

6.8. Simplicity of the Pillars of Criminal Justice

The institution of juridical ethics commonly refers to norms that ensure the independence, impartiality, and integrity of national and international criminal courts. These norms constitute part of the legal personality of courts and judges, which must be maintained at all times. They denote the core values in all courts and should be the major keys of justice in all courts in democratic, authoritarian, dictator, tyrannical, and totalitarian states. Pure justice is an essential precondition for the proper administration of justice. There is a serious difference between justice and politics, as justice is immutable and cannot be changed, while political principles are constantly changing with the times. The reason for this is that in new political systems, we do not speak about the principles of former politicians, nor do we support their politics. However, justice is separate from all this, and has to have its own permanent principles and should not change at will. In very rare situations, a principle of justice may be completely abolished as in the case of punishments such as extracting information or confessions under torture or the implementation of capital punishment.

The house of justice is the house of truth, and this house is principally based on the honesty of judges. Therefore, judges and politicians should

---

[173] Consult also Matters of Principle, Codes on the Independence and Impartiality of Judiciary. Available online at https://www.rechtspraak.nl/sitecollectiondocuments/matters-of-principle.pdf. "1. The independence of the judiciary shall be guaranteed by the State and enshrined in the Constitution or the law of the country. It is the duty of all governmental and other institutions to respect and observe the independence of the judiciary. 2. The judiciary shall decide matters before them impartially, on the basis of facts and in accordance with the law, without any restrictions, improper influences, inducements, pressures, threats or interferences, direct or indirect, from any quarter or for any reason." *Id.*, p.15.

not carry out relations with each other which could impact a case. This has to be respected at all times, as it is one of the pillars of criminal justice. The specific nature of the administration of criminal justice is its sensitivity concerning political views and its vital goal of establishing the truth as the master key of its existence. This master key is essentially in the hands of judges, and no judge in the world can assert that they have to direct this master key to match the will of politicians. In such cases, justice has not only failed, but must no longer be considered justice but rather politics. A judge who directs the life of justice with the needs of politicians, is misleading international criminal justice and abolishing the truth, thus complicating the simple principles of criminal justice.

The rules of procedural justice are established by judges who do not violate the independence of criminal jurisdiction. The function of procedural justice is not less important than the regulation of criminal justice, because justice has to be perceived as a manifestation of the consciences of the judges and their commitments. When the European Court of Human Rights emphasises that justice must not only be carried out, but it must also be seen, it does not mean that the judges should follow the orders of their politicians when carrying out their duties.[174] Judges should actually try to distance themselves from all politicians in all ways. This is what is meant with the concept of the judicial consciences of judges. In other words, the persuasive and trustworthy practice of judges constitutes the way in which a healthy form of criminal justice is established.

It is of particular significance to take into consideration the words of the Consultative Council of European Judges which declared that "the confidence in the justice system is even more important in view of the increasing globalization of disputes and the wide circulation of judgements." It goes further and clarifies that when a state has been governed by the rule of law "the public is entitled to expect the general

---

[174] Jutta Limbach, Pedro Cruz Villalón, Roger Errera, Lord Lester, Tamara Morschtschakowa, Lord Justice Sedley, Andrzej Zol., 'Judicial Independence: Law and Practice of Appointments to the European Court of Human Rights' (2003). Available online at https://www.corteidh.or.cr/tablas/32795.pdf.

principles, compatible with the notion of a fair trial and guaranteeing fundamental rights, to be set out. The obligations incumbents on judges have been put in place in order to guarantee their impartiality and the effectiveness of their action." This means that the intention of the European Council is to prevent any form of corruption in the administration of justice.[175] The intention is obviously to prevent any form of non-impartiality among judges and affirm their basic responsibility to preserve their objectivity.

Justice without the influence of politicians is indeed very difficult to achieve when criminal justice and the cases brought before the courts depend on power politics. This is particularly evident in the case of international criminal justice, which may seem to be free of politics, but is actually heavily controlled by politics. In other words, depending on the circumstances, judges may modify the major principles of criminal justice in order to align them with the will of those in power. This implies the fact that the strength of justice fails and leads to hypocrisy within the mechanism of criminal justice. Therefore, the simplicity of criminal judges in the administration of international criminal justice is not only imperative, but is also the only way to prevent the big criminality of the politicians and judges.[176] Thus, knowing how to play the game in the courtroom is an important skill for judges.[177] These are the sole factors which impact and help preserve impunity in the system of international

---

[175] However, long before the creation of European Union, Montesquieu asserted in connection to danger of the corruption of the principle of monarchical government that "The danger is not when the state passes from one moderate to another moderate government, (as from a republic to a monarchy, or from a monarchy to a republic,) but when it precipitates from a moderate to a despotic government. Most of the European nations are still governed by the principles of morality. But if, from a long abuse of power, or the fury of conquest, despotic sway should prevail to a certain degree, neither morals nor climate would be able to withstand its baleful influence: and then human nature would be exposed, for some time at least, even in this beautiful part of the world, to the insults with which she has been abused in the other three." *The Spirit of the Laws The Complete Works of M. De Montesquieu*, Translated from the French in Four Volumes: The Spirit of Laws (London, 1777), available online at https://oll.libertyfund.org/title/montesquieu-complete-works-vol-1-the-spirit-of-laws#lf0171-01_label_346.

[176] Frederik Harhoff, 'It's All in the Process: Reflections on the Relation between International Criminal Trials and International Humanitarian Law', 78 Nordic Journal of International Law (2010).

[177] *Id.* P.479.

criminal law and increase the number of victims of international crimes. We are compelled by the force of law and the true intention of accurate law to bring truth to justice. If the truth is absent in the procedures of criminal justice, and then the only alternative is that we live with lies and reject the principles of honesty with the immorality of our intentions.

Is there any difference between criminals and criminals? Is there any difference between the crimes of individuals and the crimes of a government? Is there any difference between the court of Sierra Leone in West Africa and the European or British courts? The philosophy of law is very surprised, the theory of law is in mourning, and the principles of human rights law regret to see that the big criminals of the civilisation of man are going without punishment. Here, obviously, I am not seeking to offend the good people of the world, but to call out the lacking logic of law, and the missing ethics of jurisprudence.[178] *The definition of crimes and criminality cannot, and should not, tolerate further blows to their abstract legal body. Without a doubt, we are violating the system of international criminal law, of national criminal law, of international morality, of international criminal courts, of our cultural understanding, and the system of love in criminal justice, when we bring one criminal to court while letting other big criminals get off scot-free.*

The system of International criminal justice was not created to permit the discrimination between different groups, nor to punish only Africans; nor was it constructed to tip the scales of justice in the favour of one side of the world. Surely we are offending the system of International criminal justice when we call it a system of justice when there still exists impunity for big criminals. Indubitably, we infringe upon the systems of natural law and of the natural rights of people, when we take difference stances concerning our own criminals, and violate the system of morality.[179] All this comprises the naked truth about criminal justice, and the ability of human animals to trade it. Clearly, the faculty of justice has lost sight of its mission.[180]

---

[178] Hart H.L.A., *Essays in Jurisprudence and Philosophy* (Oxford University, 1985); H.L.A. Hart, *The Concept of Law* (Oxford University Press, 1961); Hartnack Justus, *Kant's Theory of Knowledge* (Harcourt, Brace and World, 1967).

[179] Malekian, *Classical Morality in International Peremptory Criminal Law*, note 11, pp.10-18.

[180] Malekian, *Trading Virginity of International Criminal Justice*, note 1, p.152.

Chapter 7

AUTONOMY OF JUDGES OF INTERNATIONAL CRIMINAL COURTS

7.1. JUDGES SKILLS CONCERNING *JUS COGENS*

There are certain essential elements in the examination of the ethical, moral, and legal character of judges, which are indispensable for the administration of justice and indicate that a judge is capable of making correct judgements and fulfilling the expectations of their office. These required skills of judges should be considered as requirements under *jus cogens* norms, which means that all judges must fulfil these criteria in order to be recognised as proper judges.[181] Some of the most important traits/norms include:

a) being of a very high moral character
b) not having committed any crimes
c) not having been involved in corruption
d) not serving actively in a political role

---

[181] Consult also A. J. Nicolas, 'Croquet the International Criminal Court and the Treatment of Defence Rights: A Mirror of the European Court of Human Rights' Jurisprudence? *Human Rights Law Review* (2011), pp.91-131.

e) being capable of understanding legal terminology
f) not having been recommended by politicians for the position
g) having the ability to understand the metaphysics of ethics and morality
h) being responsible and having a great deal of integrity
i) not being addicted to drugs or alcohol
j) being known to be wise
k) being honest
l) not having any mental health problems
m) being impartial
n) having the capacity to analyse legal issues
o) having the ability to accurately assess legal issues
p) not being a party to any case
q) having the ability to work under duress
r) having the ability to read a large number of documents
s) having the ability to solve complicated issues
t) being capable of mediation
u) being polite
v) having the ability to write and argue
w) being able to express themselves clearly
x) being confident, trustworthy, and honest
y) being able to maintain their objectivity during a case
z) making decisions in accordance with the law
aa) not losing sight of justice in their decisions
bb) capable of issuing impartial and fair punishments

7.2. Judges Upholding Peremptory Norms

Certain international judges and scholars believe that there are several rules of international law or international criminal law which should not be violated by any state,[182]and thus have to be respected by all members of the United Nations. These rules therefore have a universal nature, and should consequently not be ignored in the international relations of states. This means that judges of national or international criminal courts should not underestimate the role of *jus cogens* norms in their decisions, as there is a great deal of evidence which speaks for their non-derogable nature. Judge Schücking of the Permanent Court of International Justice reached a similar conclusion in 1934 and mentioned the existence of the spirit of *jus cogens* norms in the following statement:

> The Covenant of the League of Nations, as a whole, and more particularly its Article 20..., would possess little value unless treaties concluded in violation of that undertaking were to be regarded as absolutely null and void, that is to say, as being automatically void. And I can hardly believe that the League of Nations would have already embarked on the codification of international law if it were not possible, even to-day, to create a jus cogens, the effect of which would be that, once States have agreed on certain rules of law, and have also given an undertaking that these rules may not be altered by some only of their number, any act adopted in contravention of that undertaking would be automatically void.[183]

The opinions of scholars have also played a significant role in the recognition of the system of international peremptory criminal law. Opposition figures, including Professor Hans Kelsen and Judge Gaetano Morelli of the International Court of Justice (ICJ), believe that international law does not possess legal force without the existence of

---

[182] It is rightly asserted that 'For the first time in history almost all jurists and almost all States were agreed in recognizing the existence of fundamental norms of international law from which no derogation was permitted, and on which the organization of international society was based. The norms of *jus cogens* had a long history but had crystallized only after the Second World War. In spite of ideological difficulties, a shared philosophy of values was now emerging and the trend had been sharply accelerated by the growth of international organizations.' UN. Conference on the Law of Treaties, Ist Sess., Vienna, 26 Mar. - 24 May, 1968, Official Records, at 297. U.N. Doc. A/Conf. 39/11.

[183] Judge Schücking's individual opinion in The Oscar Chinn Case, 63 PCIJ Rep.Ser. A/B (1934), p.149. Emphasis added.

positive law or the express consent from states. Thus, they do not put any validity on the principle of morality– however they are in the minority with this opinion.

The majority argue that the Universal Declaration of Human Rights, the United Nations Charter, and the International Covenant on Civil and Political Rights unequivocally declare that universal norms, such as the prohibition of genocide, are enforceable in any state regardless of state consent. For instance, an ICJ Judge, Fitzmaurice, has introduced a list of certain principles identified to be the most significant, consolidated naturalist-universalist elements that have to be upheld in any cooperation between members of the international legal and political community. Accordingly, these include:

> A. The rule of non-resort to the use of force and the consequent non-recognition of situations brought about by its use.
> B. The rules now contained in article 52 of the Convention on the Law of Treaties, that treaties imposed by force (sometimes called 'unequal' treaties) are void ab initio.
> C. The interdiction of crimes against peace and humanity, including genocide and acts in the nature of genocide and near genocide.
> D. The rule that the plea of 'superior orders' is prima facie no answer to a charge of crime against peace and humanity or of a war crime.
> E. The recognition, also enshrined in provisions of the Vienna Convention (articles 53 and 64) of the principle commonly known as jus cogens , of entrenched rules of law from which in principle no release or derogation is possible, so that treaties conflicting with what is designated as a 'peremptory norm of general international law' are void.
> F. Recognition of something in the nature of a 'droit de regard' by States, not in the sense of any right of intervention in one another's internal affairs, but of a right of concern over policies and actions that may have external repercussions adverse to the interests of others or to the general interest. This corollary can be deduced from several principles already discussed, and from the general duty of co-operation in matters of common concern to all countries.

G. Incipient recognition of an inchoate duty of samaritanism in international relations (aid to underdeveloped countries, etc.).[184]

The key message in the above text is that the system of international customary and conventional law dictates that certain norms in the content of treaties or customary law have the character of *jus cogens* law. Nonetheless, norms were under the yoke of the mandatory obligations of positive law. The view of the existence of *jus cogens* norms has become more important over the last few decades. The value of norms has become more essential in international relations, and therefore judges of national and international criminal courts must acknowledge the importance of protecting fundamental rights based on international peremptory law.

The most recognised part of international peremptory criminal law relates to core crimes integrated into the Statute of the ICC. These include war crimes, crimes against humanity, genocide, and aggression, as well as the prohibition of torture, rape, slavery, and any actions which hinder self-determination. These should be an integral part of the substantive knowledge of the judges of the ICC. The fact is that any attention given to core international crimes by the judges of the ICC, and even judges of national criminal courts, implies the full respect of the provisions of international humanitarian law of armed conflicts, which constitutes an integral part of international peremptory criminal law.

The judges of the ICC should be aware of the fact that there are two sides of *jus cogens* norms. One is the negative aspect which has the character of prohibition and recognition of certain acts as crimes against the foundations of the system of the international human community as a whole. The positive aspect of international peremptory criminal law suggests that part of this criminal legal system is the exact opposite of the negative aspect of the law. With this we mean that international peremptory criminal law compels all states, organs, groups, and

---

184 22 Special Report by Fitzmaurice, 'The Future of Public International Law and of the International Legal System in the Circumstances of Today', Institute de Droit International (1973), pp.323-24. Citied in Marjorie M. Whiteman, *Jus cogens* in International Law, with A Projected List' 7 (2) *Georgia Journal of International and Comparative Law* (1977), pp.609-626, at 611.

individuals to uphold legal and political morality. This duty is also included in the duties of the judges of ICC when they investigate international crimes in which their examination and arguments should be based on the positive consideration of both sides of the norms.

7.3. Basic Principles Governing the Independence of Judges

The independence of the judiciary continues to be one of the most significant topics in the system of criminal law and international criminal justice. This principle has been given particular attention in the meetings of states and under the auspices the United Nations. One document dealing with the independence of the judiciary is the Basic Principles on the Independence of the Judiciary (Basic Principles), which constitutes one of the main international documents regulating the high value of the independence of judge.[185] This document gives particular attention to the dignity of judges of national or international courts and demands that states respect the juridical independence of their judges. The intention of the Basic Principles *inter alia* is to enable judges to act in accordance with those principles and to prioritise the elaboration of guidelines relating to the independence of judges. According to one view "to disregard the judicial conscience is to compromise the dignity of the judge, the worth of her convictions, and the fullness of her humanity. Even more, it undermines the very essence of what distinguishes a democratic society characterized by diversity, inclusion, and freedom."[186]

The Basic Principles therefore underline that appropriate consideration should first be given to the role of judges in the system of justice, as well as to the importance of their selection, training, and conduct. Due to the

---

[185] Adopted by the Seventh United Nations Congress on the Prevention of Crime and the Treatment of Offenders held at Milan from 26 August to 6 September 1985 and endorsed by General Assembly resolutions 40/32 of 29 November 1985 and 40/146 of 13 December 1985.

[186] Barry W. Bussey, 'The Independence of Judicial Conscience' 9 (2) *The Journal of Christian Legal Thought* (2019), pp.34-37, at 37.

provisions and content of the Basic Principles, governments are of the view that they should take the provisions into account within the framework of their national legislation and practice them in order to promote the independence of the judiciary. They should also attempt to bring these provisions to the attention of judges, lawyers, members of the executive and the legislature, and the general public. Although the provisions of the Basic Principles were written for professional judges, they also apply to lay judges. The Basic Principles recognise that following the rules is necessary in ensuring the independence of judges and in protecting their right to freedom of expression and association.

The Basic Principles remind states that "members of the judiciary are like other citizens entitled to freedom of expression, belief, association and assembly." They nonetheless underline the values of the independence and dignity of judges, highlighting that "in exercising such rights, judges shall always conduct themselves in such a manner as to preserve the dignity of their office and the impartiality and independence of the judiciary." The Basic Principles further state that "judges shall be free to form and join associations of judges or other organizations to represent their interests, to promote their professional training and to protect their judicial independence."

The Basic Principles also deal with the qualifications, selection, and training of judges. They outline that those who are chosen to work in the judiciary, should be people of high integrity and great skill who possess the appropriate qualifications, experiences, and training regarding the law. Any method of judicial selection should safeguard and protect against judicial appointments mad with improper or inadequate motives. The Basic Principles requires that in the process of selecting judges, states should prevent discrimination against a person on the basis of race, ethnicity, sex, religion, political, or other opinion, national or social origin, property status, or any other status. However, the Basic Principles do recognise that if a nation states that a candidate for the judiciary must be a national of the relevant state, that this requirement is within the rights of the state to require and is not discriminatory.

States must also guarantee a certain level of professional secrecy and immunity for judges, including the right to immunity from civil suits or monetary suits taken against them as a result of miscarriages of justice or omissions. It is also the responsibility of states to ensure that the judiciary is bound by professional secrecy with regard to their deliberations. Accordingly, judges should not be forced to take part in public proceedings. They should also not be forced to testify about confidential matters.

Accordingly, the Basic Principles draw attention to the disciplining, suspension, and removal of judges under the following conditions:

> 17. A charge or complaint made against a judge in his/her judicial and professional capacity shall be processed expeditiously and fairly under an appropriate procedure. The judge shall have the right to a fair hearing. The examination of the matter at its initial stage shall be kept confidential, unless otherwise requested by the judge.
> 18. Judges shall be subject to suspension or removal only for reasons of incapacity or behaviour that renders them unfit to discharge their duties.
> 19. All disciplinary, suspension or removal proceedings shall be determined in accordance with established standards of judicial conduct.
> 20. Decisions in disciplinary, suspension or removal proceedings should be subject to an independent review. This principle may not apply to the decisions of the highest court and those of the legislature in impeachment or similar proceedings.

One may say that the principles introduced by the Basic Principles represent the formulation and regulation of customary attitudes towards the machinery of justice, judges, and criminal justice as a whole. The principles are therefore significant with reference to the fact that one assumes that these principles have long been exercised by states within their jurisdictions. However, their formulation is important in order to underline the way in which the judicial conscience works and identifies the ethical duties of judges as well as the ethical duties of the mechanism of justice. Judges of the court must not only be of good conscience, but the entire machinery of justice must place a high value on the integrity of justice and the personality of all those who engage with the judicial system. The intention is to preserve the common public notion of justice or other values which are significant for the honesty of criminal justice. All this means that we are looking for a way to protect the independence of judicial conscience from possible harm.

7.4. Judges of the ICC Acting in the Chambers

The decisions of the ICC should only be based on legal criteria, and therefore none of its decisions should serve a political purpose. The ICC is an independent court and it is upon this basis that the judges of the Court should keep their impartiality regarding all cases brought before their recognition. The ICC has a Presidency, the members of which should also remain objective on political matters, and should only deal with the principle of legality. The Presidency consists of up to three judges, one president and two vice presidents, who are chosen by the eighteen judges of the Court. The duty of the Presidency is concentrated on the internal and external administration of the Court. One of the important duties of the Presidency is to ensure the enforcement of sentences issued by the Court.

Additionally, judges of the ICC may work in the Pre-Trial Chambers. The Chambers can have between one and three judges working with different issues which arise before the beginning of the trial phase. The role of the judges here is basically to run the Office of the Prosecutor regarding its investigatory and prosecutorial activities in order to guarantee the rights of suspects, victims, and witnesses, which are necessary during the investigation. This is done in order to ensure the integrity of the proceedings. The judges of the Pre-Trial Chambers may decide to issue warrants of arrest or summons to appear at the Office of the Prosecutor of the ICC. In cases where the Prosecution appeals a warrant of arrest or summons to appear, the judges of the ICC must receive some of the necessary information concerning the suspect including their name, the crimes they are accused of, a short summary of the relevant evidence, and a summary of the reasons why the prosecution believes that the suspect should be arrested.

We should emphasise that all judges are people of high moral character and ought to remain impartial during all procedures. All this means that they should be qualified for their position and have the necessary experience with legal processes. [187] Judges of the ICC are elected by the Assembly of States Parties on the basis of their qualifications concerning the administration of criminal justice and their knowledge of international criminal law – including human rights law and the rights of children during war. The judges of the ICC should ensure the objectivity and fairness of all proceedings. Similarly, the ICC has a Trial Chamber which seeks to ensure that fair and full justice and impartiality are respected during proceedings in order to protect the victims, witnesses, and the accused.

The judges of the Trial Chamber decide whether the person accused of committing international crimes is innocent or guilty. If they are innocent, then they will be set free, however if they are guilty, then they will receive a punishment decided upon by the judges. The judges of a Trial Chamber also have the authority to order the convicted person to pay reparations to the victims for their suffering.[188] There is also an Appeals Chamber in the

---

[187] The conditions to be a judge in the Islamic criminal procedure deserve to be stated here. A qualified judge is:

1. a judge should be God-fearing and dignified in demeanour;
2. he should have sound common-sense and be conversant with the best of judicial literature;
3. he should bear an absolutely impeccable character;
4. he should not deliver judgements before he is satisfied that full proof has been laid before him, nor delay judgement when sufficient evidence has been produced;
5. he should be fearless in awarding what is right and due;
6. he should accept no present nor hear any recommendations;
7. he should see no party concerned in private;
8. he should really smile, and speak little;
9. he should accept no favour from any party concerned,
10. he should take great care to protect the property of orphans.

Muhammad Tal'at Al-Ghunaimi, 'Justice and Human Rights in Islam' in Gerald E. Lampe (ed.) Justice and Human Rights in Islamic Law (Washington: International Law Institute, 1997, pp.1-22, at p.2.

[188] In connection to victims' rights, "Overenthusiastically allowing victims to take part in investigations at situation level, for instance, gave rise to such hopes. In addition, a more transparent, precise and above all cohesive and consistent jurisprudence would enhance the credibility and predictability of the Court's case law, enabling victims and their representatives to estimate better whether their application has a chance at all. Otherwise,

system of ICC, comprised of the President of the Court and four other judges. The function of Appeals Chamber is to re-evaluate cases and relevant evidence if requested by the accused. The Chamber may thereafter amend the decision or judgements of the court, as well as the sentencing decisions. In certain necessary situations, the Appeals Chamber may even request the formation of a new trial before a different Trial Chamber in order to reject, mitigate, or dismiss the case against the accused.

7.5. Qualification of Judicial Conscience in the SCSL

Judges must always hold themselves to high standards of ethical reasoning and morality. They must demand the quality of judicial conscience and not vast quantities of its rules of ethical conducts. This means that they cannot pretend that they take healthy, moral approaches to criminal jurisdiction, while not doing the same in their private life. This implies the fact that they must act fairly at all times. For this reason, judges are prohibited from taking on cases where they may have a conflict of interest. Moreover, judges must be very cautious in expressing their views about political, social, or legal issues. They should also refrain from signing petitions that could be used to the advantage of parties to a criminal case. These are some of the primary requirements which are also entered into the structures of mixed international criminal courts. For example, the Special Court for Sierra Leone (SCSL) operated as a hybrid court.[189] This means that it had a mixed jurisdiction consisting of national and international provisions, principles, and judges. The Court was authorized

---

the Court is in danger of becoming paralysed by processing applications and handling purely procedural submissions without substantially advancing cases. Finally, sentencing practice needs to compensate in some way for the extremely selective character of international criminal trials, taking into consideration the effects of punishment on victims and the societies affected by the massive crimes under review, although without impeding the rights of the accused." Baumgartner, Aspects of Victim Participation in the Proceedings of the International Criminal Court', note 149, p.490.

[189] For the agreement see *Report of the Secretary-General on the Establishment of a Special Court for Sierra Leone*, 4 October 2000, U.N. Doc. S/2000/915.

under the legal and political sponsorship of the United Nations. Among the strongest reasons for the creation of this type of court was the need to resolve problems relating to the transportation of victims and witnesses, the issuance of arrest warrants for the prosecution of accused persons, and the access to evidence. These reasons imply the scope of judicial conscience for the judges of the courts/tribunals which will be discussed later.

The SCSL has been one of the most important organs of the United Nations in working to bring the perpetrators of murders, mutilation, mass rape, sexual violence, and other atrocities under an official jurisdiction. The Court was established per a request to the UN by the government of Sierra Leone. The intention of this court has been to bring the perpetrators of international crimes under criminal prosecution in order to levy punishment. The Court was established pursuant to Resolution 1315 (2000) of the Security Council. This resolution specifically recommended that three important principles be taken into account in the formulation of a statute for a special court. Some of its significant values were based on selection of its judges. The judges of the Court had to work in combination with the principles of human rights law and international criminal law standards for the prevention of impunity based on the good conscience of the judges.

The Resolution of the Security Council highlights the importance of recognising various violations and categories of crimes committed during the civil war in Sierra Leone.[190] It stated that "the subject matter jurisdiction of the special court should include notably crimes against humanity, war crimes and other serious violations of international humanitarian law, as well as crimes under relevant Sierra Leonean law committed within the territory of Sierra Leone."[191] Secondly, it placed a heavy weight on the concept of criminal responsibility. This responsibility

---

[190] See Malekian, *Jurisprudence of International Criminal Justice*, note 105, pp.34-35, 38, 45, and 74.

[191] Resolution 1315 (2000), para.2. Resolution 1315 (2000) has given a considerable number of duties to the Secretary General of the United Nations. Accordingly, the Secretary became responsible for writing a report concerning the establishment of the Sierra Leonean Court based on relations and negotiations with the government of Sierra Leone.

was to be attributed without due regard for the rank of the accused. The resolution recommended that "the special court should have personal jurisdiction over persons who bear the greatest responsibility for the commission of the crimes referred to in paragraph 2, including those leaders who, in committing such crimes, have threatened the establishment of and implementation of the peace process in Sierra Leone." According to the third principle of the resolution, the judges of the Court should conduct fair and just trials in accordance with the international standards of criminal justice. It emphasised "the importance of ensuring the impartiality, independence and credibility of the process, in particular with regard to the status of the judges and the prosecutors." This impartiality of judges was, and is echoed one of the most significant requirements for the implementation of appropriate criminal jurisdiction and the application of fair punishment.

According to the Statute of the Special Court for Sierra Leone, the Court was to consist of trial chambers, an appeals chamber, a prosecutor, and a registry. Each of these organs had their own specific function. The Statute also required that the judicial staff of the Special Court be comprised of a combination of international and domestic judges. All judges had to be individuals of high moral character and integrity who possessed the required qualifications in their respective countries. In particular, they were to be independent and not influenced by anyone regarding the outcome of the case.

7.6. Qualification of Judicial Conscience in the ICTY

The International Criminal Tribunal for Yugoslavia (ICTY) was one of several temporary organs which acted under the provisions of the United Nations until the end of 2017. It was composed of the chambers, prosecutors, and a registry, with each organ responsible for carrying out certain functions. The registry supported both of the other organs. The chambers were divided into three trial chambers and an appeals chamber. Some of the most significant conditions for the composition of the judges of chambers of the ICTY were:

1. Chambers were composed of sixteen permanent independent judges. The judges could not be of the same nationality;
2. A maximum of twelve *ad litem* independent judges were appointed at any given time;
3. Three permanent judges and a maximum of nine *ad litem* judges comprised each Trial Chamber at any given time;
4. Each Trial Chamber to which *ad litem* judges were assigned, was divided into sections of three judges each, composed of both permanent and ad litem judges, except under certain circumstances;
5. A section of a Trial Chamber had the same powers and responsibilities as a Trial Chamber under the Statute, and rendered judgement in accordance with the same rules;
6. Seven of the permanent judges were members of the Appeals Chamber;
7. The Appeals Chamber was composed of five members;
8. A person who held dual nationality was considered to be a national of the state in which they exercised their civil and political rights;
9. In accordance with the request of the President of the ICTY, the Secretary-General could appoint reserve judges, chosen from the ad litem judges, in order to replace a judge if they were unable to attend;
10. In the event that exceptional circumstances required that a permanent judge in a section of a Trial Chamber be replaced thereby resulting in a section solely comprised of *ad litem* judges, that section could continue to hear the case without issue despite not including a permanent judge.

7.7. Ethical Codes of the Extraordinary Chambers in the Courts of Cambodia

All these regulations are also entered into the statute of the Extraordinary Chambers in the Courts of Cambodia which is accompanied by a Code of Judicial Ethics. The Code particularly deals with the conscience of judges of the Extraordinary Chambers. The Chambers have a hybrid character and are comprised of national and international judges. The Code was specifically mentioned the 1985 United Nations Basic Principles on the Independence of the Judiciary. The significant articles of the Code dealing with the duties, responsibilities, independence, and impartiality of the judges of the Extraordinary Chambers state:

> Article 1. Judicial independence
> 1. Judges shall uphold the independence of their office and the authority of the Extraordinary Chambers in the Courts of Cambodia (hereinafter referred to as ECCC) and shall conduct themselves accordingly in carrying out their judicial functions.
> 2. Judges shall not engage in any activity which is likely to interfere with their judicial functions or to affect confidence in their independence.
>
> Article 2. Impartiality
> 1. Judges shall be impartial and ensure the appearance of impartiality in the discharge of their judicial functions.
> 2. Judges shall avoid any conflict of interest, or being placed in a situation which might reasonably be perceived as giving rise to a conflict of interest.
>
> Article 3. Integrity (Amended on 5 September 2008)
> 1. Judges shall conduct themselves with probity and integrity in accordance with their office, thereby enhancing public confidence in the judiciary.
> 2. Judges shall not directly or indirectly accept, offer, or provide any gift, advantage, privilege or reward that can reasonably be perceived as being intended to influence the performance of their judicial functions or the independence of their office.

Article 4. Confidentiality
Judges shall respect the confidentiality of information obtained in the discharge of their judicial functions and the secrecy of deliberations.

Article 5. Diligence
1. Judges shall act diligently in the exercise of their duties and shall devote their professional activities to those duties.
2. Judges shall take reasonable steps to maintain and enhance the knowledge, skills and personal qualities necessary for judicial office.
3. Judges shall perform all judicial duties properly and expeditiously.
4. Judges shall deliver their decisions without undue delay.

Article 6. Conduct during proceedings
1. In conducting judicial proceedings, judges shall maintain order, act in accordance with commonly accepted decorum, remain patient and courteous towards all participants and members of the public present and require them to act likewise.
2. Judges shall exercise vigilance in controlling the manner of questioning of witnesses or victims and give special attention to the right of participants to the proceedings to equal protection and benefit of the law.
3. Judges shall avoid conduct or comments which are racist, sexist or otherwise degrading and, to the extent possible, ensure that any person participating in the proceedings refrains from such comments or conduct.

Article 7. Public expression and association
1. Judges shall exercise their freedom of expression and association in a manner that is compatible with their office and that does not affect or appear to affect judicial independence or impartiality.
2. While judges are free to participate in public debate on matters pertaining to legal subjects, the judiciary or the administration of justice, they shall not comment on pending cases and shall avoid expressing views which may undermine the standing and integrity of the ECCC.

Article 8. Extra-judicial activity
1. Judges shall not engage in any extra-judicial activity that is incompatible with their judicial function or the efficient and timely

functioning of the ECCC, or that may affect or may reasonably appear to affect their independence or impartiality.
2. Judges shall not exercise any political function.

Article 9. Observance of the Code
1. The principles embodied in this Code shall serve as guidelines on the essential ethical standards required of judges in the performance of their duties.
2. Nothing in this Code is intended in any way to limit or restrict the judicial independence of the judges.192

7.8. Differences of Judges of Courts/Tribunals

The Statute of the Special Court for Sierra Leone (SCSL) was different from that of other ad hoc tribunals such as the ICTY or ICTR because of its mixed policy regarding the jurisdiction of international and national criminal courts.[193] Nevertheless, it followed the policy of other tribunals in many other aspects. The Special Court, like its predecessors the ICTY and the ICTR, was comprised of both Trial Chambers and Appeals Chambers. The Special Court consisted of eleven judges, with three judges in each of the two Trial Chambers, and five in the Appeals Chambers. The United Nations appointed two judges in each Trial Chamber and three judges in the Appeals Chamber. The remaining four judges were from Sierra Leone, and shared the seats in the Trial Chambers and the Appeals Chamber. Trial Chamber II also had an alternative judge who was appointed by the government of Sierra Leone. The judgements of the Special Court could be rendered by a majority of the judges.

[192] Adopted at the Plenary Session of the Extraordinary Chambers in the Courts of Cambodia on 31 January 2008, and amended at the Plenary Session of the Extraordinary Chambers in the Courts of Cambodia on 5 September 2008.

[193] For the court see Sriram, 'Wrong-sizing International Justice? The Hybrid Tribunal in Sierra Leone', note 76 pp.472-506; Magliveras, 'The Special Court for Sierra Leone: A New Type of Regional Criminal Court for the International Community?', note 76; Crane, The Special Court for Sierra Leone, note 76. Alison Smith, Child Recruitment and the Special Court for Sierra Leone, 2 *Journal of International Criminal Justice* 1141-1153 (2004).

Another difference was the composition of the Special Court. While the judges of the ICTY and ICTR were only international judges elected by The General Assembly of the United Nations, the judges of the Special Court were both international and Sierra Leonean judges.

7.9. Judges Affecting the Length of International Trials

The length of a trial in an inquisitorial or civil law system differs on a case-by-case basis and trials can even last more than a year. Nonetheless, the judge or the prosecutor needs several months to gather all essential documents, evidence, and certain witnesses relating to the case, based on a chain of hearings about the scenario surrounding the criminal case. The Rules of Procedure and Evidence at the ICTY, ICTR, and the Special Court for Sierra Leone included a considerable number of principles borrowed from the inquisitorial tradition under which judges are bound to follow and respect the judicial conscience in a given case.[194] Although a rule of procedure may have its origin in civil law or common law, it is neither the inquisitorial nor the adversarial procedure that impacts a fair and *expeditious* trial.[195] Rather, the requests for a fair and expeditious trial are the fundamental rights of the suspect.[196] Thus, the entire administration of criminal justice must respect these rules, and prosecutors and judges are legally required to follow the regulation of international criminal courts.

It must however be mentioned that while trial may proceed expeditiously, it may seriously violate the principles of justice and, as a result, the rights of the suspect may be ignored. There is, in fact, a relationship between the cross-examination of witnesses, haste, and the implementation of a fair trial. Moreover, ensuring fair and equal treatment is one of the duties of judges and prosecutors. For example, within the

---

194 Malekian, *Corpus Juris of Islamic International Criminal Justice*, note 3, p.129.
195 *Id.*
196 *Id.*

framework of adversarial proceedings, the prosecutor is entitled to appropriate equal treatment. Pre-Trial Chamber I of the ICC, with reference to the jurisprudence from the European Court of Human Rights, maintains that "the right to adversarial proceedings means in principle the opportunity for the parties to a criminal or civil trial to have knowledge of and comment on all evidence adduced or observations filed even by an independent member of the national legal service, with a view to influencing the court's decision." Furthermore, these requirements cannot be fixed as long as the judicial conscience of the judges of international courts remain unwise and the judges lack knowledge of national and international criminal justice, including the ability to approach a case with skill and morality.

The systems of international criminal tribunals have certain rules relating to fair and expeditious trials. For instance, the Statute of the ICTY contains certain rules dealing exclusively with delay and fairness. Article 20(1) of the tribunal provides: "Trial Chambers shall ensure that a trial is fair and expeditious and that proceedings are conducted in accordance with the rules of procedure and evidence, with full respect for the rights of the accused and due regard for the protection of victims and witnesses." Likewise, Article 21(2) provides: "In the determination of charges against him, the accused shall be entitled to a fair and public hearing, subject to Article 22 of the Statute." Furthermore, Article 21(4) provides that "in the determination of any charge against the accused pursuant to the present Statute, the accused shall be entitled to the following minimum guarantees, in full equality: (c) to be tried without undue delay."

Article 64 of the Statute of the ICC requires that the judges of the Trial Chamber ensure that trial procedures are fair and expeditious and are conducted with full respect for the rights of the accused and the protection of the victims and witnesses. These requirements of the article cannot be achieved if the judges of the ICC are incapable of rationally executing their duties. Additionally, the Rules of Procedure and Evidence of the Statute of the ICC concerning appeals goes even further and underscores the duties of judges regarding the respect of the regulations of the Statute. These rules ensure that any decision of a judge, which involves an issue that could impact the fair and expeditious conduct of the proceedings or the conclusions of the trial, should fully be respected.[197] In particular, the opinion of the judges of the Pre-Trial or the judges of the Trial Chamber may help advance proceedings.

One of the important functions of the Trial Chambers is to ensure that trials are conducted expeditiously and are reasonably fair.[198] Therefore, the right to a fair trial also equates to the right to an expeditious trial, as guaranteed by various international human rights treaties. The ICC Appeals Chamber observed that "Expeditiousness is ...an independent and important value in the Statute to ensure the proper administration of justice, and is therefore more than just a component of the fair trial rights of the accused."[199] For this reason, Article 64 (2) obliges the judges of the Trial Chamber to guarantee that trials are both fair and expeditious. Additionally, the Chamber explains further that "an expeditious trial is beneficial to victims. It ensures them of receiving justice and of going on through a healing process quickly."

For witnesses, this guarantee helps quell the anxiety that comes with being called before a court to present evidence. Unreasonable delay in commencing or concluding a trial may also diminish public interest, public support for, and cooperation with the Court. Consequently, certain provisions have been shaped and formed in the statutes of international criminal courts to ensure and guarantee the quality and fairness of the proceedings, which can only be upheld if the judges of the Chambers of the Court are legally and morally qualified and passionate. The purpose of these statutes is to review proceedings in order to encourage the expeditious trial of cases. For that reason, international courts are permitted to take measures to prevent any decision or action that may cause unreasonable delay because of the judges of the Court.

---

[197] See International Court of Justice, *Case Concerning the Arrest Warrant of 11 April 2000* (Democratic Republic of Congo v. Belgium), Judgment of 14 February.

[198] Examine also Amal Clooney, Philippa Webb, Right to a Fair Trial in International Law (Oxford Publication, 2020).

[199] "For this reason, article 64 (2) enjoins the Trial Chamber to ensure that the trial is both fair and expeditious." Prosecutor *v Katanga and Ngudjolo*, ICC - 01 - /04 - 01/07, Judgment on Unlawful Detention and Stay of Proceedings (12 July 2010), at para. 47.

7.10. WISDOM OF JUDGES

Whichever code of ethics we present, and whatever regulations we draft, the fact is that the judge is the eye, mind, and agent of criminal justice through which the wisdom of criminal justice is presented and developed.[200] Therefore, whatever the nature of our law is in the final stage, the wisdom of judges is imperative. However, there is always the question of what the requirements of wisdom for a judge are. Simultaneously, "Delivering authentic judgement and confidence in justice does not need witnesses but wisdom. This wisdom should exist in every single judge and in every lawyer. A legal representative who fights for the rights of her/his client without using her/his intuition for true and wise justice is not true to the soul of justice but a person blind to fairness."[201]

More broadly speaking, a judge presents the disputes that they then adjudicate. This means that national and international criminal communities trust the judges of the Court to hold a deep reverence for the truth regarding the case and the rules of criminal justice in their role as the purveyor of truth. It is on this account that judges of the Court are supposed to fully respect the international legal community in order to make wise decisions. Judges are thus considered to be judicial guardians operating in the sphere of the freedom of the truth in the courtroom.

The notion of wisdom in the system of international criminal justice is thus found not only within regulations or statutes, including those of international human rights law, but more significantly within actions which demonstrate to the international public that a decision was wise and not influenced by political intrigues. This means that the decisions of judges of the ICC must be free from all political ties and taken following the careful examination of the circumstances surrounding the case. With such an apparatus blowing the sails of the vessel of the International

---

200 "This wisdom should exist in every single judge and in every lawyer. A legal representative who fights for the rights of her/his client without using her/his intuition for true and wise justice is not true to the soul of justice but a person blind to fairness." Malekian, *Judgments of Love in Criminal Justice*, note 1, p.15.

201 *Id.*

Criminal Court, we believe that wisdom is usually present within the decisions of the Court. Therefore, we should not collectively lose our footing and slide unintentionally into committing further criminal acts or injustice against the victims. Thus, the wisdom of the judges of the court implies the respect of the suffering of the victims and our responsibility to help those who are suffering from atrocities of big criminals. It is our duty or the duty of our judges to be wise and to not further harm the victims by hiding the truth.

Obviously, upholding the judicial conscience with the full wisdom of our judges in the international criminal court is imperative. If the dignity of individuals is not respected with full wisdom, there is no further reason to respect the dignity of the judges of the Court. In other words, these dignities are interrelated, and thus cannot be treated in isolation from one another. The judges of the Court ought to maintain the fundamental rights and freedoms which may distinguish the system of international criminal justice from criminal courts in which the judges have lost their impartiality and their judicial conscience is occupied by political autocrats.

The judicial conscience of a judge reflects the personal assurance and obligation of the judge regarding moral integrity and moral ethics. This moral integrity is present throughout the internal codified duties of the judge, as well as in their external judicial responsibility towards the international community. The internal sphere of wisdom of the judges of the international criminal court addresses the purity of the *somebodiness* of the judge, which they must promise to uphold throughout the duration of trial.[202] This implies that the obligations of the relevant judge to manifest the ethical moralities of the codes of ethics are to be fulfilled under their authority under all circumstances, and should not be influenced by external decisions. However, the question remains:

> when ethical rules are codified, whose ethics do—or should—they reflect? There is a risk of "cultural hegemony" in the development and codification of ethical standards, to the extent that these standards

---

[202] Consult Farhad Malekian, *International Criminal Law: The Law of Somebodiness, The Law of Nobodiness* (New York: Nova Publishers, 2021).

> develop in an environment dominated by a small number of countries and legal traditions. When the Code of Conduct and Disciplinary Procedure applicable to counsel appearing before the ICC was presented to the Court in May 2003, the stated objective was to produce a code "that could be accepted and followed by Counsel from all cultures, traditions and legal systems and professional backgrounds." No matter how good the intentions, a small yet crucial piece of the puzzle seems to be missing: to be able to follow and accept such emerging ethical standards, all cultures, traditions, and legal systems need to be concretely involved in their definition. Until then, the inherently relative nature of ethics will prevail and the "international judicial culture" that the international community is struggling to build will remain nothing more than a distant dot on the horizon.[203]

We suppose that the judge demonstrates the standard of their morality free of external intrigues within the internal sphere of the ethical norms of criminal justice. The external sphere of the judicial conscience in the administration of criminal justice impacts the judge's public obligations and relationships. This implies the faithfulness of the judge or their appropriate wisdom concerning their duties to the Court and to the international community. In this way, a judge of the ICC upholds the highest ethical, conventional, and customary traditions for the understanding of the notion of criminal wisdom in the office of the judge. Thus, they must ensure that the rules of international criminal justice are being faithfully fulfilled in order to preserve the integrity of the Court.

7.11. Non-Governmental Judges Creating Nobility

Judges are usually chosen by the administration of justice based on certain requirements. They are officially given the title of "judge," and are

---

[203] Cima, *Ethical Conduct in International Criminal Courts: Whose Ethics?*, note 37, pp.300-301.

also paid for their services. They are bound by the provisions of criminal legislation to not violate the provisions of the given law. In particular, criminal judges have to be very careful when making their decisions since any wrong decision can send an innocent person to jail. This is also true in the case of judges of permanent or temporary *ad hoc* tribunals who are officially employed to work for the relevant tribunals or courts. However, private individuals dealing with the law may also be able to create international tribunals without the consent of a political authority in the name of the love for truth and justice. Such tribunals are known as non-governmental international courts; and one example of such a court is the Russell War Crimes Tribunal which was established by Bertrand Russell and was based on the model of the legislation of the Nuremberg War Crimes Tribunal. However, all the judges and members of the Russell Tribunal were volunteers and were not paid.

The Russell War Crimes Tribunal held three sessions in London, Stockholm, and Copenhagen. The latter session was supposed to be held in Paris but the French government prohibited this because they politically and militarily supported American policy in Vietnam. The French government was one of the first countries in the world to commit atrocities in Vietnam in order to possess the nation, beginning back in 1883.[204] In May 1966, Bertrand Russell addressed the first meeting of the members of the War Crimes Tribunal in London. Russell emphasised the *judicial conscience of judges* or magistrates, as well as their duty to follow the precise definitions of international crimes which were committed in Vietnam through the aggressive military conducts of the American government.[205] He particularly emphasised the duties of judges with reference to the criteria with which such actions could be judged. He also stressed the moral duty of the judges to record the horrific occurrences in Vietnam and to freely enforce a legal model in order to conduct a solemn and historic investigation without interference from politicians. The judges of the Russell War Crimes Tribunal were tasked with addressing questions

[204] Max Hastings, *Vietnam: An Epic Tragedy*, 1945-1975 (2018), p.2.

[205] On judicial conscience which was presented Vespasian Pella internationally see sub-section 4.3. *supera*.

such as: Why was the war being fought in Vietnam? And whose interests were being served with the war?

The fact was that Russell's statement added to the most significant integral part of the duties of judges in international tribunals (Nuremberg and Japan) and contributed to the idea of how the judges of a court should ethically and morally function in order to uncover the truth. The judges of the Russell Tribunal sought to understand why a small, agrarian nation had to endure the assaults of the largest industrial power on earth, which was in possession of the most advance military technology. Moreover, Russell mentioned that "it is necessary to convene a solemn Tribunal, composed of men eminent not through their power, but through their intellectual and moral contribution to what we optimistically call human civilization." The purpose of the Tribunal was to "*record the truth,*" which should be the purpose of all courts. Accordingly, the principles of truth, impartiality, and morality must be upheld by judges who in turn must remain on the side of the truth. Bertrand Russell further stated that judges must:

a) Pass judgement on what we find to be the truth;
b) Warn of the consequences of this truth;
c) Reject the view that only indifferent individuals are impartial;
d) Repudiate the degenerate concept of individual intelligence, which confuses open minds with empty ones;
e) Select individuals who respect the truth and whose life's work reflects this to be judges;
f) Pursue the truth, born of intense and unyielding inquiry.

On 13 November 1966, Russell was joined by Jean-Paul Sartre, Vladimir Dedijer, Isaac Deutscher, and Lelio Basso at the opening meeting of the Tribunal in London.[206] It was stated that the tribunal had no clear

206 Tor Krever, 'Remembering the Russell Tribunal', 5 (3) *London Review of International Law* (2017), pp.483-492. On Oct 22, 2021, the judges of the non-governmental Belmarsh Tribunal in London stated: "What, and whom are we putting on trial? The bloody crimes that have been committed by Western governments: the United States, the United Kingdom, Australia, Sweden, Ecuador and ..." It is in response to this tribunal that the British lawyer Sir Geoffrey Nice, the American Lawyer Michael Scharf, and the Swedish lawyers should

historical precedent, and was thus not supported by any state power. Therefore, although it addressed the governments responsible for crimes against the people of Vietnam, it lacked *force majeure*. The procedures of the trial were certainly impossible to execute.[207] This meant that "the tribunal lacks a concrete jurisdiction; it can impose a moral, ethical and social sanction against the defendant." The tribunal, after very long and intensive investigation and the examination of evidence concerning crimes against humanity, war crimes, aggression, and genocide and hearing witnesses, came to the conclusion that the American government had committed serious international crimes in Vietnam, with the complicity of other states.[208] The verdict of the Tribunal stated that:

> Has the Government of the United States committed acts of aggression against Vietnam under the terms of international law? Yes (unanimously).
> Has there been, and if so, on what scale, bombardment of purely civilian targets, for example, hospitals, schools, medical establishments, dams, etc.? Yes (unanimously) We find the government and armed forces of the United States are guilty of the deliberate, systematic and large-scale bombardment of civilian targets, including civilian populations, dwellings, villages, dams, dikes, medical establishments, leper colonies, schools, churches, pagodas, historical and cultural monuments.

---

reflect upon their professional licenses, including their morality of conscience, not only concerning Julian Assange but also concerning all crimes committed by big powers and their governments. See *The Belmarsh Tribunal: The War On Terror is Put on Trial*, https://www.youtube.com/watch?v=E_xxGWAxlGc. We are responsible to prevent continuation of any war by big powers against innocents. For the whole Julian Assange case consult Malekian, Allegations by Political Laundering, note 24.

[207] Consult Farhad Malekian, *International Criminal Law*, Volumes I & II (Almqvist Wiksell International, 1991).

[208] Richard Falk, *The Vietnam War and International Law* (Princeton University Press, 1968); see also Richard Falk, 'The Accountability of Leaders: A Challenge to Civil Government and Society' in Jeremy Brecher, Jill Cutler, Smith Brendan, *In the Name of Democracy: American War Crimes in Iraq and Beyond (American Empire Project)*, (New York: Metropolitan Books, Henry Holt and Company, 2005); Richard Falk, *Slouching Toward a Palestinian Holocaust*, www.transnational.org/Area.../Falk Palestine Genocide.html, 20 October 2010.

> Have the governments of Australia, New Zealand and South Korea been accomplices of the United States in the aggression against Vietnam in violation of international law? Yes (unanimously).

Bertrand Russell, the president of the Russell War Crimes Tribunal, was correct when he asserted that "good life is one inspired by love and guided by knowledge. Neither *love* without knowledge, nor knowledge without *love* can produce a good life." This is what the headline for the judges of all national, regional, and international courts, should be. Likewise,

> If the norm love is very difficult to understand and we criticise it on the basis that it has no legal dimension, legal strength, or legal validity for judges and lawyers, then the question is what is the law? Is it not the expression of our collective wishes, collective responsibility, collective duties, and the communication of our high standards of love? I am not, however, here talking about law which is dictated by different means. Nor am I concerned with law that is enforced by force and which one has to obey under threat of violence, as are the laws in some of the Islamic states. Neither am I referring to law which pretends to be law but which does not respect the rights of civilians, as is the case with many of the rules in Russia, China, the United States, Saudi Arabia. Nor am I speaking of the legislation of parliaments which apply the law with prejudice, such as the serious discrimination practised in Australia.[209]

---

[209] Malekian, *Judgments of Love in Criminal Justice*, note 1, p.75.

Chapter 8

Limits of Punishments Per Human Rights Law

8.1. Introduction to Punishment

In some countries, a majority of cases are heard by magistrates and panels who must then make a decision concerning the guilt of the accused. However, when cases concern more serious crimes, a district judge may hear the evidence in the presence of a jury. Furthermore, cases of murder or rape may be heard by other judges, such as high court judges, who are more competent regarding serious offences. This means that the relevant judges have the power to imprison anyone convicted of a crime, or sentence them to community service. The decisions of judges are very important in preventing certain crimes and teaching lessons to the accused with the hope that they will not commit another crime in the future. However, this has not always been effective, and certain situations have proven that the unwise punishment of the accused may create more problems for the greater community.

That is why the punishment of the accused also has a psychological effect on the system of criminal jurisdiction and naturally on the life of the accused. The criminal judge is also responsible for reading the case very carefully and analysing every matter in detail prior to the beginning of court proceedings. This also extends to the indictment which relates to the charges brought up against the defendant. The judge is also responsible for reading the statements of witnesses, the accused, victims, and any other relevant parties which concern the admissibility of the evidence in the trial. The high judge is also responsible for communicating with their colleagues who will also be involved in the criminal procedures. Once the trial has begun, the judge should naturally guarantee that the case is accessible for all parties and is carried out equitably. In all these situations, judges have the responsibility to apply appropriate punishment within the bounds of existing law.

8.2. SENTENCING

Judges control the sentencing in criminal cases and the amount of the fine in civil cases. It is important to note however, that judges have different duties when it comes to cases involving juveniles. The reason for this is that juveniles cannot be prosecuted for crimes due to their reduced responsibility and thus cannot be tried the same way as adults. The proceedings of investigations into crimes committed by juveniles are consequently not adversarial, and juveniles do not stand before juries. In juvenile cases, the judge examines the evidence and listens to arguments presented by the parties to the case and decides what would be the best alternative for the juvenile.

In most countries, judges are responsible for signing arrest warrants and investigating cases. In the United States and other common law legal systems, judges have the authority to punish misbehaviour happening within a courtroom. They can also punish possible violations of court orders. The judges are therefore responsible for enforcing order within the courtroom. Judges in this type of system can assert that the law is unconstitutional concerning a specific case. Moreover, judges have the right to contradict precedent, which offers some flexibility in the interpretation of the law.

In countries with juries, the condemnation of the accused is based on the decision of the jury.[210] If the jury finds the defendant guilty, then the judge will take the final decision based on their decision and determine the appropriate punishment based on the relevant criminal legislation. The nature of the punishment and sentence can change depending on certain factors relating to the parties involved in the case.

The nature of the sentence is also dependent upon the outcome of the crime and its impact on the victims. For example, if a father is killed and leaves dependent children behind, then that must be taken into consideration when determining the sentence. Additionally, the judges of a court of appeals have the same duties regarding sentencing and evaluating the circumstances of the victims of a crime. Judges should also take into account any possible mitigation of the sentence as well as any reports on the defendant. All these factors must be taken into consideration by a judge when determining the length of a sentence. These points are also significant when it comes to the victims of international crimes and the dependent children they have left behind. The judges of international criminal tribunals or courts should recognise the situation these children are in and should not ignore the power of ethical judicial conscience.

8.3. Punishment in ICC

Judges of the ICC must be very cautious when issuing decisions about cases in order to respect the provisions of the Statute of the ICC. According to Article 77 of the Statute, the judges of the Court are allowed to sanction imprisonment for the following crimes: crimes against humanity, genocide, war crimes, and aggression. This means that it is one of the duties of the judges of the Court to apply appropriate punishment for the

---

[210] "In Great Britain, lay judges sit with professional judges in some types of cases only and, where they do so, the overwhelming majority of decisions are unanimous." Burgess Pete, Susan Corby, and Paul L. Latreille, 'Lay Judges and Labour Courts: A Question of Legitimacy', 35 *Comparative Labour Law and Policy Journal* (2014), pp.191-215, at 193. Available at https://cllpj.law.illinois.edu /content/pdf/vol_35/issue_2/Burgess-et-al-35-2-FINAL.pdf.

crimes committed by different individuals of different states. It is nonetheless the case that the decisions of judges of the Court should respect certain rules and they are not permitted to impose a penalty which exceeds the limitations set by the Statute. As a result, a prison sentence issued by the ICC cannot exceed 30 years.[211]

The rationale behind this restriction is to limit the power of the judges of the Court concerning the punishment of criminals, as well as to hinder excessive punishment. This philosophy also coincides with the basic principles of human rights law which seek to prevent violations of dignity. The problem is that no minimum sentences were set in the provisions of the texts of the ICC, and there are no specific suggested sentences for particular crimes. This means that the length of a sentence is left up to the ethical discretion of the judges.

Whilst the maximum prison sentence of 30 years is written in the text of the Statute of the ICC, the expression "life imprisonment" seems to be unjustified and is recognised as violating the basic principles of human rights law. For this reason, the Statute has also foreseen situations that may reduce life imprisonment in order to mitigate its extreme harshness. Therefore, in particular situations Article 110 of the Statute has opened a window for the mitigation of the penalty according to the decisions of judges in order to ensure that the convicted person is served fair and impartial justice. As a result, when the convicted person has served two-thirds of their sentence, the ICC may re-evaluate their sentence and potentially reduce it. The decision of the judges of the Court to reduce a person's punishment may be based on several factors such as the voluntary assistance of the person in the enforcement of judgements, consistent willingness of the prisoner to work together with the Court in order to assist the relevant investigative processes, or any other reason which may justify the reduction of their sentence.

---

[211] The International Criminal Court issued its first verdict on 14 March 2012 and the first sentence on 10 July 2012 in the Lubanga case. The Prosecutor vs. *Thomas Lubanga Dyilo*, Judgment pursuant to Article 74 of the Statute, Trial Chamber I, 14 March 2012, ICC-01/04-01/06-2842; The Prosecutor vs. Thomas Lubanga Dyilo, Decision on Sentence pursuant to Article 76 of the Statute, Trial Chamber I, 10 July 2012, ICC-01/04-01/06-2901.

The judges of the Court are also allowed to review a prisoner's sentence after they have served 25 years of their sentence. Such a review is permissible if: the convicted person has cooperated with the court, assisted in the enforcement of judgements, or any other reasonable factor.[212] Accordingly, it is at the discretion of the judges to evaluate whether the evidence is strong enough to change the person's sentence.

Article 77 of the Statute also supports other provisions concerning punishment. The judges of the Court are permitted to issue a life sentence if the circumstances and gravity of the case require. Consequently, it is one of the duties of the judges of the Court to investigate and evaluate the circumstances of the case, while also keeping the gravity of the crime in mind in order to ensure a proportionate and fair penalty. This principle also relies on the proper measurement of the judicial conscience of judges and their moral and legal capacity to remain impartial while determining sentences.

While it may seem that the use of life imprisonment does not align with the principles of court, however such punishment may deliver appropriate justice in certain cases. It may then be in the best interests of the Court and international society to issue the punishment, not as a method of denying someone their natural rights, but as a method of expressing the gravity of the crime in order to prevent the crime from being repeated.

8.4. Personal Relations of Judges

Judges are people too—as a result, they may not always be able to control their personal feelings. Someone can have a relationship with a judge by knowing them personally, knowing of them, being involved in business with them, or having (secret) knowledge about them or their family. A judge could also be involved with a certain religious sect which could impact their judgements, or with a particular powerful political

---

[212] Article 110 (4).

group, which could manipulate the judge to their advantage. All these relations could potentially impact the outcome of a case.

This is regardless of the fact that a judge knows that the respect of independence, impartiality, autonomy, integrity, and legality of criminal justice is fundamental to the maintenance of justice.[213] It is also regardless of the fact that judges are aware that fairness, responsibility, equality, respect for each party, and the protection of humanity are essential to ensuring their accountability as judges. All these factors are part of the duties of a judge and an integral part of their impartiality. Certainly, judges must be tolerant, honest, and respectful of the public interest.

However, the situation in the system of international criminal court is quite different and critical when it comes to the ICC's jurisdiction. Within the jurisdiction of the ICC, a judge may not know any of the accused individuals personally, nor would they have knowledge of their lawyers or families. Nonetheless, in the system of international criminal justice, politics find their own way to influence the judges, which can lead to more serious issues than within national systems of criminal law. This is because the judge could deny the rights of a large number of victims and thus benefit the offenders with one simple mistake, or even on purpose. The latter implies that the system of international criminal justice is subservient to the personal relationships of a judge or their tendency to support certain groups or nations because of their religious beliefs.

Certainly, it would constitute serious misconduct for an attorney or politicians to attempt to influence a judge, as this violates the judicial conscience and the code of ethics of the ICC. Even influencing a judge by contacting their family or their country's political authorities constitutes an act of misconduct and a serious violation of the objectivity of the judge and the impartiality of the Court.[214] Such actions may therefore infringe

[213] Examine also Eyal Benvenisti & George W. Downs, 'Prospects for the Increased Independence of International Tribunals', 12 (5) *German Law Journal* (2011), pp.1057-1081. Available online at file:///C:/Users/admin/AppData/Local/Temp/prospects-for-the-increased-independence-of-international-tribunals.pdf; Ruth Mackenzie & Philippe Sands, 'International Courts and Tribunals and the Independence of the International Judge', 44 *Harvard International Law Journal* (2003), pp.271-285.

[214] The Appeals Chamber of the International Criminal Tribunal for the Former Yugoslavia has clarified that "the fundamental human right of an accused to be tried before an independent

upon the rules of professional conduct, the natural rights of man, and the system of international human rights as a whole. It is incumbent upon judges to maintain their integrity and independence within the jurisdiction of the ICC, in particular when making decisions concerning punishment.

Naturally, the ICC or any of its judges who become aware of the inappropriate conduct of politicians or lawyers must initiate disciplinary action against them. However, this rarely occurs in practice since law is just interpretation, codes are just words, ethical and moral theories are personal interpretations, and justice is a tool used by the strong against the weak. As a result, dutifulness, solidarity, and improvement of the system of international criminal justice remain and vary case-to-case. If a case comes before an international criminal court seeking to bring justice against big military states, history has shown that justice will not prevail.[215]

8.5. Bribery of Judges

Judges should be aware of their duties in the administration of criminal justice as outlined in the code of ethics, and thus resist all forms of bribery, including both financial and political. Judges must decisively thwart any effort to influence their decisions and thus maintain the integrity of the case and the court proceedings. Judges are obliged to report any unprofessional actions which could impact the outcome of the case and affect the gravity of punishment.

---

and impartial tribunal is generally recognized as being an integral component of the requirement that an accused should have a fair trial." Prosecutor *v. Anto Furundzija,* Case No. IT-95-71/1-A99, Appeals Chamber, Judgment, para. 177 (Int'l Crim. Trib. for the Former Yugoslavia July 21, 2000), http://www.icty.org/x/cases/furundzija/acjug/en/fur-aj000721e.pdf.

215 Impunity has been defined as "the impossibility, *de jure or de facto*, of bringing the perpetrators of violations to account—whether in criminal, civil, administrative or disciplinary proceedings—since they are not subject to any inquiry that might lead to their being accused, arrested, tried and, if found guilty, sentenced to appropriate penalties, and to making reparations to their victims." Updated Set of Principles for the Protection and Promotion of Human Rights through action to combat impunity, 8 February 2005, E/CN.4/2005/102/Add.1, p. 6. See also https://www.ohchr.org/EN/Issues/TruthJusticeReparation/Pages/InternationalInstruments.aspx.

Although one cannot say that judges are responsible for the wrongful conducts of any party, they are the only person who has read and evaluated the facts of the case. They are therefore responsible for reporting any minor influence on the proceedings, criminal justice, or the application of punishment. Therefore, judges should encourage and uphold measures and protections that they consider essential and necessary for safeguarding the integrity of criminal justice and their judgements. This means that the maintenance of objectivity is necessary, even when it comes to decisions which may not be directly connected to the relevant case but which could have an impact on the administration of justice and the parties to the case.

In the end, these discussions and arguments relate to the principle of impartiality and the preservation of its ethical integrity regarding all matters. Bribery is a crime within all systems of law; however it is still commonly seen at all levels of governance in the majority of countries. As a result, bribery in the administration of criminal justice is not only a crime, but represents the mistreatment of the independence of criminal jurisdiction. Bribery may even occur in international criminal courts if a case could reveal the truth about the permanent members of the Security Council.

8.6. Criminality of Judges Permitting Capital Punishment

As a rule, punishments of all types have to be replaced with the force of love if our intention is to decrease violations and increase the effect of rehabilitation when it comes to the decisions of judges.[216] Love is the only legal medicine for healing which should be expressed and shown in the opinions or decisions of a judge. This has to be understood by all legal systems, judges, prosecutors, and lawyers. Nevertheless, I am also fully conscious of the fact that most of us, including the layman, lawyers,

---

[216] Adopted from the author's book Malekian, *Judgments of Love in Criminal Just*ice, note 1, with full modifications.

prosecutors, judges, and students of law, when coming across the word love, think first of romantic love. This is the love which is articulated by individuals to the person they adore, who they might sacrifice their lives for, and with whom they may share intimacy, feelings of isolation, and interconnectedness.[217] However, with the love in the system of criminal justice which should be respected by a judge we are referring to:

> Impartial sympathy judgement is the major implication of the principle of love. It requires the judges to take the moral perspective of all the parties to legal process. A judge has to use all her or his ability of imagination and intuition to penetrate the inner world of these who will be affected by judicial decision. A judge must endeavour to understand their motives and emotions. Sympathy does not require the judge to deny or disregard their own moral beliefs and convictions. What it does require is that a judge should not accept his on moral convictions as the only true and correct ones, but be ready to engage into dialogue with the moral world of another. The essence of sympathy judgement lies in genius willingness to do good to the persons affected by judicial decisions through understanding and critical acceptance of the moral perspective of those persons. Only though having such understanding and acceptance is a judge able to give a proper evaluation of the facts and interpretation of the relevant legal rules.[218]

It is also obvious that most buildings, rooms, walls, doors, and windows have been constructed to keep our sensual feelings private between ourselves and the person with whom we have chosen to share our physical movements, sentimental experiences, and love. Nonetheless, let me make it clear here that with the notion of love in this context, we are speaking about the justice within the naked judgement of law for the effective implementation of the requirements of the basic principles of humanity in order to qualify the decision of a judge not to commit crimes

---

[217] *Id.*, p.121.

[218] Alexander Nikolaevich Shytov, Conscience and Love in Making Judicial Decisions (2001), p.xiv.

by permitting the application of capital punishment.[219] There are a number of judges in the world who commit this crime, such as "the hanging-judge," who is one of the notorious Iranian judges who bends to the Islamic regime's criminal system. Cases in which other judges would not dare to be involved are addressed to his office.

The "hanging-judge" sentences almost every offender to death before even hearing the case as required. The rights of the accused are reduced to the lowest degree possible.[220] Likewise, there have been similar allegations about the notorious judges Gholam-Hossein Mohseni-Eje'I and Abolqasem Salavati and their decisions to kill. There are also similar accusations concerning the new president of Iran who asserts that he has protected international human rights principles through his decisions. However, his decisions have not only violated the norm of love, but also the norms of morality and legality.

> A judge may give a considerable number of reasons for her/his engagement in criminal cases which lead to the death penalty. Nevertheless, the jus cogens law accepts no excuse. This legal philosophy of jus cogens is quite exceptional in that it does not treat the relevant judges by means of argumentum ad hominem, but as an ex concessis of what has been consolidated in the system of international human rights law. Furthermore, the decision of a judge, which gives permission for the application of capital punishment, goes strongly against the principles of jus naturale. Human beings should not avert the principles of jus naturale and neither can jus naturale follow human being's natural rights. A reason given by a judge in self-defence is simply not to be found guilty of international crimes. Obviously, the written judgement of a judge is an intentional erratum carried out with full consent with due regard for the principle of mens rea. A reason is often an explanation that is expressed by most of us in order to justify our wrongful conduct or fault. Its basic intention is to minimise the borderline of responsibility by freeing ourselves from moral accountability. Most judges of those states that have implemented capital punishment give

---

219 Malekian, *Judgments of Love in Criminal Justice,* note 1, pp.120-121; Gerald Gardiner, *Capital Punishment as a Deterrent: And the Alternative* (London: Victor Gollancz, 1956).

220 *Id.*

> amnesty and forgiveness to themselves by reasoning that they were carrying out their duties. This is particularly notable in the case of replacing the old regime with a new one.[221]

A newly-constructed synonym for the development of the principle of the right to love is the phrase: "right to hope." This means that capital punishment should not be allowed under any circumstances. In the case of *Vinter and Others v. the United Kingdom*, the concurring judgement of the Grand Chamber of the European Court of Human Rights voiced clearly that the European Convention on Human Rights in its Article 3, which governs the implementation of the prevention of inhumane or degrading treatment, clearly preserves the right to hope for every human being. The Court in its significant decision clarifies:

> The judgement recognises, implicitly, that hope is an important and constitutive aspect of the human person. Those who commit the most abhorrent and egregious of acts and who inflict untold suffering upon others, nevertheless retain their fundamental humanity and carry within themselves the capacity to change. Long and deserved though their prison sentences may be, they retain the right to hope that, someday, they may have atoned for the wrongs which they have committed. They ought not to be deprived entirely of such hope. To deny them the experience of hope would be to deny a fundamental aspect of their humanity and, to do that, would be degrading.[222]

As I have emphasized elsewhere, capital punishment is an abolished institution, just like the institutions of torture and slavery. One may even conclude that since *jus cogens* law prohibits the application of capital punishment, any judgement made by a judge which results in capital punishment violates international law-making treaties, customary international law, general principles of law, the law of the permanent

---

[221] *Id.*, note 1, p.124.

[222] Concurring Opinion of Judge Power-Forde, the Grand Chamber of the European Court of Human Rights (9 July 2013) (Applications nos. 66069/09, 130/10 and 3896/10) http://hudoc.echr.coe.int/fre?i¼001-122664#{%22itemid%22:[%22001-122664%22]} (Accessed October, 2015).

International Criminal Court, the law of the ICTY, the law of the ICTR, the law of the SCSL, European Union law, African laws, most Asian laws, Australian law, and most North and South American laws.

8.7. Capital Punishment Constituting a Universal Crime

A judge who permits capital punishment and justifies it by stating that the provisions of the relevant legislation permit it commits crimes against the basic rights of man. In other words:

> A duty which goes against the pure philosophy of love for justice, love for the implementation of jus cogens law, love for the application of the basic principles of human rights law, and love for the appropriate application of European criminal law can no longer be called a duty. It is instead a serious violation of the principle of universality of abolition of capital punishment. The term love here means a norm that is clearly the intention of a particular norm of law presented in the substance of the relevant law for the proper implementation of the purpose of its object. These are the non-derogable purpose of prohibition of capital punishment, non-excusable implementation of torture, or non-acceptable impunity in the case of sexual offences in war and peacetime. All these mean a borderline between what is permitted and what is not permitted by international law. Here, I am not only focusing on the law of all states—Western or non-Western—but also those cruel Islamic provisions that have become reasons for the application of capital punishment, stoning, cutting off hands and entire arms.[223]

Authorised judges who sanction cruel capital punishment are guilty of violating the rules of national criminal jurisdictions and the statutes of international criminal law and justice.[224] The respective judges should bear

---

[223] Malekian, *Judgments of Love in Criminal Justice*, note 1, p.124.

[224] Such violations of the basic principles of law can be seen in the provisions of Iranian criminal legislation.

criminal responsibility, not only before their national criminal courts, but also before the jurisdiction of other national courts.[225] In other words, a judge who permits the application of capital punishment has seriously violated the system of international human rights law and the rules of universal natural law, and has thus committed an international crime against the value of man.[226] Such judges can be arrested by any state by evoking the universality principle and be brought under the procedures of criminal justice in order to receive appropriate punishment.

This principle also applies to the judges who participated in the Saddam Hussein Tribunal and the subsequent execution of Hussein and others. Furthermore, the international criminal lawyers who were working with the Statute of the Iraqi Special Tribunal and were involved in drafting its provisions under CIA supervision are certainly criminally responsible for supporting a constitution of a court which gave permission to ignore the *jus cogens* principle of the abolition of capital punishment.[227] The

---

[225] Nandor Knust and Kettuli Lingenfelter. Individual Criminal Responsibility beyond the State: Trafficking as Both a Transnational and an International Crime (Palgrave Macmillan, 2020).

[226] Gerald Gardiner, *Capital Punishment as a Deterrent: And the Alternative* (London: Victor Gollancz, 1956). William A Schabas, The Abolition of the Death Penalty in International Law (Third Edition: Cambridge UP, 2002), 373; Eric Prokosch, 'The Death Penalty versus Human Rights' in Death Penalty: Beyond Abolition (Council of Europe Publishing: Strasbourg, 2004), 3-35, 7.

[227] Consult Farhad Malekian, 'Conundrums of *Jus cogens:* In Case Law' (Part II), No.13 *Вісник Південного регіонального центру Національної академії правових наук України, No.13 Journal of the South regional Center of National Academy of Legal Sciences of Ukraine (*2017), pp.12-21; Farhad Malekian, 'Conundrums of *Jus cogens*: in International Criminal Law' (Part I), *Вісник Південного регіонального центру Національної академії правових наук України No.12 Journal of the South regional Center of National Academy of Legal Sciences of Ukraine (*2017), pp.8-16; A Cassese, 'For an Enhanced Role of *Jus cogens*' in A Cassese, (ed.), *Realizing Utopia* (2012); Antônio Augusto *Cançado Trindade* '*Jus cogens* in Contemporary International Law', UN Audiovisual Library, (http://www.un.org/law/avl); M. Byers 'Conceptualising the Relationship Between *Jus cogens* and *Erga Omnes Rules*' 66 *Nordic Journal of International Law* (1997); J. Brunnée, 'The Prohibition on Torture: Driving *Jus cogens* Home?' 104 *Proceedings of the Annual Meeting of the American Society of International Law* (2010); A. Bianchi, 'Human Rights and the Magic of *Jus cogens*', 19 *European Journal of International Law* (2008), pp.491-508; C. Chinkin, '*Jus cogens*, Article 103 of the UN Charter and other Hierarchical Techniques of Conflict Solution' *Finnish Yearbook of International Law* (2006); C. Chinkin, '*Jus Cogens*, Article 103 of the UN Charter and Other Hierarchical Techniques of Conflict Solution', 17 *Finnish Yearbook of International Law* (2008), pp.63-90;, A. D. Amato, 'It's a Bird, It's a Plane, It's *Jus Cogens*' 6 *Connecticut Journal of International*

abolition of capital punishment is a peremptory norm and should not be ignored in order to benefit politics, personal interests, or economic interests.[228] This is not to say that we are protecting the notorious Iraqi criminals, but we are emphasising that justice has to be carried out on an equal footing and with love for justice and the full respect of international human rights law.[229]

The plea of superior order should no longer be tolerated as a justification for permitting the impunity of judges who issue capital punishment. This means that the judges of courts in Iran, Iraq, Yemen, Saudi Arabia, China, Libya, the United States, North Korea, Syria, Somalia, Afghanistan, Pakistan, Vietnam, and Bangladesh who order the application of capital punishment are considered to be *hostis humani generis*. They are subsequently to be prosecuted and punished under any jurisdiction which does not permit the application of capital punishment.[230] In addition,

> As I have emphasized elsewhere, capital punishment is an abolished institution, as are torture and slavery. One may even conclude that since jus cogens law prohibits the application of capital punishment, any judgement which permits such inhuman conduct violates the following legal orders too. These are law-making treaties, customary international law, general principles of law, the law of the permanent International Criminal Court, the ICTY, the ICTR, the SCSL, European Union law, African laws, Antarctica laws, most Asian laws, Australian law, most North American and South American law. Evidently, the authorised judges in charge who sanction such cruel punishment are guilty of violating international criminal law. This means without any hesitation, the respective judges should bear criminal responsibility, not only before their wrongful national criminal courts but also before the jurisdiction of other national courts… This principle also applies to those judges who

---

Law (1990); C Bassiouni, 'International Crimes: *Jus cogens* and *Obligatio Erga Omnes*' 59 *Law and Contemporary Problems* (1996).

[228] Consult Malekian, 'Emasculating the Philosophy of International Criminal Justice in the Iraqi Special Tribunal', note 28, pp.673-723.

[229] *Id*. See *also* Malekian, 'Judging International Criminal Justice in the Occupied Territories', note 71, pp.627-869.

[230] Malekian, *Judgments of Love in Criminal Justice*, note 1, p.123.

> contributed to the Saddam Tribunal and ordered his and other persons' executions. This is not to say that we are protecting, by one means or another, the notorious Iraqi criminal, but we are emphasising that justice has to be carried out on an equal footing and with love for justice. The plea of superior order or order of the law should no longer be tolerated as a reason to permit the impunity of those judges.[231]

Our theory is based on very simple reasoning: judges should not work in a criminal court which supports capital punishment. Judges that do violate the conscience of judicial independence of criminal jurisdiction and permit non-impartiality in the matter of criminal jurisdiction by being employed by a system which is not impartial in its basic legal system and which violates the fundamental principles of natural and international human rights law. How can a judge condemn a criminal to capital punishment, while turning a blind eye to the crimes of super powerful states which violate international criminal law and the basic principles of humanity? Are these actions correct from an ethical or judicial conscience point of view, or are such judges violating the international legal order?

A judge may present a considerable number of arguments concerning their engagement in criminal cases which lead to the death penalty, including that they were simply following the legal order. The ethical question to ask however, is whether the national legal order of a state supersedes the international criminal order of *jus cogens* law or vice versa. A legal order which contains provisions against the common moral unity of an individual and their existence is certainly a violative legislation, and judges in such criminal jurisdictions should be aware of this fact. *Jus cogens law* accepts no excuse.[232] This legal philosophy of *jus cogens* is

---

[231] *Id.*

[232] Consult Malekian, *Classical Morality in International Peremptory Criminal Law*, note 11. See further O'Connell, ME 'Jus cogens: International Law's Higher Ethical Norms' in Childress, DE III (ed.), *The Role of Ethics in International Law* (2012); Orakhelashvili, *A Peremptory Norms in International Law* (2006); A. Pellet, 'Comments in Response to Christine Chinking and in Defense of *Jus cogens* as the Best Bastion against the Excesses of Fragmentation' *Finnish Yearbook of International Law* (2008), p. 83; Paust, J 'The Reality of Jus cogens' 7 *Connecticut Journal of International Law* (1991), p. 81; Saul, M 'Identifying Jus cogens Norms: The Interaction of Scholars and International Judges' *Asian Journal of International Law* (2014); Shelton, D 'Normative Hierarchy of International

quite exceptional in that it does not treat the relevant judges by means of *argumentum ad hominem*, but as an *ex concessis* of what has been consolidated in the system of international human rights law.[233]

8.8. JUDGES VIOLATING THE PRINCIPLE OF *JUS NATURALE*

The decision of a judge who consents to the implementation of capital punishment violates the principles of *jus naturale*. Human beings should not subvert the principles of *jus naturale*. Obviously, the written judgement of a judge is an intentional error carried out with clear *mens rea*. A reason given by a judge is often a justification that is articulated in order to rationalise unlawful criminal conduct or fault. Its basic purpose is to reduce the scope of responsibility by freeing ourselves from moral accountability. We should remember that a judge works for justice and they are therefore responsible for following the natural rights of man in order to promote justice.

> If justice be not a natural principle, it is no principle at all. If it be not a natural principle, there is no such thing as justice. If it be not a natural principle, all that men have ever said or written about it, from time immemorial, has been said and written about that which had no existence. If it be not a natural principle, all the appeals for justice that have ever been heard, and all the struggles for justice that have ever been witnessed, have been appeals and struggles for a mere fantasy, a vagary of the imagination, and not for a reality.
>
> If justice be not a natural principle, then there is no such thing as injustice; and all the crimes of which the world has been the scene, have been no crimes at all; but only simple events, like the falling of the rain, or the

---

Law' 80 *American Journal of International Law* (1986), p. 1; Suy, E 'Article 53: Treaties Conflicting with a Peremptory Norm of General International Law ('jus cogens')' in Corten, O and Klein, P (Eds.) *The Vienna Convention on the Law of Treaties: A Commentary*, Vol.II (2011); Tomuschat, C and Thouveinin, JM (eds.) *The Fundamental Rules of the International Legal Order: Jus cogens and Obligations Erga Omnes* (2006).

[233] *Id.*

> setting of the sun; events of which the victims had no more reason to complain than they had to complain of the running of the streams, or the growth of vegetation.
>
> If justice be not a natural principle, governments (so-called) have no more right or reason to take cognizance of it, or to pretend or profess to take cognizance of it, than they have to take cognizance, or to pretend or profess to take cognizance, of any other nonentity; and all their professions of establishing justice, or of maintaining justice, or of regarding justice, are simply the mere gibberish of fools, or the frauds of imposters.[234]

It has been proven that most judges of states which allow capital punishment grant amnesty and forgiveness to themselves by reasoning that they were fulfilling their duties. This is particularly notable in cases where the old regime has been replaced with a new one. A duty which violates the pure philosophy of love for justice, love for the implementation of *jus cogens* law, love for the application of the basic principles of human rights law, and love for the appropriate application of European criminal law can no longer be called a duty; rather, it is instead a serious violation of the universal abolition of capital punishment.

The notion of love for the appropriate application of criminal justice with full conscience of humanity here indicates a norm which seeks to promote the proper implementation of its intent. These norms include the non-derogable prohibition of capital punishment, non-excusable implementation of torture, and the non-acceptable impunity in the case of sexual offences, both in times of war and of peace. Thus, there is a border between what is permitted and what is not permitted by international law. Here, I am not only focusing on the law of all states—Western or non-

---

[234] Lysander Spooner, Natural Law; or the Science of Justice: A Treatise on Natural Law, Natural Justice, Natural Rights, Natural Liberty, and Natural Society; showing that all Legislation whatsoever is an Absurdity, a Usurpation, and a Crime. Part First. [1882], 11. Available online at https://oll.libertyfund.org/title/spooner-natural-law-or-the-science-of-justice-1882.

Western—but also on cruel Islamic provisions which promote the application of capital punishment, stoning, and mutilation.

> A criminal judge is therefore duty bound by moral, legal, and love norms to examine her/his decision under power of reason of judgement and the strength of the quintessence of the law to arrive at the essence of justice under consideration of all motives. A rule of law that permits cutting of members or parts of the body as its penal sanction is not law but a terrible statement, and a judge who applies such law is not a judge but a butcher of humanity and justice. A law which permits marriage of a nine-year-old girl in its legal provisions is obviously not a law but a misunderstanding of culture and therefore unjust. A professor of criminal law criminologist who teaches such a law as a part of his lecture, with the reasoning that he has no alternative and is forced by rules to follow legislation, is not a tutor of justice but a servant of the relevant legal system. Even if her/his motivation is not to lose his job or position. As a whole, one who works for any reason within the criminal justice system of such legislation or society is the violator of the rules of ethics of morality, justice, and philosophy and of the dignity of human beings.[235]

I really wonder what the nature of law is. Is law the manifestation of the concept of morality? Or is morality the law? Can a violation of law qualify as a violation of a legal system? Or can the non-violation of law qualify as a violation of moral norms? Obviously, the law may not represent morality and may violate its objective substance, but morality unquestionably symbolizes the real virtue of the law, and in particular, the qualifications of the judge.[236] By all this, I mean that the norms of law which present injustice, and even those norms which seem to present justice, may not be considered the obvious norms of legality if they do not fulfil the standard of proportionality of the rules of law or if they violate the basic principles of international human rights law.

---

235 Malekian, *Judgments of Love in Criminal Justice*, note 1, pp26-27.
236 Consult Lon L. Fuller, *The Morality of Law* (Yale Law University, 2nd ed., 1969).

8.9. Conscience Modifying Punishment

Moral responsibility in criminal justice constitutes one of the vital questions of criminal jurisdiction and implies to what extent if any, a judge has moral responsibility for criminal justice is a matter of ethical and legal understanding and the way in which we interpret the legal discipline. The question becomes more serious when we consider that judges of a court should not follow positive law too literally since it may contain provisions which violate the principles of human rights law. The situation therefore creates conflict between different opinions and the strict question of legality. The principle of legality requires that judges follow the philosophy of the given legislation and obey its provisions. This means that we should follow the strict philosophy of legality and positivism and should not impact the principle of morality or the moral consideration of the case. We are aware of the fact that courts ought to decide cases according to the given law, although a judge may also see that the application of the given law or strict positivism may violate the moral requirements or the ethical standards of criminal justice. These principles require the fair implementation of criminal rules and the correct examination of evidence with regard to the principle of proportionality.

The situation requires further examination when the moral aspect of the law exceeds the ethical responsibility of a judge and ethical responsibility becomes superior in the inner conscience of the judge. This means that the relevant judge seriously interferes with the law in order to modify its flawed application without breaking the law. Thus, a judge may consciously decide against the provisions of the given law. Here, however, we are only discussing the consequences of the decisions made by a judge who does not obey the law in order to preserve the integrity of the legal discipline.

In certain situations, a judge may give greater weight to their own understanding of the provisions of the law if the legal principles of their nation are based on harsh religious norms. Here, the judge may apply their own understanding of legal norms if this interpretation can decrease the severity of punishment. In other words, in such situations, the judgement may be based on morally legitimate principles and values and the intention of the legislator and the connection between them. We have even seen that in Christianity and Islam, morality comes before revenge, and forgiveness becomes dominant. For our purposes, forgiveness means that a judge may adopt lighter punishment for the accused because they are morally required to do so since the legislation they have to work with is fundamentally flawed. Additionally, the legitimate principles of morality, which seek to find humanity between the rules of immorality, have a high value of recognition in order to trump the notion of criminal jurisdiction.

The body of criminal jurisdiction may not have a clear answer to the limit of the consciences of judges and whether or not judges can go beyond the normal independence of the administration of criminal jurisdiction and bring more independence than that which has been artificially promulgated.[237] Here, it is a matter of the practical personal wisdom of the relevant judge and their will to cope for the sake of justice with the values of humanity. As previously mentioned, a wise judge does not order the implementation of lashes, torture, dismemberment, or capital punishment as sentences. Obviously, an intelligent and wise judge would not put a person on trial if they have not carried out criminal conduct as per international regulations–even if it would be allowed under the relevant national legislation. This includes punishing women for not wearing headscarves or for posting on YouTube. The discussions on such matters are so low and preposterous that the decision of a judge against the provisions of a criminal legislation should not be recognised as a violation of their given responsibility under the law. This means that human values should be regarded as the primary values of criminal law, and criminal law should be based on morality.

---

237 "Obviously, only the second type of lawmaking reflects what most commentators would regard as compatible with democratic principles. It is doubtful that surrogate lawmaking can ever be wholly democratically legitimated. A given decision may happen to be good law (e.g., ending impunity to war criminals, improved protection of global commons, etc.), but judicial independence is a necessary condition for legitimacy and surrogate lawmaking fails this test by definition. Moreover, it is doubtful whether opening up the international tribunal for public participation and reason-giving could remedy the inherent deficiencies of a dependent tribunal." Examine also Benvenisti & George W. Downs, 'Prospects for the Increased Independence of International Tribunals', note 213 p.1059

8.10. IMPERATIVE MORAL FIGHTS IN THE HEART OF THE JUDGE

Judges must be very careful not to let their personal feelings interfere with proceedings– although this is one of the most difficult obligations for judges to uphold, as it is sometimes very difficult to remain impartial. It is the very question of "of how to play the game in the courtroom and a consensus on basic standards for ethical and professional conduct."[238] However, the interference of personal feelings may not be interpreted as a violation of the impartiality of the judge, as long as they are controlling the case with complete independence of judicial conscience. It may just be a matter of personal honesty about a particular case and its circumstances and the facts or the law which are applicable in a given case. This is particularly notable in countries where the judge may be frustrated about a ruling due to their past experience. A judge may hold the personal belief that moral rules are imperative for the continuation of the court. This situation mostly arises when judges face difficulty in accepting the monopolised or unfair rules of punishment, or when someone is punished for a conduct which is not considered a crime in most other nations.

Such circumstances occur when a judge of a court foresees that the delivery of justice is not wise and the intention of justice may disappear. Thus, in such situations the law permits and requires the proper consideration of the conscience of the judges although the provisions of the law are unfair and violate the integrity of man. Similarly, a number of Islamic countries which apply traditional Islamic punishments promote flawed justice and violate the essence of the law through their brutal interpretation of the law. This is where the law seeks to find how it can apply practical wisdom through the authority, experience, knowledge, and skill of the judge. In other words, if the punishment is certainly wrong, such as with the application of capital punishment or cutting off the hands of the offender, the judge must follow their conscience in order to make

---

[238] Harhoff, 'It's All in the Process: Reflections on the Relation Between International Criminal Trials and International Humanitarian Law', note 176, p.479.

wise decisions or apply practical wisdom and fulfil the intention of the law. Thus, the wisdom of the judge should overcome flawed, immoral criminal law in order to benefit the judicial system and prevent the application of harsh punishments.

Additionally, it is true that the development of the principles of human rights requires the prevention of the application of certain punishments which violate the international standard for the conscience of individuals and which explicitly require that all judges follow those fundamental principles. In such situations, there may be no disagreement concerning the intention of said principles, but rather about how judges from certain regions can motivate their decisions concerning the non-application of the relevant punishment. Thus, the expression of the personal conscience of the judge may not be really personal, but rather an expression of the international standards of justice. In such circumstances, the judges have to choose between the national or international legal system, and pure and practical wisdom which protects humanity. This represents the imperative moral fight in the heart of the judge who has the responsibility to create balance between the harsh positive legality and the morally acceptable and fair application of the law.

8.11. Ethical Principles of Justice

A judge is assumed to have a clear understanding of criminal conscience in order to prevent unlawful conduct per the provisions of the law. This means, *inter alia*, good faith in the natural substance of the law, the intention of achieving good results regardless of the purpose of the law, demanding the full standard of human justice for the subjects of the law, and creating an atmosphere of fairness for the law. The standard of the international legalisation of law also means ensuring the absence of any political deception, while also ensuring the creation of a justice with tolerance for other ideologies. It also means that the quality, not the quantity of the provisions of human rights law should be a decisive factor. The standard of international legalisation of law also prevents criminal justice from committing crimes against the mechanism of judgement. Thus, a true pillar of love in accordance with the true ethical principles of justice must be established.

It is true that the ethical principles reflect the basic values of the judiciary and inject soul into the conduct of the court and to individual judges. The intention of the ethical principles is to determine the proper definition of the application of criminal justice and not to prevent morality. The purpose of this is to create a common good within all aspects of criminal jurisdiction and not for the immoral aspects of the rule of the law. This implies the fact that the proper application of good ethics is the most significant intention of the law. In other words, we should not promote immoral rules of the law against the moral rules of humanity or international human rights law.[239] This is the principal duty of a judge.

Humanity is a process and not something static. Ethical principles embody constitutional and lawful obligations of judges and describe how they must be administered. In addition, the principles set the standards of qualified ethics for judges and describe the main duties of a professional judge. The ethical principles enlighten the society through the way in which the administration of justice is directed and provides judges with the necessary confidence to be on the side of the truth and justice. Understanding these principles in the appropriate direction of humanity is one of the duties of judges. In particular, the intentions of ethical principles are especially significant when it comes to the unlawful application of capital punishment by a judge.

In the system of judicial conscience, the efficient building of ethical norms constitutes one of the primary issues that most courts in the world face in connection with the evaluation of the moral understanding of their judges. A judge who does not realise that a system which allows capital punishment should be hindered and changed lacks legal and moral capacity. The principles of judicial ethics therefore have a strong connection with the morality of judges, which relates to their practical

---

[239] Examine Farhad Malekian, *Documents on the Principles of International Human Rights* (Stockholm: Norstedts Juridik, 2007).

experiences and ought to be based on the knowledge of the essence of humanity.[240] Moreover:

> The Court is not under obligation to love justice, but it is certainly under serious obligation to act for true international justice. If, by reason, we mean that international criminal justice is unable to bring all criminals under its jurisdiction because of their military and political powers, and is consequently unable to require accurate accountability by an inductive and efficient process of criminal justice, the Court will face many problems in the establishment of moral obligations. It will then follow that moral judgment is not a pressing act of the Statute of the Court, and therefore the true nature of its judgment remains short of morality. The fact is that morality of truth should be a faculty within the Court's jurisdiction, as it is within us for discovering of the truth, seeing the truth, and dealing with the truth. This is the substance of all morality. The Court should not separate its conclusions from the truth. If a single judgment of the Court is correct, this does not necessary mean that the moral policy of the Court is correct. This is what we may call the faculty of understanding of the truth in all relevant cases. It includes cases which are submitted to the Court and cases which are not submitted to the Court. The duties of this faculty are the notions from which we form solidarity, equality, equivalent accountability, receiving compensation, dealing with the substance of morality, and full understanding of the position of victims. A Court without the real power of accusation, its humanity with the principles of limitation, the Statute without equal, and understanding of the Prosecutor and judges without scarification of their positions is doing nothing more than encouraging violence. Obviously, I am not, at any degree or at any level, presenting and supporting the plea of *tu quoque* for the criminal conduct of criminals who have been brought before the jurisdiction of the Court. Their prosecutions and punishments have certainly been correct. But, I am asking why the Court itself is arguing with the ban principle of *tu quoque* when it comes to the establishment of the principle of ethical obligations of the Court?[241]

The independence of judges also implies independence from unlawful legal force. The impartiality of judges denotes the true legal analysis of norms and accepting responsibility.[242] Equally, the integrity of judges deals

---

[240] Examine also, S. L. Pepper 'The Lawyer's Amoral Ethical Role: A defence, a Problem, and Some Possibilities, *American Bar Foundation Research Journal*, (1986), 613.

[241] Malekian, *Judgments of Love in Criminal Justice*, note 1, p. 288.

[242] Joseph Hoover, Moral Practices: Assigning Responsibility in the International Criminal Court, 76 *Law and Contemporary Problems* (2014), pp.263-86; see also Vischer K. Robert,

with the personal comprehension of the integrity of decisions. The principle of equality demonstrates there is something wrong with the death penalty. Similarly, respectability or politeness in the house of criminal jurisdiction implies the existence of propriety in the mind of judge to respect human personality without harsh punishment. These are all integral parts of the competence and conscience of the *somebodiness* of judges.

8.12. Power of Judges Invalidating Legislation

Although judges are obliged to follow the legislation and its provisions, in certain circumstances judges may have the ability to denounce a provision if it violates human rights law or the ethics of natural law. In other words, we fully understand that the ratification of laws by the government of a state has a highly significant function in the implementation of an international convention, however this does not automatically mean that an act of non-ratification subverts the positive nature or substance of the relevant law, its meaning, its goodwill, its essence of purity, and its service for human beings. That is why in some states, a *judge* is permitted to declare a national rule invalid if it contradicts with international obligations, as seen in Germany.[243]

According to German legislation, treaties are recognised as an integral part of its domestic legislation. Therefore, the principle of *lex posterior derogat priori* is in effect, which means that new laws can nullify old ones. This principle comes from the provisions of Article 32 of the 1969 Vienna Convention on the Law of Treaties. Thus, the provisions of a treaty may take precedence over pre-existing national provisions. It is also possible that the judicial conscience of the judge requires that if they are not empowered to declare provisions invalid, they may still open up a

---

Martin Luther King Jr. and the Morality of Legal Practice: Lessons in Love and Justice (2014); L. M. Baum, 'Pursuing Justice in a Climate of Moral Outrage: An Evaluation of the Rights of the Accused in the Rome Statute of the International Criminal Court,' 19 *Wisconsin International Law Journal* (2001), 197.

243 Malekian, *Judgments of Love in Criminal Justice*, note 1, p.56.

discussion and bring the case to a higher court or authorities in order to modify the flawed provision. This has been seen in the case of the European Court of Human Rights, where national law has been identified as violating the provisions of regional or international treaties.[244]

In several countries, judges can create case law which then becomes part of criminal law. This is evident in the practice of certain member states of the European Union and the United Kingdom. Thus, judges may invalidate previous written or unwritten provisions of the law and promote the legal discipline according to a certain standard of internationalisation. Additionally, the judges of Islamic courts are responsible for adjusting the law of their courts to meet the standard of international law and if necessary, to bring cases to the recognition of authorities. This power/duty of the judge is particularly imperative if a judge realises that the nation's provisions violate the basic rules of criminal justice.

> An Islamic judge is even responsible for the development of the law, although it has to be within the framework of Islamic provisions. This means that a judge of an Islamic court who applies the provisions of European Union criminal law does not by any means violate the criminal provisions of Islamic law; instead, he has developed the standard of law to the stage of internationalisation. This is because Islamic law does not insist on the development of Islamic law, as many lawyers understand it, but on the universalisation of humanity from all aspects of the law. This can be taken into recognition from the provisions of any law, as long as the law does not go against the principles of humanity. For instance, Islamic nations have adopted various international human rights instruments but do not implement their aims regarding certain significant matters of freedom and liberty…a wise Islamic judge or jurist realises the

[244] Consult also B. Wägenbaur, *Court of the European Union* (Hart, 2013); On 17 occasions, Sweden came under the lens of the European Commission and the European Court of Justice in 2014. Available at http://www.eu-upplysningen.se/Sverige-i-EU/EU-lagargaller-framfor-svenska-lagar/Sverige-i-EU-domstolen/ (Accessed September 24, 2015); See also http://www.dagensjuridik.se/2013/10/skatteverkets-vrakningar-kan-ga-emot-fns-barnkonventionfragan-provas-av-hd.

> fact that most punishments under Islamic criminal law are not compatible with the principles of humanity and cannot therefore be enforced.[245]

We are not encouraging the application of monist or dualist theory, nor are we arguing that one theory is better than the other. Both theories are dependent on the political powers of a state. The monist state believes international law does not necessarily need to be converted into national law and they simply incorporate it automatically into national law through ratification of international legislation. This means that judges are permitted to apply international law and customary international law to their decisions. However, the dualist approach to the system of international law is the exact opposite of the monist approach. This means that they believe that there should be an official transfer of international law into national legislation.

Thus, we argue that there are certain situations where the provisions of modern law violate the natural rights of man or international human rights law, and that judges should keep this in mind while performing their duties. I draw this conclusion specifically regarding the international human rights law, international criminal law, international criminal justice, and the international humanitarian law of armed conflict. Thus, a judge is not only responsible for protecting the rule of law, but also for protecting the rules of human beings as the subjects of the law. A judge is also responsible for the protection of the subjects of the law during court proceedings:

---

[245] *Id.*, p.78, 79. Yet, "Islamic law requires the principle of love to be respected in all aspects of criminal justice *but not just by legal phenomena* and *not by the understanding of Islamic law*, but also *by the wisdom and vision of the judge. This means that certain punishments, assured penalties or certain actions are not judicious, and therefore the order of the law should not be a reason for their severe implementation. The legal authorities should respect the proper application of the principle of humanity*. As is rightly asserted, "there are good reasons for arguing that the presumption of innocence is inherent in any proper conception of the relationship between the state and its citizens in an open and democratic society." Malekian, *Judgments of Love in Criminal Justice*, note 1, pp.77-78. Quotation in the end from A. Ashworth, Four Threats to Presumption of Innocence' *South African Journal* (2006), pp.63–97, at 73.

> Human rights and humanitarian treaties do not represent an Exchange of interests and benefits between contracting States in the conventional sense, and in this respect may also be distinguished from the generality of multilateral treaties, many of which are concerned with the economic, security or other interests of States. Human rights and humanitarian treaties represent, rather, a commitment of the participating States to certain norms and values recognized by the international community. Stated another way, the personality of the sovereign is not the essence of such an agreement. Multilateral treaties are most often concluded with the object of protecting and benefiting the international community as a whole, and for the maintenance of world order and co-operation, rather than of protecting and advancing one particular State's interests.[246]

This situation implies the fact that it is a recognised duty of judges to not ignore the provisions of international human rights law, even if doing so would violate national legislation. Without a doubt, an international convention may invalidate national provisions which violate its basic substance. However, none of these situations have any effect on the substance of law and the maintenance of the purity of the law which has to be sound and serve justice. A pure law which serves individuals should foresee the situation in which the development of international rules can better protect its citizens. This means that a good law or wise legislation does not prevent judges from increasing their knowledge and applying positive international norms when deemed necessary.

---

[246] Application of the Convention on the Prevention and Punishment of the Crime of Genocide (Bosnia and Herzegovina v. Serbia and Montenegro). Separate Opinion of Judge Weeramantry, http://www.icj-cij.org/docket/files/91/7361.pdf, 55.

Chapter 9

The Puppets of Ventriloquist Politicians

9.1. Judges as the Puppet of Ventriloquist Politicians

Ventriloquy is a profession in which a person speaks a message through an actor in order to convince their audience of something. Historically, there have been many ventriloquists across the globe who have performed puppet shows. Ventriloquists have even forgone using a puppet to convince others of their message by asserting that they were speaking with the voice of a god, prophet, or a deceased individual. However, the history of ventriloquism is quite different from that of judges who are the instruments of politicians or dictatorial authorities, but still pretend to be trustworthy.[247] The judge or "*Puppets's on Bench*"[248] is in fact the tool of the politicians who then speak through the judge to carry out their vendettas against their political enemies. In return, the puppet on the bench i.e., the judge, is protected or supported either financially or in their career by political authorities. The judge may even be assisted in becoming the president of a nation.[249]

There are a considerable number of judges around the world who are controlled by ventriloquists, especially in dictatorial nations where only those who comply with the regime are protected. In certain cases, dissenters may even be arrested at the order of a judge or prosecutor and placed in jail to suffer further humiliation of their freedom and human rights. Within such authoritarian regimes, a considerable number of judges have received their education, academic positions, and even their positions as high judges exclusively through social connections. There are a number of such judges in Iran, Saudi Arabia, Russia, China, Italy, Romania, Egypt, the United States, and Hungary for example. These judges mostly function as the voices of politicians and carry out their final wishes. However, these judges believe they are doing the right thing and are able to convince others of the same.

The situation is similar when it comes to judges of the ICJ and ICC who are elected based on politics and not on their legal knowledge and accomplishments. These national or international puppets are conniving, and are able to get others to support their education, social life, and political standing by abandoning the principles of truth and impartiality. Here, judicial conscience is not measured upon honesty, uprightness, or decency, but on how well the puppet judge is able to convince others that

---

247 This also holds true with international politics. For instance, the following dictators were considered American puppets or a "Washington Choice": Rafael Trujillo (1930-1961) (Dominica Republic); Augusto Pinochet (1973-1990) from Chile who tortured more than 80,000 people and killed more than 3,000 of his critics; Fulgencio Batista (1952 -1959) from Cuba who was also supported by the Cuban Mafia; Mohammed Reza Pahlavi (1953-1979) from Iran who protected US and British oil interests; Saddam Hussein (1979-2003) from Iraq; and Ashraf Ghani (2014-2021) from Afghanistan. Available online at https://www.youtube.com/watch?v=elWD1rwWG6w.

248 See *infra* note 250.

249 This may be examined in the case of position of the contemporary president of the Islamic Republic of Iran.

their conclusions are their own and not those of the ventriloquist politicians. This means that their responsibilities decrease, and if the puppet runs into problems, the politicians will help them without hesitation. The situation becomes precarious at the international level when those who are guilty are found to be innocent, and the innocent are found to be guilty, as has been seen in recent cases in the ICC where judges voted against the innocent and wrote dissenting opinions.

Regrettably, under the national systems of China and the Islamic Republic of Iran, a large number of innocent people have been wrongly found guilty. The judges have enforced the legal order and rules of the ventriloquist politicians. Thus, innocent people have been punished, tortured, murdered, hanged, and forced to commit suicide. These puppets of the regimes are not ashamed that they have sold the judicial independence of justice, and are even honoured by politicians and receive career boosts as well. Puppet judges have been seen throughout the history of the US judicial system. In 1935, the President of Fordham University correctly alerted the public to the fact that *"unprincipled judges serving as political puppets and the trend of legal theory away from the natural law toward pragmatism are reasons for a growing distrust of the judiciary."*[250]

It has been frequently seen that corrupt judges have sold the judicial independence of their courts and have taken the advantage of their positions to serve their personal interests, which is not permitted. For instance, corruption has been identified in Spanish, Turkish, Hungarian, Iranian, Chinese, Russian, Romanian, American, and Latin American criminal courts.

Despite it being obvious that judges must exercise their judicial functions objectively and resist material or social influence, the lack of impartiality has been seen time and again in certain countries. However, the same has not been seen within in the system of international criminal courts or the ICC. The judges of certain pretend courts which deal with the

---

[250] Puppets's on Bench Assailed at Mass: Judges Who Serve Politicians Cause Distrust of Judiciary, Father Gannon Asserts. PRAGMATISM IS SCORED Annual Service for Lawyers Attended by High Officials of All Courts Here. Very Rev. Robert I. Gannon, president of Fordham University. https://www.nytimes.com/1936/10/14/archives/puppets-on-bench-assailed-at-mass-judges-who-serve-politicians.html.

questions of international criminal law may be purchased, not with money, but with the temporary satisfaction of the wills of the victims and by permitting certain judges to have authority over serious criminals such as Saddam Hussein. Although the judges involved in the Saddam Hussein tribunal may not have been bribed, they were given career and ego boosts by the United States in that they were permitted to preside over a case which should have been brought before an ad hoc tribunal or the ICC. Therefore, the judges felt psychologically empowered to prosecute Saddam Husain for his grave crimes against humanity in Iraq and against the Kurds. However, this significant fact was ignored by those who established the court in order to hide their own involvement in Hussein's crimes. The power of the ICC was therefore denied by the US and the UK in order to hide the truth and ensure that their own savage and uncivilised crimes would not be revealed.[251]

9.2. Puppets on the Bench of International Criminal Courts

It is of the utmost importance that judges are just, ethical, and morally strong. Additionally, judges should not be involved in political intrigues as that violates the obligations of their duties. Therefore, appointing judges based on their political connections and ability to advance political goals is not permitted and is unethical and immoral. Such appointments also violate judicial independence and cannot be permitted, especially if a judge

[251] "Since its establishment in 1946, the Security Council has been faced with considerable criticism and since that time there have been many suggestions for the reform of the Council. A large part of the criticism is due to the structure of the Council that many believe is undemocratic especially because it gives considerable power and privileges to certain countries of the world. The main example is the veto power of the Permanent Five. As Robert Hill, former Australian ambassador to the United Nations, summarises, '*the Security Council is a club and P5 is a club within a club*'." Sahar Okhovat, 'The United Nations Security Council: Its Veto Power and Its Reform' CPACS Working Paper No. 15/1 December 2011, p.9. Available online at https://sydney.edu.au/arts/peace_conflict/docs/working _papers/UNSC_paper.pdf.

is appointed in order to ensure impunity for an offender. Therefore, adding any personal bias to any court is wrong–particularly when a judge is chosen by certain members of the Assembly of States Parties of the ICC to assist them in difficult situations.

Judges of any court should not be instrumentalised by political influence and politicians. This constitutes an element of an independent judiciary in both national and international criminal jurisdictions. An American judge stated that in order to uphold the judicial conscience, judges must remain independent from politics, and that "judicial independence is critical to liberty and to justice," based on the significant imperative rule of law. Accordingly, "in our great country, the judiciary is not a puppet of those in power, nor is it the engine for pioneering social change. Rather, it is a safeguard against tyranny and an assurance of neutral arbiters for those seeking the protection of the law." If the judge is a puppet, then it is even more common for public opinion to galvanize behind specific notorious outcomes. Thus, "advancing a narrative all too often becomes more important than the rule of law." Moreover, "it can be tempting for us as judges to want to fit into that narrative or to confuse what we perceive as a just outcome with the justice that the law requires and that flows from being fair and impartial. As judges we have a sacred duty to resist that temptation."[252]

Whether or not the ICC has puppet judges on its bench is hard to discern definitively, however it is likely. There is also proof that certain judges of the ICJ have also been the puppets of politicians at times. Although both bodies are supposed to keep their impartiality regarding all the cases, the reality is certainly different in the heart of the judges when it comes to their own personal and national interests. In connection with the work of international courts, Karen Alter of Northwestern University correctly stated:

---

[252] Justice Clarence Thomas. Justice Thomas says judiciary 'is not a puppet of those in power', *Aba Journal* (22 Oct. 2018), available online at https://www.abajournal.com/news/article/justice_thomas_says_judiciary_is_not_a_puppet_of_those_in_power.

> The thrust of this argument is that the presumption should be in favour of IC independence rather than Principal control. Giving up the idea that states are the hidden puppet masters of ICs allows us to instead focus on how international politics is being transformed by the existence of an alternative venue of international politics – namely international legal arenas.[253]

The legal question surrounding the judges of the ICC is also very controversial and may not always meet the requirements of *de lege lata*, especially when cases are political in nature and relate to state power. It is here that confusion arises concerning the credibility of the judicial conscience of the judges of the ICC, as well as the independence of the decisions of the Court. It is important to remember that the ICC has no power of its own to arrest criminals and it must thus rely on states and their politicians to bring criminals to the court. While police forces are able to enforce arrest warrants under national criminal jurisdiction, the ICC has no such system and lacks an apparatus with which to direct criminal justice.

9.3. ICC Judges as Puppets of the Security Council

The fact is that national criminal courts do not need to obtain permission from any authority to carry out their duties, while the ICC is obliged to negotiate the arrest of suspects, who may themselves be politicians who are still in office, such as with the cases of politicians in Libya, Kenya, Uganda, and Sudan. Therefore, the ICC is unable to proceed with trials without political negotiation, and thus politicians must be cautious concerning the appointment of ICC judges.

The Rome Statute is the legal basis for the administration of criminal justice in the ICC and provides guidance for how legal proceedings should be conducted. However, the problem here is that the due process

---

[253] Karen J. Alter (2008), p.55; quoted in https://www.peio.me/wp-content/uploads/2014/04/Conf4_Elsig-Pollack-24.01.2011.pdf.

guaranteed in the Statute may be interpreted as a balance between the ICC's administration of criminal justice and how a state understands its provisions. In addition, the Statute introduces the principle of complementarity, which ensures the creation of greater political ties between the ICC and states involved in trials. Therefore, wherever criminal jurisdiction of a state fails, the ICC is permitted to exercise jurisdiction pursuant to Articles 15–17. The provisions of Article 15 indicate that the court must demonstrate that there is a reasonable basis, or adequate evidence and information, for commencing an investigation into a given state. Here, the ICC cannot act alone because of its limited power of implementation. The Court therefore depends on political negotiations between the ICC and the diplomats of the state in question.

Article 17(1) sets forth the conditions under which the ICC cannot exercise jurisdiction or determining the inadmissibility. These include when: a) the case is being inspected or prosecuted by a State which has jurisdiction over it, unless the State is unwilling or unable to sincerely carry out the investigation or prosecution, b) the case has been examined by a State which has jurisdiction over the case and the State has decided not to continue the prosecution, unless the decision resulted from the unwillingness or inability of the State to genuinely prosecute. The provisions addressed in Article 17(2) speak about the authority of the judges of the Court to determine the unwillingness of a state, the government or superiors of which have committed serious international crimes and fulfil the criteria for inadmissibility. Therefore, if the Court determines that a state has not conducted its proceedings without prejudice or that objectivity has not been maintained, or if the legal process was delayed or hidden, then the ICC can take over the case. This is a process which creates certain unwanted conditions for the Court, for the victims, and for the witnesses, and which can also lead to the destruction of evidence by states which have committed serious international crimes.

9.4. Instance of Political Control

One of the most recent examples of the legal-ethical views of judges, is the recent dissent of Judge Péter Kovács from Hungary regarding a case concerning the barbarous crimes committed by the government of Israel in Palestine. Reading the dissenting view of the judge reveals the political influence on this case and the judge's unwillingness to prosecute crimes against the Palestinian population.[254] Kovács' dissent rejects any form of admissibility for the most serious crimes committed under the authority of the Israeli government. Additionally, Kovács rejects Palestinian's statehood. However, this is a serious mistake, as rejecting the Security Council's resolution concerning the territorial integrity of Palestine simultaneously rejects Israel's statehood.[255] His dissent, which reveals his support of the criminal activities of the Israeli government, includes further conclusions concerning international peremptory law and the value of the principles of *jus cogens* and *erga omnes*. The dissent has therefore confirmed the impunity of criminals. Moreover, I hesitate to accept that the long dissenting view of the judge was written independently without the involvement of the super powers.

As we have thus seen, judicial independence has not been maintained in the process of criminal justice. This problem does not just rely on the lacking enforceability of the ICC, but on the fact that the ICC is under the full control of the Security Council, even though the ICC is legally an independent international organisation with its own international legal

---

[254] https://www.icc-cpi.int/RelatedRecords/CR2021_01167.PDF.

[255] In addition, the recent report on complicity of governments shows that "672 European financial institutions have financial relationships with 50 businesses that are actively involved with illegal Israeli settlements. These financial institutions provided US$ 114 billion in the form of loans and underwritings and held investments to the amount of US$ 141 billion in shares and bonds of these companies. This is the key finding of a new research report published today by a cross-regional coalition of Palestinian and European NGOs, which looked at financial flows between January 2018 and May 2021", 'New Report Exposes Billions in European Financial Support to Companies in Illegal Israeli Settlements', *International Federation for Human Rights* (fidh, 29th September 2021), available online at https://www.fidh.org/en/issues/globalisation-human-rights/business-and-human-rights/new-report-exposes-billions-in-european-financial-support-to.

personality.[256] Thus, there is no value in remaining under the control of the Security Council members and their allies Saudi Arabia, Israel, Egypt, France or the United Kingdom, which are continuously committing international crimes and violating international human rights law. The fact is that the political efficacy of the ICC and its political struggles with the politicians of the world cannot be denied, considering the reality that the ICC and the Court are first to satisfy global politics. Therefore, the Court is always at the risk of dealing with the somebodiness of individuals when cases concern the deaths of victims of the big criminals.[257]

Although the ICC has the ability to carry out pure negotiations, their negotiations are tainted by politics, despite the fact that seeking justice for crimes against humanity, war crimes, genocide, and rape should not be political. The result has been that the ICC has lacked credibility since its establishment due to its inability to prosecute criminals from militarily powerful states. This has been further solidified by the ICC's compliance with Security Council case referrals, and thus impunity prevails in the international system. Therefore, individuals such as George W. Bush, Tony Blair, and Barak Obama have received impunity for their crimes.[258]

---

[256] For example, the United States President states that "Today, the International Criminal Court (ICC) announced its unanimous rejection of a request to investigate American military and intelligence professionals who served in Afghanistan. This is a major international victory, not only for these patriots, but for the rule of law. We welcome this decision and reiterate our position that the United States holds American citizens to the highest legal and ethical standards. Since the creation of the ICC, the United States has consistently declined to join the court because of its broad, unaccountable prosecutorial powers; the threat it poses to American national sovereignty; and other deficiencies that render it illegitimate. Any attempt to target American, Israeli, or allied personnel for prosecution will be met with a swift and vigorous response." Statement from the President (Law & Justice, White House, 12 April 2019). Available online at https://www.whitehouse.gov/briefings-statements/statement-from-the-president-8/.

[257] It is correctly stated by Michael Lynk, UN Special Rapporteur on the situation of human rights in the Palestinian Territory occupied since 1967 that ""The involvement of these corporations with the settlements – through investments, banking loans, resource extraction, infrastructure contracts and equipment and product supply agreements – provides them with the indispensable economic oxygen they require to grow and thrive." 'New Report Exposes Billions in European Financial Support to Companies in Illegal Israeli Settlements', *International Federation for Human Rights* (fidh, 29th September 2021), available online at https://www.fidh.org/en/issues/globalisation-human-rights/business-and-human-rights/new-report-exposes-billions-in-european-financial-support-to.

[258] Consult Malekian, *Trading Virginity of International Criminal Jus*tice, note 1.

Moreover, the International Court of Justice (ICJ) forms one of the organs of the United Nations under the authority of which judges may deliver dissenting views regarding judgements of the Court. One of the most recognised dissenting views was written for a case concerning genocide. Therefore, it is highly relevant to view the dissenting opinion of another judge in another case here. Judge Weeramantry, in his separate opinion concerning the Convention on Genocide in the case brought before the ICJ relevant to Bosnia and Herzegovina v. Serbia and Montenegro, argued:

> The Genocide Convention does not come to an end with the dismemberment of the original State, as it transcends the concept of State sovereignty. An important conceptual basis denying continuity to treaties is that the recognition of the continuity of the predecessor State's treaties would be an intrusion upon the sovereignty of the successor State. This would be so if it were a matter confined within the ambit of a State's sovereignty. But with human rights and humanitarian treaties, we are in a sphere which reaches far beyond the narrow confines of State sovereignty, and enters the domain of universal concern. In its ongoing development, the concept of human rights has long passed the stage when it was a narrow parochial concern between sovereign and subject. We have reached the stage, today, at which the human rights of anyone, anywhere, are the concern of everyone, everywhere. The world's most powerful States are bound to recognize them, equally with the weakest, and there is not even the semblance of a suggestion in contemporary international law that such obligations amount to a derogation of sovereignty.[259]

---

[259] Emphasis added. Application of the Convention on the Prevention and Punishment of the Crime of Genocide (Bosnia and Herzegovina v. Serbia and Montenegro). Separate Opinion of Judge Weeramantry, available at http://www.icj-cij.org/docket/files/91/7361.pdf, 55–56 (Accessed June 20, 2015).

9.5. Judges as Dummies of Superior Powers

Many believe that the Special Court for Sierra Leone was also controlled by big political powers in order to hide the truth. Here, we are discussing the famous criminal Charles Taylor and his trial, as well as the possible falsification of evidence to hide Taylor's relationship with the CIA. This was asserted by the Senegalese judge, Justice El Hadji Malick Sow, who served as an alternate judge for Trial Chamber II of the Special Court of Sierra Leone, which tried the former Liberian president, Charles Taylor. The judge, who held a dissenting view, believed that the three elementary principles of justice, i.e., legality, morality, and love, were absent from the Court's decision due to the corruption of evidence and judges through the influence of *Western money*.

While the Court declared a unanimous decision, Sow expressed his dissenting view because of information which came to him just before delivering the judgment. Remarkably, one of the three judges of the case was purposefully absent. Sow's microphone was turned off before he could begin to issue his dissent, and he was forcefully removed from the Court. However, the judge was able to issue the following dissent opinion in the Court, while they were taking him out of the SCSL by force (unlike the Hungarian judge who was allowed to deliver his dissenting view without issue since he was not speaking against big powers of the world but rather supporting them). The voice of Judge Sow reverberated in the Court:

> The only moment where a Judge can express his opinion is during the deliberations or in the courtroom, and pursuant to the Rules, when there are no serious deliberations, the only place left for me in the courtroom. I won't get — because I think we have been sitting for too long but for me I have my dissenting opinion and I disagree with the findings and conclusions of the other Judges, because for me under any mode of liability, under any accepted standard of proof the guilt of the accused from the evidence provided in this trial is not proved beyond reasonable doubt by the Prosecution. And my only worry is that the whole system is not consistent with all the principles we know and love, and the system is not consistent with all the values of international criminal justice, and

> I'm afraid the whole system is under grave danger of just losing all credibility, and I'm afraid this whole thing is headed for failure.[260]

Moreover, Sow was not just a judge, but a judge with an exceedingly positive reputation in his home state. A Senegalese professor of law familiar with the merits of the case emphasised that:

> ...judge Sow is a judge of repute in Senegal. He is very well known in the Senegalese judiciary for his integrity, fierce honesty and scrupulous attachment to principles. He is known for a man of courage who will always stand up for what he believes is right, no matter what. As a Senegalese citizen I am proud that judge Sow showed abroad the same hardcore qualities for which is known and respected in his home country.[261]

This is unfortunately the reality of international criminal justice and its hidden features. The problem is that the influence of the big political powers does not end with court proceedings as exemplified by the Saddam Husain Tribunal during which the big political powers managed to conceal the truth and their involvement in the crimes. Thus, judicial conscience was absent during this tribunal. Obviously, the responsibility of the show tribunals is not only based on the judges of the relevant international criminal courts, but on the fact that we aide the big political powers in their crimes out of the fear of losing our positions. In reality, we have limited the freedom of our writings to the point that there may be no freedom left at all today.

---

260 http://www.africalegala*ld*.com/IManager/MailingWeb/7332/yfPhhp5EuNMX/129684/2349472; http://www.ejiltalk.org/the-verdict-in-the-charles-taylor-case-and-the-alternate-judges-dissentingopinion/ (Accessed May 8, 2020).

261 Professor Fatou Camara statement. See http://www.google.de/imgres?imgurl¼http://3.bp.blogspot.com/-tZpcSA79PSM/T5s0vwdK2cI/AAAAAAAAAEs/DnrHzGRVamk/.s1600/elhadjimalick.bmp&imgrefurl¼http://www.intlawgrrls.com/2012/04/judge-sows-struck-statement-reflections. html&h¼150&w¼100&tbnid¼udh-CEEja-DsEM:&zoom¼1&tbnh¼95&tbnw¼63&usg¼_mhl1Kk9x735LAyXFQ-98-SFxUyo¼&docid¼6vcUXgC0f9uAxM (Accessed May 8, 2021).

9.6. Unbiased Independence of Judges

Bias can be seen in cases where judges allow their decisions to be influenced by a party to the case. This means that the court procedures, the judges, and the decisions lose their independence. Independence denotes freedom in the presentation of the law by the court, and certainly by its judges. The principle of independence is a basic requirement of the court not only for the judges, but also for the outcome of the decision. If the court is not independent, the judicial system will be dependent and it will become difficult for judges to make impartial decisions. The principle of independence also reflects the guarantee which exists in the statutes of courts and their validity as authoritative organs of a given community.

A judge of a non-independent court cannot appropriately handle different cases in their office if the decision of the relevant judge relies on the decisions of another court. The question of the independence of a court, as we have mentioned earlier, is also addressed in Article 6 of the European Convention as one of the criteria required for a reasonable and fair trial. Additionally, one can determine whether or not a court is independent by looking at how judges are chosen or appointed to their positions. This also includes the length of the appointment, and what guarantees there exist concerning exterior influence on the judges and any situations which could impact their independence.

The fact is that a judge has an external independence, which means that the judge must be free from any undue guidance or influence coming from other bodies or individuals. This means the respect of judicial ethics.[262] External independence also refers to the fact that the

[262] "The set of norms and values that regulate judicial conduct are referred to as judicial ethics. Three key values are fundamental in guiding judicial conduct: independence, impartiality, and diligence. Independence refers to the lack of external forms of influence on adjudication, whether direct or indirect, while impartiality concerns the internal predisposition of the adjudicator, requiring fair and balanced treatment of the parties and forbidding any bias or personal prejudice. Diligence, finally, refers to the faithful fulfillment of duties and can include integrity, confidentiality, propriety, equality, competence, and diligence *stricto sensu*." Cima, 'Ethical Conduct in International Criminal Courts: Whose Ethics?', note 37, p.297; see *also* 'The Burgh House Principles on The Independence of The International Judiciary: The Study Group of the International Law Association on the Practice and Procedure of International Courts and Tribunals, in

administration of the courts as well as judges must be self-governing. Therefore, the court and judges must not be dependent on any private or public bodies either. As a result, the constitution and related legislation must be expressed in a way which safeguards independence. All this also points to the freedom of the courts and judges from any imaginable dependency. The internal independence of a judge refers to the fact that the judges of courts are self-sufficient and discharge their duties independently.

The next stage for the nature of independence of judges and their unbiased position is the question of impartiality. A judge cannot have any legal or moral value if they allow personal interests to influence their decisions. In order to remain ethical, judges must value all individuals equally and treat them as such. A judge is supposed to honour the equal rights of all individuals while discharging their duties in order to ensure that they are not being discriminatory in their actions.

The impartiality of the judge must therefore be guaranteed in order to uphold moral and ethical standards, as well as to preserve public confidence in the courts. All this requires the maintenance of an unbiased position. For instance, under the Swedish system the term "bias can be expressed in different ways. The Supreme Court has defined bias as when a judge allows the position of the parties to influence the outcome of the case. If the judge were to adjudicate in the same way even if the composition of the parties had been the reverse, the judge is not biased. Nor of course must the judge appear to be biased."[263] This means that judges must respect ethical rules in order to prevent biased decisions.

Additionally, by identifying ethical rules, judges establish a framework regulating judicial conduct in order to avoid bias. This framework also encourages the fundamental values of jurisdiction in order to promote impartial, nonbiased, and acceptable behaviours, conducts, acts, and decisions. These principles are part of the principle of juridical

---

association with the Project on International Courts and Tribunals', available online at burgh_final_21204.pdf (ucl.ac.uk).

263 Johan Hirschfeldt, Good Judicial Practice - https://johanhirschfeldt.files.wordpress.com/2019/02/goodjudicialpratice.pdf.

independence which is all essential for the judiciary in the administration of justice. Moreover, judicial ethics support the legislative and executive powers to improve and foster understandings of the specificity and thoughtfulness of judicial activity in order to promote justice within appropriate ethical measures. This is very essential for the application of the principle of the separation of powers, promoting cooperation between state powers, and particularly in judicial processes which may be connected to politics in order to alter the rules. If the intention of law is to create and implement democratic rules, this must then be seen in the practice of legislators and the judges.[264]

Impartiality here means that the judge does not enthusiastically support any particular party. Therefore, judges must keep their impartiality in relation to parties and counsel. This basic principle could also at times affect the judge's approach to the subject matter in a case. In the administration of justice, judges must deal with matters while remaining objective. In order for the independence of judges to be maintained, they must not be influenced by external considerations, biases, or prejudices made prior to hearing the case. In general, a judge must have a secure, independent, and unbiased position when delivering justice. As a rule, there must not be any doubt that the judge in a case is unbiased. Launching good standards for ethical conduct of judges and their moral approach to the problems of justice therefore seems impossible to ignore when the question of ethical conscience exists. Moreover, creating the possibility for the appropriate guidance of judges is an autonomous mechanism for the judges themselves, and also the judges who will be in charge in the future.

9.7. Dealing with an Accused Judge

It should be taken into consideration that judicial ethics essentially guarantee the protection of the rights of judges and prevent any possible violation of the independence and impartiality of the court. Hence, the

---

[264] Malekian, *Trading Virginity of International Criminal Justice*, note 1, p.2.

observation of judicial ethics should be faithful and promote the independence of judges, both nationally and internationally. The system of criminal justice must be sure that it has a good number of judges who have professional respect for the implementation of justice as a prerequisite for the appropriate internal administration of criminal courts. There is no doubt that a highly qualified internal administration of criminal courts constitutes a major core pillar in certifying the control of judicial ethics as a whole.

It is also very essential that surveys of violations of judicial ethics under the power of a judge should be based on procedures that can ensure the judicial independence and human rights of judges who have been suspected of infringing upon judicial ethics in any way. Additionally, violations of judicial ethics are also violations of judicial conscience, and a violation of judicial conscience constitutes a violation of moral law or the independence of justice. However, such violations cannot take away the right of a judge to defend themselves before a court if they are accused of committing criminal violations. All this means that there should be proper sanctions and proper engagements of a court when they attempt to deal with an accused judge.

It is also important to emphasise that judicial ethics not only govern the methods for appropriately prosecuting the lies of false victims, but also judges and their immoral conducts, economic interests, and political intrigues. The examination of judges concerning how they deal and/or sell justice, usually leads to judges being chastised, although one cannot reject the fact that any immoral conduct or behaviour of a judge tarnishes the good reputation of the administration of criminal justice and creates serious problems.

For example, in United States, "Judges have made racist statements, lied to state officials and forced defendants to languish in jail without a lawyer – and then returned to the bench, sometimes with little more than a rebuke from the state agencies overseeing their conduct."[265] In Iran, China, Russia, Romania, and Hungary judges are able to commit serious

[265] Thousands of U.S. Judges who Broke Laws or Oaths Remained on the Bench. Visited online at https://www.reuters.com/investigates/special-report/usa-judges-misconduct/.

violations of moral ethics without consequence. The Council of Europe Group, for instance, is worried "because of insufficient measures taken to prevent corruption," in the offices of judges in Hungary.[266] Politicians in all these nations are aware of the problems plaguing the justice system as a result of the conducts of the judges and their criminal involvement, and yet the judges remain in office. This phenomenon can also be seen to a lesser degree in other nations.

For instance, in Sweden purchasing sex is illegal. A Swedish judge, who was presiding over cases where the offenders were accused of purchasing sex, was himself purchasing sex every weekend from a boy. When the case became known, he simply defended his position by stating that he was not purchasing sex but was just helping this man because of his poor economic condition. This is the expression of the judicial conscience of a judge in practice. In another case, judges who were prosecuting two young ladies for their involvement in sex trafficking took both ladies back to their office for drinks on the weekend. All these judges have retained their positions and have not suffered any consequences for their actions. However, the machinery of criminal justice in any country should recognise that dealing with accused judges is more important than dealing with ordinary criminals because the sole function of judiciary conscience is based on the moral, ethical, and legal responsibility of the judges. Thus, if any of these principles are violated by a judge, then the pillars will collapse.

9.8. Obligation of Judges to Love the Truth

The independence of judicial conscience spurs competition surrounding who gets to work in the ICC. This is certainly a dangerous situation, which in the end denies proper justice to the victims. We need to establish immunity for the judicial conscience of all courts. However, this

---

266 Pablo Gorondi, Judicial credibility in Hungary worries corruption expert (2019), https://apnews.com/article/e88a1133d0f5491c9409e9b3bd22868b.

immunity is not easy to establish if we confuse the dignity, legality, and the protection of victims. In other words, establishing an outline regulating trustworthy judicial conduct and promoting a better understanding of judicial conscience and the tasks of judges must be the main requirements of criminal justice. This is particularly important when we talk about the impartiality of judges of national and international criminal courts. If the love for justice does not exist in the hearts of the judges of our criminal courts, justice can never be served properly.

> A duty which goes against the pure philosophy of love for justice, love for the implementation of jus cogens law, love for the application of the basic principles of human rights law, and love for the appropriate application of European criminal law can no longer be called a duty. It is instead a serious violation of the principle of universality of abolition of capital punishment. The term love here means a norm that is clearly the intention of a particular norm of law presented in the substance of the relevant law for the proper implementation of the purpose of its object. These are the non-derogable purpose of prohibition of capital punishment, non-excusable implementation of torture, or non-acceptable impunity in the case of sexual offences in war and peacetime. All these mean a borderline between what is permitted and what is not permitted by international law. Here, I am not only focusing on the law of all states—Western or non-Western—but also those cruel Islamic provisions that have become reasons for the application of capital punishment, stoning, cutting off hands and entire arms.[267]

We may therefore need to establish a court in which judges not only work with the application of the words of law, but also with the requirement of the words of the love for justice, love for the truth, and love to preserve the judicial conscience. The expression 'court of love' is the appellation for a court that is not ruled by the law of a sovereign, but by the law of conscience. This is where the law is silent and cannot, for one reason or another, investigate moral and oral contracts between parties. The purpose of a court is not to gain profit from conflicts. The 'court of

---

[267] Malekian, *Judgments of Love in Criminal Justice*, note1, p.123.

love' deals with conflicts between individuals as they are integral parts of human society and not just subjects of the law. This does not mean that this court and its judges ignore law; on the contrary, it places a heavy emphasis on the law of morality, which is the primary source of the legal discipline in the system of criminal justice.[268]

Most modern regulations of criminal law are also based on this source and not only on harsh passivism. That is why we have established "the right of hope." The intention is not to say that morality should be the first step in the creation of new rules because if this were the case, many laws would not make it past the drafting phase. When we say that torture, slavery, and capital punishment are prohibited, this is partially based on the expansion of the law and partially on a modification of morality resulting from judges promoting moral love and ethics in order to pursue the truth. The intention is to reduce human suffering and prohibit impunity as a result of our judgements or dissents. Over the last century, millions of children, elderly individuals, women, and men have been the victims of unimaginable atrocities that have deeply shocked the conscience of humanity.[269]

> This means that there is a strong interconnectedness between the entire machinery of justice and the whole intention of the injured society to express their love for the victims. We did not establish international criminal courts simply because we wanted to establish such courts; the reason for the establishment of the courts was the implementation of our sincere love for justice to be done.40 This implies the fact that there is an interconnectedness among human spirits to discover the cause of the actions. What is the nature of this interconnectedness, which exists in our mind, in our heart, in our actions, or in our essence? Should we call it law? However, the law does not exist as long as we have not drafted its shape. It is still an abstract form of existence. There must be another matter which is surrounded by our law, by our regulations, by our courts,

---

[268] *Id.*, p.137.

[269] Susie Woo, *Framed by War: Korean Children and Women at the Crossroads of US Empire* (New York University Press, 2019). The book should also be located in the bibliography: Woo Susie, Framed by War: Korean Children and Women at the Crossroads of US Empire (New York University Press, 2019).

> and by our judgments. This is what I call the norm of love. In other words, a judgment is not the heart of justice, but if love for justice is done with the sole intention of fairness, it constitutes the heart of pure judgment.[270]

Many of these victims suffered as the result of crimes such as genocide, crimes against humanity, war crimes, and aggression. One of the main problems plaguing the system of the ICC is its lack of an enforcement mechanism. The court is thus unproductive when issuing arrest warrants for individuals who have committed or are actively committing brutal crimes. The ICC lacks international respect when it comes to the prosecution of serious international criminals. This means that in practice, prosecutors and judges of the Court must wait for permission to launch investigations. This is also the case in many states where cases can only be tried if state authorities allow them to be. The ICC certainly needs more international acknowledgment, appreciation, and support in order to properly execute its criminal jurisdiction. In other words, the ICC is a forum which was established to try crimes committed by the members of weak nations. The judges of the ICC are not only powerful, but may lose the protection of judicial conscience when it comes to certain authoritarian states. Several of the big nations of the world have committed serious international crimes but were still granted impunity because they were able to prevent the ICC from investigating their crimes.[271] Therefore, the ICC

---

[270] *Id.*, p.145.

[271] My point relates to the impunity of political authorities of powerful governments. The dissenting opinion of Judge Weeramantry on the Nuclear Case in the International Court of Justice, along with the prohibition on genocide, clearly suggests that acts which are essentially immoral and incorrect violate the independence of the conscience of the jurisdiction and the judges of the courts. Judge Weeramantry asserts that "The Court's treatment of the relevance of genocide to the nuclear weapon is, in my view, inadequate (paragraph 26 of the Opinion). Nuclear weapons used in response to a nuclear attack, especially in the event of an all-out nuclear response, would be likely to cause genocide by triggering off an all-out nuclear exchange, as visualized in Section IV below. Even a single 'small' nuclear weapon, such as those used in Japan, could be instruments of genocide, judging from the number of deaths they are known to have caused. If cities are targeted, a single bomb could cause a death toll exceeding a million. If the retaliatory weapons are more numerous, on WHO'S estimates of the effects of nuclear war, even a billion people, both of the attacking State and of others, could be killed. This is plainly genocide and, whatever the circumstances, cannot be within the law. When a nuclear weapon is used, those using it must know that it will have the effect of causing deaths on a scale so massive as to wipe out entire populations. Genocide, as defined in the Genocide Convention (Art.

and its judges and prosecutors are essentially wingless doves of peace. The systems of international criminal conscience, international human rights law and international criminal justice are indeed just mirages.[272]

II), means any act committed with intent to destroy, in whole or in part, a national, ethnical, racial or religious group, as such. Acts included in the definition are killing members of the group, causing serious bodily or mental harm to members of the group, and deliberately inflicting on the group conditions of life calculated to bring about its physical destruction in whole or in part. In discussions on the definition of genocide in the Genocide Convention, much play is made upon the words 'as such'. The argument offered is that there must be an intention to target a particular national, ethnical, racial or religious group qua such group, and not incidentally to some other act. However, having regard to the ability of nuclear weapons to wipe out blocks of population ranging from hundreds of thousands to millions, there can be no doubt that the weapon targets, in whole or in part, the national group of the State at which it is directed. Nuremberg held that the extermination of the civilian population in whole or in part is a crime against humanity. This is precisely what a nuclear weapon achieves." Dissenting opinion of judge Weeramantry - CIJ/ICJ, available online at https://www.icj-cij.org/files/case-related/95/095-19960708-ADV-01-12-EN.pdf, pp.279-80 (501-2).

[272] Malekian, *The Mirage of International Criminal Law,* note 22; p.104; Mona Rishimawi, 'A Reality or a Mirage: Judicial Review of Detention,' in Charles Riziki Majinge (ed.), *Rule of Law Through Human Rights and International criminal justice: Essays in Honour of Adama Dieng* (Cambridge Scholars publishing, 2015), pp.507-522; Parish Matthew, *International criminal law – Justice or Mirage?* Transconflict (2013). Available online at http://www.transconflict.com/2013/05/international-criminal-law-justice-or-mirage-025/.

Chapter 10

CONCLUSION

The theory of judicial conscience is as old as the theory of criminal justice and represents the way in which society evaluates the value of the administration of criminal justice as a whole. The enshrined rules, provisions, norms, and principles of criminal justice work to provide access to justice for everyone. The intention of having high standards of judicial conduct which promote compassion and plurality/diversity in the administration of (criminal) justice, is therefore to achieve fairness, honesty, and pure justice for all parties involved, and to decrease the severity of punishments. These high standards are determined by the expectations of the international community. Here, we are discussing the professional activities of the judiciary and judges which are considered essential for maintaining healthy and powerful judicial ethics at all times.

The rule of law must be applied and respected to the same degree as the principles of international human rights law. In other words, the rule of law should not violate the basic principles of international human rights law. Thus, the rule of law must remain pure and not harm its subjects. That is why we have created and spoken about the judicial conscience of judicial administration, and specifically of judges. *Laws which do not protect their subjects or which are enforced by political powers seeking to protect their interests are no longer laws, but rather the principles of autocracy which lack judicial conscience and enforce undemocratic principles.* Therefore, in order to ensure the appropriate operation of legal disciplines, certain primary requirements of criminal justice need to be present including: judicial ethics, judicial morality, judicial understanding, objective judicial behaviour, and clarity.

The duty of all judges in the world, in particular criminal judges, is to accurately investigate the wrongful or criminally wrongful conducts of suspects, while at the same time not violating the rights of any bodies involved in the administration of criminal justice. This means that judges function as the eyes and minds of jurisdiction in their pursuit of the truth. It is based on this account that the judges of a court have important duties within the administration of criminal justice, and therefore must maintain their impartiality at all times. Any acts of violence committed by a judge may give rise to the establishment of a disciplinary hearing, which could lead to a loss of credibility as well as an increase in public mistrust of the criminal justice system. The impartiality of judges therefore constitutes a major element of judicial integrity and honesty. It is consequently of great importance to protect the independence of the judicial administration of criminal justice through guaranteeing that judges of the courts are impartial and do not use the power of the court to their advantage. However, we must remember that this impartiality must also be respected by all parties involved in a criminal case, and the enshrined principles of judicial ethics or judicial conscience should not be abused by anyone.

The question of the impartiality of judges and their judicial conscience is without a doubt an integral part of international criminal justice, specifically concerning the independence of the system of international criminal justice in the ICC. The fact is that the Statute of the ICC has led to the unification of the standards of judicial ethics, if not in practice, at least at different points of its legislation history. There is actually an international tendency among judges to increase the significance of judicial ethics in the administration of justice in the courts of all states, and particularly in the system of international criminal courts established under the power of the United Nations Charter. However, this tendency may still be controlled by the political powers, which brings the ethical independence of the courts and judges into question. Although we understand that all judges must obtain and demonstrate high moral ethics, this is not always easy to implement and enforce. Moral theory says that we should take steps to implement criminal justice which is based on the purity and honesty of the judges. While this may not always be possible, it may help to significantly reform and improve systems of judicial ethics in the world– slowly but surely.

The fact is that we should not only look at examples of ethical conscience, but also at how we can prevent the impunity of criminals. We are, however, aware of the fact that the accuracy of judges is not a gift, and no judge can ensure that they will promote morality and the principles of humanity within their jurisdiction. However, we have to work hard for the establishment of true wisdom within the hearts of all judges and representatives of our criminal jurisdictions. The severity of this issue is very tangible and demands more attention in the case of international crimes and the newly orchestrated dance under the notion of diversity or pluralism.[273] Certainly, the complexity of judicial ethics, particularly in the system of criminal law and international criminal law, is determined by specific constitutional statutes which deal with the responsibility of judges before the law or before the international community as a whole.

We surely need to establish a consolidated system of judicial conscience such that all judges possess the same moral standard of understanding concerning judicial conscience– at least on paper. This is especially necessary in the system of international justice, which is lacking in this regard considering that the most dangerous international criminals are granted impunity and control the principles of international criminal justice. The fact is that the judicial conscience of judges has become a game, and there is serious competition among international judges concerning the chance to be recommended to serve on the ICC.

The sensitivity of the system of criminal justice, and in particular international criminal justice, should not undermine the value of the objectivity of judicial ethics. It is normal that national and international

---

[273] Farhad Malekian, *Orchestrating Diversity in International Criminal Justice* (New York: Nova Publishers, 2021).

criminal jurisdictions are criticised by individuals, in particular concerning the impunity of big super powers. This should be welcomed and indicates the presence of inequality and wisdom in justice.[274] Naturally, in order to establish fundamental standards concerning the ethical conduct of judges, to deliver guidance to judges, and to compensate for the shortcomings of morality of criminal justice, we ought to believe in the capacity of our administration of criminal justice and not ignore the criminal conducts of the big super powers by empowering the ICC to enforce their jurisdiction and decisions. As long as the incapability of the system of criminal justice is directly or indirectly acknowledged by ignoring the truth, the irrationality of certain conducts of big criminals will remain uninterrogated. The recent examples of genocide in many nations in the presence of the ICC, and the accompanying inability of the Court to present the truth within its jurisdiction, are examples of situations in which judges are instrumental. In fact, there was a recent case in the ICC where a judge issued a dissent which supported the strong states while dismissing the rights of the victims.

The assumption that the legal grounds for adopting a good code of judicial ethics have already been legislated within our rules of law is false, and will remain false as long as the positive aspect of the legislation has not been evaluated concerning its morality and utility in the promotion of justice. Norms of judicial ethics are based on the consciences of our judges, and as long as the judges of the courts are not capable of bringing criminals under the jurisdiction of criminal courts, the theory that judicial ethics represent a self-governing institution remains false.

Our actions are surely condemned along with the wise men, our actions are certainly wrong, our conclusions are surely irrational, and our commitments obviously reflect our personal interests and social priorities. We are all criminals in the eyes of the law and justice as long as we do not see the truth, do not fight for the truth, continue to hide the truth, and fail to promote the truth. Judicial conscience, ethical conscience, and moral conscience are nonsensical principles if there are millions of law books

---

[274] Malekian, *Gravity of Wisdom in International Criminal Law*, note 24, pp.13,19, 20, and 43-44, for example.

speaking about the ethical codes of justice for judges. Furthermore, if we are pure judges of our own actions and demands ourselves, it will be very difficult to request practical conscience from judges. These concluding words do not reflect the emotions of the author, nor do they seek to simply fill a page. Duties within criminal justice, criminal politics, and international politics must be based on the truth and on seeking the truth in order to prevent widespread suffering among victims, who thus represent the consequences of our personal, public, and judicial intrigues.

APPENDIX

CODE OF JUDICIAL ETHICS OF INTERNATIONAL CRIMINAL COURT
ICC-BD/02-01-05

Table of contents

Preamble

The judges of the International Criminal Court;

Noting the solemn undertaking required by article 45 of the Rome Statute of the International Criminal Court (the "Statute") and rule 5 (1) (a) of the Rules of Procedure and Evidence (the "Rules");

Recalling the principles concerning judicial independence, impartiality and proper conduct specified in the Statute and the Rules;

Recognising the need for guidelines of general application to contribute to judicial independence and impartiality and with a view to ensuring the legitimacy and effectiveness of the international judicial process;

Having regard to the United Nations Basic Principles on the Independence of the Judiciary (1985) and other international and national rules and standards relating to judicial conduct;

Mindful of the international character of the Court and the special challenges facing the judges of the Court in the performance of their responsibilities;

Have agreed as follows:

Article 1

Adoption of the Code

This Code has been adopted by the judges pursuant to regulation 126 and shall be read subject to the Statute, the Rules and the Regulations of the Court.

Article 2

Use of terms

In this Code of Judicial Ethics the terms "Court," "Statute," "Rules" and "Regulations" shall have the meaning attached to them in the Regulations of the Court.

Article 3

Judicial independence

1. Judges shall uphold the independence of their office and the authority of the Court and shall conduct themselves accordingly in carrying out their judicial functions.

2. Judges shall not engage in any activity which is likely to interfere with their judicial functions or to affect confidence in their independence.

Article 4

Impartiality

1. Judges shall be impartial and ensure the appearance of impartiality in the discharge of their judicial functions.

2. Judges shall avoid any conflict of interest, or being placed in a situation which might reasonably be perceived as giving rise to a conflict of interest.

Article 5

Integrity

1. Judges shall conduct themselves with probity and integrity in accordance with their office, thereby enhancing public confidence in the judiciary.

2. Judges shall not directly or indirectly accept any gift, advantage, privilege or reward that can reasonably be perceived as being intended to influence the performance of their judicial functions.

Article 6

Confidentiality

Judges shall respect the confidentiality of consultations which relate to their judicial functions and the secrecy of deliberations.

Article 7

Diligence

1. Judges shall act diligently in the exercise of their duties and shall devote their professional activities to those duties.

2. Judges shall take reasonable steps to maintain and enhance the knowledge, skills and personal qualities necessary for judicial office.

3. Judges shall perform all judicial duties properly and expeditiously.

4. Judges shall deliver their decisions and any other rulings without undue delay.

Article 8

Conduct during proceedings

1. In conducting judicial proceedings, judges shall maintain order, act in accordance with commonly accepted decorum, remain patient and courteous towards all participants and members of the public present and require them to act likewise.

2. Judges shall exercise vigilance in controlling the manner of questioning of witnesses or victims in accordance with the Rules and give special attention to the right of participants to the proceedings to equal protection and benefit of the law.

3. Judges shall avoid conduct or comments which are racist, sexist or otherwise degrading and, to the extent possible, ensure that any person participating in the proceedings refrains from such comments or conduct.

Article 9

Public expression and association

1. Judges shall exercise their freedom of expression and association in a manner that is compatible with their office and that does not affect or appear to affect judicial independence or impartiality.

2. While judges are free to participate in public debate on matters pertaining to legal subjects, the judiciary or the administration of justice, they shall not comment on pending cases and shall avoid expressing views which may undermine the standing and integrity of the Court.

Article 10

Extra-judicial activity

1. Judges shall not engage in any extra-judicial activity that is incompatible with their judicial function or the efficient and timely

functioning of the Court, or that may affect or may reasonably appear to affect their independence or impartiality.

2. Judges shall not exercise any political function.

Article 11

Observance of the Code

1. The principles embodied in this Code shall serve as guidelines on the essential ethical standards required of judges in the performance of their duties. They are advisory in nature and have the object of assisting judges with respect to ethical and professional issues with which they are confronted.

2. Nothing in this Code is intended in any way to limit or restrict the judicial independence of the judges.

REFERENCES[*]

Allison Henry, *Kant's Theory of Freedom* (Cambridge University Press, 1990).

Andreopoulos George J. (ed.), *Genocide: Conceptual and Historical Dimensions* (Philadelphia, 1994).

Annacker C 'The Legal Régime of erga omnes Obligations in International Law' 46 *Austrian Journal of Public International Law* (1994), pp.131–66.

Aquila Richard E., *Matter in Mind: A Study of Kant's Transcendental Deduction*. (Indiana University Press, 1989).

Araujo, 'Anti-Personnel Mines and Peremptory International Law: Argument and Catalyst' 30 *Vanderbilt J Transnat'l L* (1997).

Arif Sardar MA, Waqar Khan, 'Judicial precedent and its authority under international law', 3 (6) *International Journal of Law* (2017), pp.75-81.

Arthur Naiman, '*9/11: The Simple Facts -- Why the Official Story can't Possibly be True*', (US: Soft Skull Press, 2011).

Arts Karin and Vesselin Popovski (eds.), *International Criminal Accountability and the Rights of Children* (Heidelberg: Springer, 2006), pp. 37–52 and 53–65.

* Mention here neither includes nor excludes in the text.

Ashman Allan and David L. Lee, 'Non-Lawyer Judges: The Long Road North' 53 (3) *Chicago Kant Law Review* (1977), pp.565-595.

Ashworth A., Four Threats to Presumption of Innocence' *South African Journal* (2006), pp.63–97.

Baderin Mashood A., *International Human Rights and Islamic Law* (New York, NY: Oxford University Press, 2005).

Baderin Mashood, A., 'A Comparative Analysis of the Right to a Fair Trial and due Process under International Human Rights Law and Saudi Arabian Domestic Law', 10 (3) *The International Journal of Human Rights* (2006).

Baderin Mashood A., 'Effective Legal Representation in '*Shariah*' Courts as a Means of Addressing Human Rights Concerns in the Islamic Criminal Justice System of Muslim States.' 11 *Yearbook of Islamic and Middle Eastern Law* (2006), pp. 135-167.

Baderin Mashood A., *International Law and Islamic Law* (Ashgate, 2008).

Ballin Ernst Hirsch, 'The Value of International Criminal Justice: How Much International Criminal Justice Can the World Afford?' *International Criminal Law Review* (online publication, 2019), pp.201-213, available online at https://brill.com/view/journals/icla/19/2/article-p201_201.xml?language=en.

Bantekas Ilias and Susan Nash, *International Criminal Law* (2007).

Bartlett Eva, *How We Were Mislead about Syria*, available at https://timhayward.wordpress.com/2017/02/06/how-we-were-misled-about-syria-channel-4-news/.

Bartlett Eva, *What's Happening in Syria? The Media 'Kills the Truth', 'Terrorism' is Described as 'Moderate Opposition.'* (Global Research, February 05, 2017).

Bassiouni M. Cherif, Islam: Concept, Law and Word *Habeas Corpus*, 2 *Rutgers Camden Law Journal* (1970).

Bassiouni M. Cherif (ed.), *International Terrorism and Political Crimes* (1975).

Bassiouni M. Cherif, *Studies in Early Hadith Literature* (Indianapolis, 1978).

Bassiouni M. Cherif, 'Protection of Diplomats under Islamic Law', 74 *American Journal of International Law* (1980), pp.609-655.

Bassiouni M. Cherif, (ed.), *The Islamic Criminal Justice System* (London, Rome, New York, Oceana Publications, 1982).

Bassiouni M. Cherif, 'A Comprehensive Strategic Approach on International Cooperation for the Prevention, Control and Suppression of International and Transnational Criminality, Including the Establishment of an International Criminal Court', 15 *Nova Law Review* 353 (1991).

Bassiouni M. Cherif, 'Draft Statute of International Criminal Tribunal', 9 *Nouvellese Etudes Penales* (1993).

Bassiouni M. Cherif, 'International Crimes: *Jus cogens* and *Obligatio Erga Omnes*' 59 *Law and Contemporary Problems* (1996) 63.

Bassiouni M. Cherif (ed.), *International Criminal Law* (US: Ocean Publication, 3 vols., 1999).

Bassiouni M. Cherif, *Crimes Against Humanity in International law* (1999).

Bassiouni M. Cherif, *Introduction to International Criminal Law* (2005).

Bassiouni M. Cherif, 'International Recognition of Victims' Rights,' in Bassiouni (ed.), III *International Criminal Law* (2008).

Bassiouni M. Cherif, 'The Discipline of International Criminal Law', in M. Cherif Bassiouni (ed.), *International Criminal Law*, Vol. 1 (2008), pp.5-40.

Bassiouni M. Cherif, 'The Subjects of International Criminal Law: Ratione Personae' in M. Bassiouni Cherif (ed.), *International Criminal Law*, Vol. 1 (2008) pp.41-70.

Bassiouni M. Cherif, *Criminal Justice in the Time of War and Peace* (Cambridge University Press, Cambridge, 2014).

Bassiouni M. Cherif, *The Shariah and Islamic Criminal Justice in the Time of War and Peace* (Cambridge University Press, Cambridge, 2014).

Bassiouni M. Cherif and Benjamin B. Ferencz, *The Crime Against Peace and Aggression: From Its Origins to the ICC, in International Criminal Law*, vol. I, (M. Cherif Bassiouni, ed. 2008).

Bassiouni M. Cherif & Christopher Blakesley, 'The Need for an International Criminal Court in the New International World Order', 25 *Vand. J. Transnat'l* 151 (1992).

Bassiouni M. Cherif & Daniel Derby, 'Final Report on the Establishment of an International Criminal Court for the Implementation of the Apartheid Convention and Other Relevant Instruments', 7 *Hofstra Law Review* 525 (1981).

Bassiouni M. Cherif and Ved P. Nanda (eds.), *A Treatise on International Criminal Law: Crimes and Punishment* (2 vols. 1973).

Baum L. M., 'Pursuing Justice in a Climate of Moral Outrage: An Evaluation of the Rights of the Accused in the Rome Statute of the International Criminal Court,' 19 *Wisconsin International Law Journal* (2001), 197.

Baumgartner Elisabeth, 'Aspects of Victim Participation in the Proceedings of the International Criminal Court', 90 (870) *International Review of the Red Cross* (2008), pp.409-440. Available online at https://www.corteidh.or.cr/tablas/R21692.pdf.

Beattie J. M., *Policing and Punishment in London, 1660-1750: Urban Crime and the Limits of Terror* (Oxford: Oxford University Press, 2001).

Beccaria Cesare, *On Crimes and Punishments* (1764).

Beccaria Il caso. *A 250 anni dalla pubblicazione del "Dei delitti e delle pene"* [*250 years after the publication of "Crimes and Punishment"*] (Società editrice il Mulino, 2016).

Beck Lewis White, *Kant Studies Today* (Open Court, 1969).

Bekker P. M., 'The undefended accused/defendant: a brief overview of the development of the American , American Indian and South African Positions' *XXIV CILSA* (1991), pp. 151-188.

Bell Richard, *Introduction to the Quran* (Edinburgh University Press, 1955).

Bellamy A., *Responsibility to Protect: the Global Effort to End Mass Atrocities* (Polity Press, Cambridge, 2009).

Bellamy R (ed.), C Beccaria, *On Crimes and Punishments*, (1995).

Benazir Bhutto, Reconciliation, Islam, Democracy, and the West (Simon & Schuster, 2008).

Benneh, EY 'Sovereignty Immunity and International Crimes' 22 *Ghana Law Journal* (2002–2004), 112.

Bennett Jonathan, *Kant's Analytic* (Cambridge University Press, 1966).

Bennett Jonathan, *Kant's Dialectic* (Cambridge University Press, 1974).

Bennoune Karima, 'As-Salamu 'Alykum? Humanitarian Law in Islamic Jurisprudence', 15 *Michigan Journal of International Law* (1994), pp. 605-643.

Benny Philip Berger, *Criminal Code of the Jews: According to the Talmud* (New Jersey: The Law Book Exchange, LTD., 2005).

Bentley D., *English Criminal Justice in the Nineteenth Century* (London: Bloomsbury Academic, 1998).

Benvenisti Eyal & George W. Downs, 'Prospects for the Increased Independence of International Tribunals', 12 (5) *German Law Journal* (2011), pp.1057-1081.

Benvenisti Eyal and George W. Downs, Prospects for the Increased Independence of International Tribunals (2019).

Berman Schiff (ed.), *The Oxford Handbook of Legal Pluralism* (Oxford University Press, 2019).

Berman Schiff, Global *Legal Pluralism: A Jurisprudence of Law Beyond Borders* (2012).

Bernstein Richard J, *Radical Evil: A Philosophical Interrogation* (New York: Blackwell Publisher, 2002).

Bianchi A., 'Human Rights and the Magic of *Jus cogens*', 19 *European Journal of International Law* (2008), pp. 491-508.

Bigi Giulia, 'Joint Criminal Enterprise in the Jurisprudence of the International Criminal Tribunal for the Former Yugoslavia and the Prosecution of Senior Political and Military Leaders: The Krajišnik Case' 14 *Max Planck United Nations Yearbook* (2010), pp.51-83.

Bird Graham, *Kant's Theory of Knowledge* (Humanities Press, 1962).

Bix Brian, 'Natural Law: The Modern Tradition' in Jules Coleman and Schott Shapiro (eds.), *The Oxford Handbook of Jurisprudence and Philosophy of Law* (2002).

Blackstone W., COMMENTARIES (reprint 1978), pp. 66-7.

Bloxham Donald, *Genocide on Trial: War Crimes Trials and the Formation of Holocaust History and Memory* (2001).

Boas Gideon, *International Criminal Law Developments in the Case Caw of the ICTY* (2004).

Boas Gideon, *International Criminal Justice: Legitimacy and Coherence* (2012).

Boerefijn Ineke, 'Towards a Strong System of Supervision: The Human Rights Committee 's Role in Reforming the Reporting Procedure under Article 40 of the Covenant on Civil and Political Rights', *Human Rights Quarterly* 17.4 (1995), pp.766-793.

Boot Machteld, *Genocide, Crimes against Humanity, War Crimes: Nullum Crimen Sine Lege and the Subjective Matter of Jurisdiction of the International Criminal Court* (2002).

Bosworth-Smith R, *Mohammad and Mohammadanism* (London, 1889).

Boyle James D. A., 'Is Subjectivity Possible? The Postmodern Subject in Legal Theory', 62 *University of Colorado Law Review* 489 (1991).

Boyle James D. A., ed., *Critical Legal Studies* (1992).

Browning Christopher, *The path to genocide: Essays on Launching the Final Solution* (2002).

Browning Don (eds.), *Universalism vs. Relativism: Making Moral Judgements in a Changing, Pluralistic, and Threatening World* (Rowman and Littlefield Publishers, United Kingdom, 2006).

Brownlie, Ian, *International Law and the* Use of Force *by States* (Oxford: Oxford University Press, 1996).

Brownlie Ian, *Principles of Public International Law* (Oxford: Clarendon Press, 5th ed., 1998).

Brunnée J, 'The Prohibition on Torture: Driving *Jus cogens* Home?' 104 *Proceedings of the Annual Meeting of the American Society of International Law* (2010).

Brunstetter Daniel R. and Arturo Jimenez-Bacardi, 'Clashing over Drones: The Legal and Normative Gap between the United States and the Human Rights Community,' 19 (2) *International Journal of Human Rights* (2015), pp. 176–198.

Buchanan Allen, 'Toward a Drone Accountability Regime,' 29 (1) *Ethics and International Affairs (2015)*, pp. 15–70.

Burke-White William W., 'Implementing a Policy of Positive Complementarity in the Rome System of Justice,' 19 *Criminal Law Forum* (2008), 59-89.

Burgess Pete, Susan Corby, and Paul L. Latreille, 'Lay Judges and Labour Courts: A Question of Legitimacy', 35 *Comparative Labour Law and Policy Journal* (2014), pp.191-215.

Burns Peter, 'An International Criminal Tribunal: The Difficult Union of Principle and Politics', 5 *Criminal Law Forum* (1994).

Byers M, 'Conceptualising the Relationship Between *Jus cogens* and *Erga Omnes Rules*' 66 *Nordic Journal of International Law* (1997).

Byrd B. Sharon and Joachim Hruschka, *Kant and Law* (Ashgate, 2005).

Caenegem R. C. van, *European Law in the Past and the Future: Unity and Diversity over Two Millennia* (Cambridge: Cambridge University Press, 2001).

Cançado Trindade, A '*Jus cogens* in Contemporary International Law', UN Audiovisual Library, (http://www.un.org/law/avl).

Cannizzaro E., 'A Higher Law for Treaties?', in E. Cannizzaro (ed.), *The Law of Treaties Beyond the Vienna Convention* (2011).

Carvin Stephanie, 'Getting Drones Wrong', 19 (2) *International Journal of Human Rights* (2015), pp. 127–141.

Cassese Antonio (ed.), *The New Humanitarian Law of Armed Conflict* (Naples: Editoriale Scientifica, 1979).

Cassese Antonio, 'First Annual Report of the ICTY', *Yearbook* of *International Law Commission* (1994).

Cassese Antonio, *International Criminal Law* (Oxford: Oxford University Press, 2nd, ed., 2008).

Cassese Antonio, 'For an Enhanced Role of *Jus cogens*' in Cassese, A (ed.), *Realizing Utopia* (2012).

Chinkin Christine, '*Jus cogens*, Article 103 of the UN Charter and other Hierarchical Techniques of Conflict Solution' *Finnish Yearbook of International Law* (2006).

Chinkin Christine, '*Jus cogens*, Article 103 of the UN Charter and Other Hierarchical Techniques of Conflict Solution,' 17 *Finnish Yearbook of International Law* (2008), pp. 63-90.

Chinkin Christine, Mary Kaldor, *International Law and New Wars* (New York: Cambridge University Press, 2017).

Chossudovsky Michel, *War and Globalisation: The Truth Behind September 11* (Global Outlook, *2002).*

Christian Wolff., *Jus Gentium Methodo Scientifica Pertractatum* translated by Joseph H. Drake (Oxford: Clarendon Press at London (1934).

Cicero, *De Finibus Bonorum et Malorum*, Book V, XXIII.

Cima Elena, 'Ethical Conduct in International Criminal Courts: Whose Ethics?', *American Journal of International Law*(2019), pp.296-301. Available online at https://www.researchgate.net/publication/335848353_Ethical_Conduct_in_International_Criminal_Courts_Whose_Ethics.

Clooney Amal, Philippa Webb, *Right to a Fair Trial in International Law* (Oxford Publication, 2020).

Cohen Morris, 'Moral Aspects of the Criminal Law,' 49 *Yale Law Journal* (1949), pp. 987-1026.

Colbran Stephen, 'Diligent as a Criterion for Judicial Performance Evaluation', 11 (1) *Griffith Law Review* (2002), pp.198-222Coleman Francis, X. J., *The Harmony of Reason: A Study in Kant's Aesthetics*. (University of Pittsburgh Press, 1974).

Combs Nancy, *Fact-Finding Without Facts* (Cambridge: Cambridge University Press, 2010).

Combs Nancy, 'Grave Crimes and Weak Evidence: A Fact-Finding Evolution in International Criminal Law' 38 *Harvard International Law Review* (2016), pp.47-125.

Corten Olivier, 'La rébellion et le droit international: Le principe de neutralité en tension' ['Rebellion and International Law: The Principle of Neutrality in Tension'], 374 *Recueil des Cours: Académie de Droit International de la Haye* (2014), pp. 53–312.

Coulson, N. J, *Conflict and Tensions in Islamic Jurisprudence* (University of Chicago Press, 1969).

Cox, J. Gray, *The Will at the Crossroads: A Reconstruction of Kant's Moral Philosophy* (University Press of America, 1984).

Crane David M., 'The Special Court for Sierra Leone, in International Criminal Law', Vol. III (M. Cherif Bassiouni, ed. 2008) pp. 195-218.

Craven Sarah M. R., *In Good Conscience: Expressions of Judicial Conscience in Federal Appellate Opinions,* (Akron Law Publication, 2012), pp.1-67.

Crawford J and S Olleson 'The Continuing Debate on a UN Convention on State Responsibility' *54 ICLQ* (2005) 959–71.

Crawford J., *The ILC's Articles on State Responsibility: Introduction, Text and Commentaries* (CUP Cambridge 2002).

Cryer Robert, *Prosecuting International Crimes, Selectivity and the International Criminal Law Regime* (Cambridge University Press, Cambridge, 2005).

Cryer Robert, 'The Doctrinal Foundations of International Criminalization,' in *International Criminal Law*, Vol. 1 (M. Cherif Bassiouni, ed., 2008), pp. 107-128.

Cummings Scott L, 'Introduction: What Good are Lawyers?' in Scott L. Cummings (ed.), *Paradox of Professionalism Lawyers and the Possibility of Justice* (2011).

D'Amato A., 'The Moral Dilemma of Positivism', 20 *Valparaiso University Law Review* (1985-86), 43-53.

D'Amato A., 'It's a Bird, It's a Plane, It's *Jus cogens'* 6 *Connecticut Journal of International Law* (1990).

Danilenko G, 'International *Jus cogens*: Issues of Law-Making' 2 *European Journal of International Law* (1991).

Danilenko G. M., 'International *Jus cogens*: Issues of Law Making', *European Journal of International Law* (1991).

David Eric, 'The Belgin Experince', in M. Cherif Bassiouni, *International Criminal Law*, Vol. III (Netherlands: Brill, 2008), pp.359-384.

David Lyons, 'Moral Aspects of Legal Theory' in Kenneth Himma and Brian Bix (eds) *Law and Morality* (2005).

David MacGregor, "September 11 as 'Machiavellian State Terrorism'", in Paul Zarembka, *The Hidden History of 9-11-2001* (New York: Seven Stories Press, 2008).

Davis Michael C., Dietrich Wolfgang, Bettina Schoolman and Sepp. Dieter, *International Intervention in the Post-Cold War World: Moral Responsibility and Power Politics* (M. E. Sharpe, Inc., 2003).

de Hoog AJJ, 'The Relationship between *Jus cogens*, Obligations *Erga Omnes* and International Crimes: Peremptory Norms in Perspective' 42 *Österreichische Zeitschrift für öffentliches Recht und Völkerrecht* (1991).

de Hoogh A, *Obligations erga omnes and International Crimes: A Theoretical Inquiry into the Implementation and Enforcement of the International Responsibility of States* (Kluwer The Hague , 1996).

de Wet, Erika '*Jus cogens* and Obligations Erga Omnes' in de Wet, E and Vidmar (eds.), J *Hierarchy in International Law: The Place of Human Rights* (2012).

de Wet Erika, 'The Prohibition of Torture as an International Norm of *Jus cogens* and its Implementation for National and Customary Law,' 15 (1) *European Journal of International Law* (2014), Vol. 15, No.1, 97-121.

Delmas-Marty Mireille, The Contribution of Comparative Law to a Pluralist Conception of International Criminal Law, 1 *Journal of International Criminal Justice* (2003), pp. 13-25.

DeSon Jason S., 'Automating the Right Stuff? The Hidden Ramifications of Ensuring Autonomous Aerial Weapon Systems Comply with International Humanitarian Law,' 72 *Air Force Law Review* (2015), pp. 85–122.

Despland Michael, *Kant on History and Religion* (McGill-Queen's University Press, 1973).

Detmold M. J., *The Unity of Law and Morality: A Refutation of Legal Positivism* (Canada: Law Book Co. of Australasia, 1984).

Dhanapala Jayantha, *Under-Secretary-General for Disarmament Affairs United Nations, International Law, Security, and Weapons of Mass Destruction* (New York, 9 May 2002).

Dhokalia, 'Problems Relating to *Jus cogens'*, in S. Agrawala (ed.), *Essays on the Law of Treaties* (1972).

Dickson Julie, *Evaluation and Legal Theory* (2001).

Don Paul and Jim Hoffman, Waking Up from Our Nightmare, the 9/11/01 Crimes in New York City (New York: I/R Press, 2004).

Drost Pieter Nicolaas, *The Crime of State: Genocide* (Original from Indiana University, 1959).

Drost Pieter Nicolaas, *The Crime of State: Humanicide* (Original from Indiana University, 1959).

Dryer Douglas P., *Kant's Solution for Verification in Metaphysics* (Allen and Unwin, 1966).

Dugard John, 'Lifting the Guise of Occupation and Recourse to Action before the ICJ and ICC', Palestine Yearbook of International Law, Vol. 17, 2013–14, pp. 9–27.

Duncan A. R. C., *Practical Reason and Morality* (Nelson, 1957).

Dupuy P. M, 'Reviewing the Difficulties of Codification: On Ago's Classification of Obligations of Means and Obligations of Result in Relation to State Responsibility' 10 *EJIL* (1999), pp. 371–85.

Dupuy, P 'Some Reflections on Contemporary International Law and the Appeal to Universal Values: a Response to Marti Koskenniemi' 16 *European Journal of International Law* (2005), 131.

Duțu Mircea, Vespasian V. Pella (1897-1952): *Founder of International Criminal law, Promoter of the Unification of the Criminal Law, Architect of the International Criminal Justice* (Universul Juridic, Bucharest, 2012).

Eberle Edward J., 'The German Idea of Freedom', 10 *Orgon Review of Int'L Law* (2008), pp. 1-76.

Edgeworth F. Y., *Mathematical Psychics: An Essay on the Application of Mathematics to the Moral Sciences*, (London: C. Kegan Paul & Co. 1881).

Emil L., 'Fackenheim, Kant and Radical Evil', in Immanuel Kant: *Critical Assessments.* 3 ed., Chadwick Ruth. (Routledge, 1992), 259-273.

Engelhardt Jordan, *The Pre-eminent State: National Dominance in the Effort to Try Saddam Hussein*, *Cornell Journal of International Law*, (2009).

Eric David, *Principes de Droit des Conflits Armés* [*Principles of the Law of Armed Conflict*] (2nd, ed. 1999).

Ewald F., 'Unger's Philosophy: A Critical Legal Study' 5 *Yale Law Journal* (1988), 665.

Ewing A. C., *A Short Commentary on Kant's 'Critique of Pure Reason'* (Methuen, 1978).

Falk Richard, *The Vietnam War and International Law* (Princeton University Press, 1968).

Falk Richard, 'The Accountability of Leaders: A Challenge to Civil Government and Society' in Jeremy Brecher, Jill Cutler, Smith Brendan, *In the Name of Democracy: American War Crimes in Iraq and Beyond (American Empire Project)*, (New York: Metropolitan Books, Henry Holt and Company, 2005).

Falk Richard, *Slouching Toward a Palestinian Holocaust*, www.transnational.org/Area…/Falk Palestine Genocide.html, 20 October 2010.

Farmer John, *The Ground Truth: The Story behind America's Defense on 9/11* (New York: Riverhead Books, 2009).

Fein Bruce, 'Hillary Clinton's 5 lies about Syria, Terror Threat,' The *Washington Times* (25 October, 2016).

Ferencz Benjamin, *International Criminal Court* (2 vols. 1980).

Ferencz Benjamin, *An International Criminal Code and Court: Why They Stand and Where They're Going,* 30 *Columbia Journal of Transnational Law* (1992), 375.

Ferencz Benjamin B., 'Ending Impunity for the Crime of Aggression,' 41 *Case W. Res. J* (2009), pp.281-290.

Finch George Augustus, 'The Nuremberg Trial and International Law,' 41 *American Journal of International Law* (1947), 20.

Finch George A., 'Draft Statute for an International Court', editorial comment 46 *American Journal of International Law* (1952), pp. 89-98.

Finch George A., 'Draft Statute for an International Criminal Court,' 46 *American Journal of International Law* (1990), 67.

Findlay Escrito por Mark J., *International and Comparative Criminal Justice: A Critical Introduction* (Routledge, London, 2013).

Finnis John (ed.), *Natural Law* (1991).

Finnis John, *Fundamentals of Ethics* (1985).

Finnis John, *Aquinas: Moral, Political and Legal Theory* (1998).

Fischer-Lescano A. and G. Teubner, 'Regime Collision: The Vain Search for Legal Unity in the Fragmentation of Global Law,' 25 *Michigan Journal of International Law* (2004), pp. 999-104.

Fitzmaurice Gerald, 'The General Principles of International Law Considered from the Standpoint of the Rules of Law,' 92 *Recuel des Cours* (1957).

Focarelli C, 'Promotional *Jus cogens*: A Critical Appraisal of *Jus cogens*' Legal Effects' 77 *Nordic Journal of International Law* (2008), 429.

Fouladvand, S. *Complementarity and cultural sensitivity: Decision-making by the International Criminal Court (ICC) Prosecutor in Relation to the Situations in the Darfur Region of the Sudan and the Democratic Republic of Congo (DRC)* (2012).

Fuller Lon Luvios., The Morality of Law (Yale Law University, 2nd ed., 1969).

Gardiner Gerald, *Capital Punishment as a Deterrent: And the Alternative* (London: Victor Gollancz, 1956).

Garland David; Randall McGowen; Michael Meranze, *America's Death Penalty: Between Past and Present* (2011).

Gavison Ruth (ed.), *Legal Philosophy: The Influence of H.L.A. Hart* (1987).

George Robert P., *Natural Law Theory: Contemporary Essays* (1994).

George Robert P. (ed.), *The Autonomy Of Law: Essays On Legal Positivism* (1995).

Gideon Boas and William A. Schabas (eds.), *International Criminal Law Developments in the Case Law of the ICTY* (2005).

Glennon, MJ "De l'Absurdité du Droit Impératif (*Jus cogens*)' 110 *Revue Générale de Droit International Public* (2006), 529.

Gómez Robledo, A "Le *Jus cogens* International: Sa Genése, sa Nature, ses Fonctions' 172, *Recueil des Cours de l'Académie de Droit International de la Haye* ["*Jus cogens* International: Its Genesis, its Nature, its Functions' 172, *Compendium of Courses of the Hague Academy of International Law*] (1982), 9.

Gottfried Martin, *Kant's Metaphysics and Theory of Science* (Manchester University Press, 1974).

Gram Moltke S. (ed.), *Kant: Disputed Questions* (Quadrangle, 1967).

Gray C., *International Law and the Use of Force* (2000).

Grayeff Felix, *Kant's Theoretical Philosophy* (Barnes & Noble, 1970).

Greenawalt Alexander K. A., The Pluralism of International Criminal Law, 86 *Indiana Law Journal* (2011), 1063-1130.

Gross Michael L., 'Nonlethal Weapons, Non-Combatant Immunity, and the Principle of Participatory Liability', 47 *Case Western Reserve Journal of International Law* (2015), pp. 201–216.

Grover Sonja, *Prosecuting International Crimes and Human Rights Abuses Committed Against Children – Leading International Court Cases* (2010), pp. 169–279.

Guyer Paul, *The Cambridge Companion to Kant* (1992).

Guyer Paul, *Kant and the Experience of Freedom* (Cambridge University Press, 1993).

Haas Jacob De, *History of Palestine - The Last Two Thousand Years* (USA: Macmillan, 1934).

Hacker P. M. S. and J. Raz, (eds.), Law, *Morality and Society: Essays in Honour of H. L. A. Hart* (1977).

Hakim Khalifa Abdul, *Fundamental Human Rights* (1952).

Hall W. A., *Treatise of International Law* (8th ed., 1924).

Hannikainen, L., *Peremptory Norms (jus cogens) in International Law: Historical Development, Criteria, Present Status* (1988).

Harees Lukman, *The Mirage of Dignity on the highways of Human 'Progress': - the Bystanders Perspective* (2012).

Harhoff Frederik, 'It's All in the Process: Reflections on the Relation between International Criminal Trials and International Humanitarian Law', 78 Nordic Journal of International Law (2010).

Harle Vilho, *Ideas of Social Order in the Ancient World* (1998).

Harrit, Niels H. Jeffrey Farrer, Steven E. Jones, Kevin R. Ryan, Frank M. Legge, Daniel Farnsworth, Gregg Roberts, James R. Gourley, Bradley R. Larsen, 'Active Thermitic Material Discovered in Dust from the 9/11 World Trade Center Catastrophe' in http://911review.com/evidence/wtcexplosives.html and www.benthamopen.org/pages/content.php?TOCPJ/2009/00000002/00000001/7TOCPJ.SGM.

Hart H. L. A., *The Concept of Law* (1961).

Hart H. L. A., *Essays in Jurisprudence and Philosophy* (1985).

Hart H. L. A., *The Concept of Law,* 2nd ed., (P.A. Bulloch and J. Raz, eds., 1994).

Hartnack Justus, *Kant's Theory of Knowledge* (Harcourt, Brace and World, 1967).

Head Michael, *The Legal Power to Launch War: Who Decides?* (2009).

Head Michael, *Domestic Military Powers, Law and Human Rights: Calling out the Armed Forces* (2021).

Head Michael; Kristian Boehringer, *Domestic Deployment of the Armed Forces: Military Powers, Law and Human Rights* (Routledge, 2019).

Heidegger Martin, *Kant and the Problem of Metaphysics* (Indiana University Press, 1962).

Heikkilä Mikaela, International Criminal Tribunals and Victims of Crime: A Study of the Status of Victims before International Criminal Tribunals and of Factors affecting this Status (Institute for Human Rights, Abo Akademi University, Turku, 2004).

Heller Kevin Jon, *The Nuremberg Military Tribunals and the origins of international criminal law* (2010).

Heller Kevin Jon, 'What Is an International Crime? (A Revisionist History)', 58 *Harvard International Law Journal* (2017), pp. 353-420.

Hendeled C. W., (ed.), *The Philosophy of Kant and Our Modern World* (Liberal Arts, 1957).

Hersh Seymour M., *The Killing of Osama Bin Laden (2016).*

Higgins, 'Derogations under Human Rights Treaties' *BYIL* (1976–1977), 282.

Hoffe Otfried, *Immanuel Kant* (State University of New York Press, 1994).

Hoover Joseph, Moral Practices: Assigning Responsibility in the International Criminal Court, 76 *Law and Contemporary Problems* (2014), pp.263-86.

Hugo Adam Bedau, Paul G. Cassell, *Debating the Death Penalty: Should America Have Capital Punishment? The Experts on Both Sides Make Their Best Case* (2004).

Huntington Cairns, *Plato's Theory of Law*, 56 Harvard Law Review (1942), pp. 559-587.

Husabø Erling Johannes and Ingvild Bruce, *Fighting Terrorism through Multilevel Criminal Legislation: Security Council Resolution 1373, the EU Framework Decision on Combating Terrorism and their Implementation in Nordic, Dutch and German Criminal Law* (Martinus Nijhoff Publishers, 2009).

Hutchings Patricia A. E., *Kant on Absolute Value* (Wayne State University Press, 1972).

Jacovides A., *Treaties Conflicting with Peremptory Norms of International Law and the Zurich-London 'Agreements'* (1966).

James Paul, Jonathan Friedman, *Globalization and Violence, Vol. 3: Globalizing War and Intervention* (London: Sage Publications, 2006).

Janis, MW 'The Nature of *Jus cogens*' 3 *Connecticut Journal of International Law* (1988) 59.

Jeffreys-Jones Rhodri, In *Spies We Trust: The Story of Western Intelligence* (Oxford: Oxford University Press, 2013).

Jevons W. S., *The Theory of Political Economy* (London: Macmillan and Co., 1871).

Jones Hardy E., *Kant's Principle of Personality* (University of Wisconsin Press, 1971).

Jørgensen, *The Responsibility of States for International Crimes* (OUP Oxford 2000).

Jori Mario (ed.), *Legal Positivism* (1992).

Kant Immanuel, *The Only Possible Argument in Support of a Demonstration of the Existence of God* (1763).

Kant Immanuel, *Critique of Pure Reason* (1781).

Kant Immanuel, *Prolegomena to Any Future Metaphysics* (1783).

Kant Immanuel, *Answering the Question: What is Enlightenment?* (1784).

Kant Immanuel, *Perpetual Peace, and Other Essays on Politics, History, and Morals* (1784).

Kant Immanuel, *Groundwork of the Metaphysic of Morals* (1785).

Kant Immanuel, *Metaphysical Foundations of Natural Science* (1786).

Kant Immanuel, *The Critique of Practical Reason* (1788).

Kant Immanuel, *Critique of Judgment* (1790).

Kant Immanuel, *The Science of Right* (1790).

Kant Immanuel, *Religion within the Bounds of Bare Reason* (1793).

Kant Immanuel, *Perpetual Peace: A Philosophical Sketch* (1795).

Kant Immanuel, *The Metaphysics of Morals* (1797).

Kant Immanuel, *Opus Postumum* (1995).

Kant Immanuel, 'Religion within the Limits of Reason Alone,' in *Religion and Rational Theology*, ed. and transl. Allen Wood and George di Giovanni (Cambridge University Press, 1996), 93.

Kant Immanuel, *Practical Philosophy* (editor: Mary J. Gregor, 1999).

Kawasaki KYOJI, 'A brief Note on the Legal Effects of *Jus cogens* in International Law', 34 *Hitotsubashi Journal of Law and Politics* (2006), pp. 27-43.

Kelsen Hans, 'Will the Judgement of the Nürenberg Trial Constitute a Precedent in International Law,' 1 *International Law Quarterly* (1947), 153.

Kelsen Hans, *What is Justice? Justice, Law and Politics in the Mirror of Science* (1957).

Kelsen Hans, *Pure Theory of Law* (transl. Maz Knight, 1967).

Kemal Salim., *Kant's Aesthetic Theory: An Introduction* (St. Martin's Press, 1992).

Kennedy D, 'Law and Ideology' 5 *Tikkun* (1988).

Kent Greenawalt, *Statutory and Common Law Interpretation* (Oxford: Oxford University Press, 2013).

Khadduri Majid, (ed.), (transl.) *The Islamic Law of Nations: Shaybani's Siyar* (Transl. with an introduction, notes, and appendices, Baltimore, 1966).

Khadduri Majid, (ed.), *War and Peace in the Law of Islam* (Baltimore: The Johan Hopkins Press, 1955).

Khadduri Majid, 'The Islamic Theory of International Relations and its Contemporary Relevance in Proctor' in J. Harris Protector, *Islam and International Relations* (New York, 1965), pp. 24-39.

Khadduri Majid, *Major Middle Eastern Problems in International Law* (1972).

King Martin Luther, *The Quest for Peace and Justice, a Nobel Lecture delivered by Martin Luther King in December* 11, 1964.

Kitcher Patricia, *Kant's Transcendental Psychology* (Oxford University Press, 1990).

Klamberg Mark, 'The Alternative Hypothesis Approach, Robustness and International Criminal Justice: A Plea for a "Combined Approach" to Evaluation of Evidence', 13(3) *Journal of International Criminal Justice* (2015), pp. 535-553.

Klein A., Theory for the Application of the Customary International Law of Human Rights by Domestic Courts 13 *Yale Journal of International Law* (1988).

Klein David F., 'A Theory for the Application of the Customary International Law of Human Rights by Domestic Courts,' 13 (2) *Yale Journal of International Law* (1988), pp. 332-365.

Klincewicz Michal, 'Autonomous Weapons Systems, the Frame Problem and Computer Security,' 14 (2) *Journal of Military Ethics* (2015), pp. 162–176.

Kolb, R *Théorie du Jus cogens International: Essai de Relecture du Concept* [*Jus cogens International Theory: Concept Proofreading Essay*] (2001).

Kolb, Robert 'Observations sur l'évolution du concept de jus cogens' ['Observations on the evolution of the concept of jus cogens'] in *Revue générale de droit international public* (2009), pp. 837-850.

Kolb, Robert "*Jus cogens*, Intangibilité, Intransgressibilité, Dérogation 'Positive' et 'Négative'" 109 *Revue Générale de Droit International Public* ["*Jus cogens*, Intangibility, Intransgressibility, Derogation

'Positive' and 'Negative'"] 109 *Revue Générale de Droit International Public*] (2005).

Komicker Uhlmann, EM 'The State Community Interests, *Jus cogens* and the Protection of the Global Environment: Developing Criteria for Peremptory Norms' *Georgetown International Environmental Law Review* (1998), 101.

Kornicker, 'State Community Interests, *Jus cogens* and Protection of the Global Environment' 11 *Georgetown Int'l Environmental L Rev* (1998).

Koskenniem Martti, *The Politics of International Law* (Hart, 2011).

Koskenniemi M. Martti, 'Solidarity Measures: State Responsibility as a New International Order?' 72 *BYIL* (2001), pp. 337–56.

Koskenniemi Martti, Mónica García-Salmones Rovira, and Paolo Amorosa, *International Law and Religion: Historical and Contemporary Perspectives* (2017).

Koskenniemi Martti, *The Gentle Civilizer of Nations: the Rise and Fall of International Law*, 1870-1960 (Cambridge University Press 2002).

Kress Claus, 'Aggression and the Use of Force in International Law', *Proceedings of the 108th Annual Meeting of the American Society of International Law* (2014), pp. 325–346.

Kuper Leo, *International Action against Genocide* (Minority Rights Group Report No. 53, London, 1982).

Kuper Leo, *The Prevention of Genocide* (New Haven and London, 1985).

Lefenya Kesolofetse, 'Use of Explosive Weapons in Densely Populated Areas: Implications for International Humanitarian Law,' *African Yearbook on International Humanitarian Law* (2014), pp. 68–86.

Legal Consequences of the Construction of a Wall in the Occupied Palestinian Territory (I.C.J. Reports, 2004).

Leiboff Marett and Mark Thomas, *Legal Theories in Principle* (2004).

Limbach Jutta, Pedro Cruz Villalón, Roger Errera, Lord Lester, Tamara Morschtschakowa, Lord Justice Sedley, Andrzej Zol., 'Judicial Independence: Law and Practice of Appointments to the European Court of Human Rights' (2003). Available online at https://www.corteidh.or.cr/tablas/32795.pdf.

Linderfalk Ulf, 'The Creation of *Jus cogens* – Making Sense of Article 53 of the Vienna Convention,' Max-Planck-Institut für ausländisches öffentliches Recht und Völkerrecht (2011), pp.259-278.

Luper-Foy, Steven 'Introduction: Global Distributive Justice' in Steven Luper-Foy (ed.), *Problems of International Justice* (London: Westview Press, 1988), pp. 1-24.

MacGregor, 'State Immunity and *Jus cogens*' 55 *International & Comparative Law Quarterly* (2006), 437.

MacIntyre Alasdair, *A Short History of Ethics: A History of Moral Philosophy from the Homeric Age to the Twentieth Century* (1965).

MacIntyre Alasdair, *After Virtue: A Study in Moral Theory* (University of Notre Dame Press, 1982).

Madsen Wayne, Jean-Charles and Guillaume Dasquie, *Forbidden Truth: U.S.-Taliban Secret Oil Diplomacy, Saudi Arabia and the Failed Search for bin Laden* (2002).

Magliveras Konstantinos D., 'The Special Court for Sierra Leone: A New Type of Regional Criminal Court for the International Community?' 17 *International Enforcement Law Rep*orter (Feb. 2001).

Majd Mohammad Gholi, T*he Great Famine & Genocide in Iran: 1917-1919* (2nd ed., University Press of America, 2013).

Majd Mohammad Gholi, *Victorian Holocaust Iran in the Great Famine of 1869-1873* (Hamilton Books, 2018).

Majinge Charles Riziki, 'Peaceful Settlement of Disputes among States and the Rules of Regional Judicial Institutions in Africa ' in Charles Riziki Majinge (ed.), *Rule of Law Through Human Rights and International Criminal Justice : Essays in Honour of Adama Dieng* (Cambridge: Cambridge Scholars publishing (Cambridge Scholars Publishing, 2015), pp. 523-52.

Malekian Farhad, *International Criminal Responsibility of States: A Study on the Evolution of International Responsibility of States with particular Emphasis on the Concept of Crime and Criminal Responsibility* (Stockholm, 1985).

Malekian Farhad, *System of International Law: Formation, Treaties, Responsibility* (Uppsala, 1987).

Malekian Farhad, *International Criminal Law: The Legal and Critical Analysis of International Crimes* (Stockholm: Almqvist & Wiksell International, 2 vols. 1991).

Malekian Farhad, *Condemning the Use of Force in the Gulf Crisis* (Almqvist & Wiksell International, 1st ed., 1992).

Malekian Farhad, *The Monopolization of International Criminal Law in the United Nations, A Jurisprudential Approach* (Almqvist Wiksell International, 1st ed., 1993).

Malekian Farhad, *Condemning the Use of Force in the Gulf Crisis* (Almqvist & Wiksell International, 2nd ed. 1994).

Malekian Farhad, *The Concept of Islamic International Criminal Law, A Comparative Study* (Netherlands: Brill, 1994).

Malekian Farhad, *The Monopolization of International Criminal Law in the United Nations, A Jurisprudential Approach* (Almqvist Wiksell International, 2nd ed., 1995).

Malekian Farhad, '*International Criminal Responsibility', in International Criminal Law* (M. Cherif Bassiouni, 2ed, ed., 1999).

Malekian Farhad, 'International Criminal Responsibility: International Criminal Responsibility of Individuals' in M. Cherif Bassiouni, *International Criminal Law,* Vol. *Crimes* (2ed, ed., New York: Transnational Publishers, 1999).

Malekian Farhad, 'Emasculating the Philosophy of International Criminal Justice in the Iraqi Special Tribunal,' *Cornell International Law Journal*, 58/5 (2005), pp.675-725.

Malekian Farhad, *Prohibition Governing Child Soldiers Constituting an Integral Part of Jus cogens and Obligatio Erga Omnes*, XVII *World Congress of the International Association of Youth and Family Judges and Magistrates*, Belfast, Northern Ireland, 27 August – 2 September (2006).

Malekian Farhad, 'Armenian Genocide and the Questions of Responsibility of the Turkish Government,' *House of Commons Conference on the Armenian Genocide, Armenian Solidarity, British-Armenian All-Party Parliamentary Group, No Security Publication* (2007), pp.31-9.

Malekian Farhad, *Documents on the Principles of International Human Rights* (Stockholm: Norstedts Juridik AB, 2007).

Malekian Farhad, 'Mutilating the Philosophy of Justice in the Time of Armed Conflicts,' *Contemporary Journal of International Criminal Law* (Publication of the Institute of International Criminal Law, Uppsala, 2007).

Malekian Farhad, 'The Functions of International Criminal Law and the Problem of Positivism and Neutralism Philosophy', *Contemporary Journal of International Criminal Law* (Publication of the Institute of International Criminal Law, Uppsala, 2007).

Malekian Farhad, 'The Homogeneity of International Criminal Court with Islamic Jurisprudence,' 9 (4) *International Criminal Law Review* (2009), pp.595-621.

Malekian Farhad, 'The Miserable Wedding of Naturalism into Positivism,' 2 *ID EST Journal* (2009).

Malekian Farhad, *Principles of Islamic International Criminal Law: A Comparative Search* (Netherlands: Brill & Nijhoff, 2011).

Malekian Farhad, 'The Laws Governing Crimes against Women Constituting *Obligatio Erga Omnes*' in David Wingeate Pike, *Crimes Against Women* (New York: Nova Science Publishers, 2011).

Malekian Farhad, 'Judging International Criminal Justice in the Occupied Territories,' 12 *International Criminal Law Review* (2012), pp.627-869.

Malekian Farhad, 'The Child as an Autonomous Subject of Justice' in Farhad Malekian, Kerstin Nordlöf, *Sovereignty of Children in Law* (Cambridge: Cambridge Scholars Publishing, 2012), pp. 2-55.

Malekian Farhad., *'Islamic Law Justice Systems' in* Jay S. Albanese, *The Encyclopaedia of Criminology and Criminal Justice* (United States: Wiley-Blackwell (5 volumes, 2013), vol. III, pp.1220-1225.

Malekian Farhad, *Jurisprudence of International Criminal Justice* (Introduction by Professor Benjamin B. Ferencz, the former Prosecutor of the Nuremberg Tribunal (Cambridge: Cambridge Scholars Publishing, 2014).

Malekian Farhad, 'Consolidating the International Criminal Law of Children', 26, (3) Criminal Law Forum (2015), pp. 569-593.

Malekian Farhad, 'The Canon of Love against the Use of Force in Islamic and Public International Law: Part II: The Anatomy of Love Against Violations,' 15 *International Criminal Law Review*, 2015), pp. 861-895.

Malekian Farhad, 'The Canon of Love against the Use of Force in Islamic and Public International Law: Part I: The Chamber of Love within Legal Discipline,' 15 *International Criminal Law Review*, 2015), pp. 591-628.

Malekian Farhad, 'Comparative Substantive International Criminal Justice,' in Ronald Slye (ed.), *The Nuremberg Principles in Non-western Societies: A Reflection on their Universality, Legitimacy and Application* (2017), pp. 10-44.

Malekian Farhad, 'Conundrums of *Jus cogens:* In Case Law' (Part II), No. 13 *Вісник Південного регіонального центру Національної академії правових наук України,* [No. 13 *Journal of the South regional Center of National Academy of Legal Sciences of Ukraine*] (2017), pp. 12-21.

Malekian Farhad, 'Conundrums of *Jus cogens*: in International Criminal Law' (Part I), *Вісник Південного регіонального центру Національної академії правових наук України* [*No.12 Journal of the South regional Center of National Academy of Legal Sciences of Ukraine*] (2017), pp. 8-16.

Malekian Farhad, *Corpus Juris of Islamic International Criminal Justice* (Newcastle: Cambridge Scholars Publishing, 2017).

Malekian Farhad, *Judgments of Love in Criminal Justice* (Switzerland: Springer: 2017).

Malekian Farhad, 'The Heaven of Justice with Love,' *The Journal of the Henry Martyn Institute* (2017), pp. 5-29.

Malekian Farhad, *Classical Morality in International Peremptory Criminal Law* (Newcastle: Cambridge Scholars Publishing, 2018).

Malekian Farhad, *Judgments of Love in Criminal Justice* (Switzerland: Springer: 2018).

Malekian Farhad, *The Mirage of International Criminal Law: Kant Metaphysics of Mens Rea* (Newcastle: Cambridge Scholars Publishing, 2018).

Malekian Farhad, *Allegations by Political Laundering* (Newcastle: Cambridge Scholars Publishing, 2019).

Malekian Farhad, *Trading Virginity of International Criminal Justice* (New York, Nova Science Publishers, 2020).

Malekian Farhad, *Classical Morality in International Peremptory Criminal Law* (Newcastle: Cambridge Scholars Publishing, 2021).

Malekian Farhad, *Conscience of Judges in International Criminal Law, the Heart of Judgements* (New York: Nova Science Publishers, 2021).

Malekian Farhad, *Conscience of Lawyers in International Criminal Law, the Burden of Doppelgängers* (New York: Nova Science Publishers, 2021).

Malekian Farhad, *Conscience of Prosecutors in International Criminal Law, the Heart of the Matter* (New York: Nova Science Publishers, 2021).

Malekian Farhad, *Gravity of Wisdom in International Criminal Law* (New York: Nova Science Publishers, 2021).

Malekian Farhad, *International Criminal Law of Children* (New York: Nova Science Publishers, 2021).

Malekian Farhad, *International Criminal Law, the Law of Somebodiness, the Law of Nobodiness* (New York, Nova Science Publishers, 2021).

Malekian Farhad, *Orchestrating Diversity in International Criminal Justice* (New York: Nova Science Publishers, 2021).

Malekian Farhad, *Paralysing International Criminal Justice* (New York: Nova Science Publishers, 2021).

Malekian Farhad and Kerstin Nordlöf, *Confessing the International Rights of Children: The Basic documents with Analysis* (Newcastle: Cambridge Scholars Publishing, 2012).

Malekian Farhad, Kerstin Nordlöf, *The Sovereignty of Children in Law* (Newcastle: Cambridge Scholars Publishing, 2012).

Malekian Farhad and Kerstin Nordlöf,'International Legal Status of Children' in Jay S. Albanese (ed.), *The Encyclopaedia of Criminology*

& Criminal Justice (United States: Wiley-Blackwell (5 volumes, 2013), vol. III, pp. 1173-1178.

Malekian Farhad, Kerstin Nordlöf, *Prohibition of Sexual Exploitation of Children Constituting Obligation Erga Omnes* (Newcastle: Cambridge Scholars Publishing, 2013).

Manacorda Stefano, '*Cesare Beccaria e la pena dell'ergastolo.' Jus* [*Cesare Beccaria and the sentence of life imprisonment*] (2015), pp. 165–182.

Marc Weller, *Iraq and the Use of Force in International Law* (Oxford: Oxford University Press, 2010).

Markovic Milan, 'International Criminal Trials and the Disqualification of Judges on International Criminal Trials and the Disqualification of Judges on the Basis of Nationality the Basis of Nationality', 13 (1) *Washington University Global Studies Law Review* (2014), pp.1-48. Available online at https://openscholarship.wustl.edu/cgi/viewcontent.cgi?article=1472&context=law_globalstudies

Maxwell Max, *A Socratic Perspective on the Nature of Human Evil*, available online at http://www.socraticmethod.net/socratic_essay_nature_of_ human_evil.htm.

May Lary, *'Habeas Corpus as* Jus cogens *in International Law' 4 (3)* Criminal Law and Philosophy *(2010), 249–265.*

McAuley Finbarr and J Pail McCutcheon, *Criminal Liability* (Round Hall Sweet and Maxwell, 2000).

McDermott, Yvonne 'Strengthening the Evaluation of Evidence in International Criminal Trials' 17(4) *International Criminal Law Review* (2017), pp. 682-702.

McInerny Ralph, 'Thomistic Natural Law and Aristotelian Philosophy' in John Goyette, Mark Latkovic and Richard Myers (eds.) *St Thomas Aquinas and the Natural Law Tradition: Contemporary Perspectives* (2004).

Mendus Susan, 'The Importance of Love in Rawls's Theory of Justice' 29 (1) *British Journal of Political Science* (1999), pp. 57-75.

Meron, Theodor, 'On Hierarchy of International Human Rights' 80 *American Journal of International Law* (1986).

Meron Theodor, 'Judicial Independence and Impartiality in International Criminal Tribunals'. 99 (2) *American Journal of International Law* (2005), pp.359-369.

Meron Theodor, *The Humanization of International Law* (Netherlands: The Hague Academy, 2006).

Meyssan Thierry, *11 September 2001: L'effroyable Imposture* (2002).

Mill J. S., *Collected Works of John Stuart Mill*, Gen. Ed. J. M. Robson, Toronto: University of Toronto Press, 1963-91).

Milmed Bella K., *Kant and Current Philosophical Issues* (New York University Press, 1961).

Mokhtar Ali, '*Nullum Crimen, Nulla Poena, Sine Lege*: Aspects and Prospects', 26 *Statute Law Review,* pp. 41-55.

Moyn Samuel, *Not Enough: Human Rights in an Unequal World* (2018).

Muchnik Pablo, *Kant's Theory of Evil: An Essay on the Dangers of Self-love and the Aperiodicity of History* (Lexington Books, 2010).

Mueller Gerhard O. W., 'International Criminal Law: Civitas Maxima,' 15 *Case Western Reserve Journal of International Law* (1985).

Murphy Peter, 'No Free Lunch, No Free Proof: The Indiscriminate Admission of Evidence is a Serious Flaw in International Criminal Trials', 8(2) *Journal of International Criminal Justice* (2010), pp. 539-573.

Murphy S., 'Nation-Building: A Look at Somalia,' 3 *Tul J Int'l & Comp L* (1995).

Nafeez Mosaddeq Ahmed, *'Terrorism and Statecraft: Al-Qaeda and Western Covert Operations after the Cold War,'* in Paul Zarembka (ed.), pp. 143-182.

Neal J., *Principles of Legislation: From the Ms. of Jeremy Bentham; By M. Dumont … With Notes and a Biographical Notice of Jeremy Bentham and of M. Dumont*, Boston, MA: Wells and Lilly, 1830).

Newton Michael A., 'Back to the Future: Reflections on the Advent of Autonomous Weapons Systems', 47 (1) *Case Western Reserve Journal of International Law* (2015), pp. 5–23.

Nicolas A. J., 'Croquet the International Criminal Court and the Treatment of Defence Rights: A Mirror of the European Court of Human Rights' Jurisprudence?', *Human Rights Law Review* (2011), pp.91-131.

Nieto-Navia, R *International Peremptory Norms (Jus cogens) and International Humanitarian Law* (2011).

Nikam N. A. *Sense, Understanding and Reason* (Asia Publishing House, 1966).

Noone Gregory P. and Diana C. Noone, 'The Debate over Autonomous Weapons Systems', 47 (1) *Case Western Reserve Journal of International Law* (2015), pp. 25–35.

O'Connell, '*Jus cogens*: International Law's Higher Ethical Norms' in Childress, DE III (ed.), *The Role of Ethics in International Law* (2012).

O'Connor Susan, 'Up in Arms: A Humanitarian Analysis of the Arms Trade Treaty and Its New Zealand Application,' *11 New Zealand Yearbook of International Law* (2013), pp. 73–105.

Ogletree Charles J., Austin Sarat, *The Road to Abolition? The Future of Capital Punishment in the United States* (2009).

Ogunfolu Adedokun and Oludayo Fagbemi, 'I Have a Drone: The Implications of American Drone Policy for Africa and International Humanitarian Law,' 23 (1) *Revue Africaine de Droit International et Comparé* (2015), pp. 106–128.

Oliver Covey, 'The Attorney-General of the Government of Israel v. Eichmann,' 56 (3) *The American Journal of International Law* (1962), pp. 805-845.

Oliver Covey, 'Attorney-General of the Government of Israel v. Adolf Eichmann,' 36 *Israeli Law Review* (1968).

Olson Peter M., 'The Lawfulness of Russian Use of Force in Crimea', 53 (1) *Revue de Droit Militaire et de Droit de la Guerre* (2014), pp. 17–40.

O'Neill Onora, *Constructions of Reason: Explorations of Kant's Practical Philosophy* (Cambridge University Press, 1989).

Orakhelashvili Alexander, 'The Impact of Peremptory Norms on the Interpretation and Application of United Nations Security Council

Resolutions,' 16 (1) *The European Journal of International Law* (2005), pp. 59-88.

Orakhelashvili Alexander, *Peremptory Norms in International Law* (2006).

Oriolo Anna, 'Codes of Conduct for International Prosecutors', *Max Planck Encyclopaedias of International Law*, https://opil.ouplaw.com/view/10.1093/law-mpeipro/e2656.013.2656/law-mpeipro-e2656.

Pardo Pilar Villanueva Sainz, 'Is International Criminal Law a living discipline?', 3:4 *The International Journal of Human Rights* (1999), pp. 92-100.

Parish Matthew, *International criminal law – Justice or Mirage?* Transonflict (2013). http://www.transconflict.com/2013/05/international-criminal-law-justice-or-mirage-025/.

Paton Herbert James, *Kant's Metaphysic of Experience* (Humanities Press, 1961).

Patrides C. A. and Joseph Anthony Wittreich, *The Apocalypse in English Renaissance Thought and Literature: Patterns, Antecedents, and Repercussions* (Manchester University Press, 1984).

Patterson Dennis (ed.), *Postmodernism and Law* (1994).

Paul Roberts, 'The Priority of Procedure and the Neglect of Evidence and Proof: Facing Facts in International Criminal Law', 13(3) *Journal of International Criminal Justice* (2015), pp. 479-506.

Paulus A., '*Jus cogens* in a Time of Hegemony and Fragmentation', 74 *Nordic Journal of International Law* (2005), pp. 297-334.

Paust, J 'The Reality of *Jus cogens,*' 7 *Connecticut Journal of International Law* (1991), 83.

Pella V. Vespasian, *La criminalité collective des états et le droit pénal de l'avenir* [*The collective criminality of states and the criminal law of the future*], Bucarest: Imprimerie de l'état, (1925).

Pella Vespasian V., *Revue Internationale de Droit Penal* (1928).

Pella Vespasian V., *La Guerre-Crime et les Criminels de Guerre* [*War-Crime and War Criminals*] (Paris, 1946).

Pella Vespasian V., Plan for World Criminal Code, 17 *Revue Internationale de Droit Penal* (1946).

Pella Vespasian V., "Fonctions Pacificatrices du Droit Pénal Supranational et Fin du Système Traditionnel des Traités de Paix" ["Peacemaking Functions of Supranational Criminal Law and End of the Traditional System of Peace Treaties"], 1 *Le Droit Internationale Public* (1947).

Pella Vespesian V., 'Towards an International Criminal Court', 44 *American Journal of International Law* (1950), 57.

Pella Vespasian V., Plan d'un Code Répressif Mondial [Plan of a Global Repressive Code], 6 *Rewe International de Droit Pénal* 1948 (1955).

Pellet A, 'Vive le crime! Remarques sur les degrés de l'illicité en droit international' in United Nations /International Law Commission (ed.), *International Law on the Eve of the Twenty-first Century: Views from the International Law Commission* (United Nations New York 1997), pp. 287–315.

Pellet A, 'Comments in Response to Christine Chinkin and in Defense of *Jus cogens* as the Best Bastion against the Excesses of Fragmentation' 83 *Finnish Yearbook of International Law* (2006).

Penrose Mary Margaret, 'Lest We Fail: The Importance of Enforcement in International Criminal Law: An Essay on the Nature and Immutability of Truth', 15 (2) *American University International Law Review* (1999), pp. 321-394.

Pepper S. L. 'The Lawyer's Amoral Ethical Role: A defence, a Problem, and Some Possibilities, *American Bar Foundation Research Journal*, (1986).

Peterson Jeremy, 'Unpacking Show Trials: Situating the Trial of Saddam Hussein,' 48 *Harvard International Law Journal* (2007).

Plaw Avery and João Franco Reis, 'Learning to Live with Drones: Answering Jeremy Waldron and the Neutralist Critique', 14 (2) *Journal of Military Ethics*, 2015, pp. 128–145.

Posner Eric A., A. O Sykes, *Economic Foundations of International Law* (Cambridge: Harvard University Press, 2013).

Potter R. B., War and Moral Discourse (Richmond, Va., John Knox Press, 1969).

Power Jonathan, *Conundrums of Humanity: The Quest for Global Justice* (2007).

Protector J. Harris, *Islam and International Relations* (New York, 1965).

Quadri Kafayat Motilewa, Hunud Abia Kadaouf, Mohammad Naqib Ishan Jan, Mohd. Iqbal AbdulWahab and Haniff Ahama, 'Adquisitorial: The Mixing of Two Legal Systems' 3 (1) *International Journal of Humanities and Management Sciences* (2015), pp.31-36.

Ragazzi M The Concept of International Obligations erga omnes (Clarendon Press Oxford 1997).

Rahmdel Mansour, 'Money Laundering in Iranian Law: Present and Future,' *Journal of Money Laundering Control* (2002).

Rahmdel Mansour, 'The Ne Bis In Idem Rule in Iranian Criminal Law,' *Journal of Financial Crime* (2004).

Rahmdel Mansour, The Role of the Courts in the Reform of Iranian Criminal Law Policy,' *Criminal Law Forum* (2006).

Ramadan Tariq, *Radical Reform: Islamic Ethics and Liberation* (Oxford: Oxford University Press, 2009).

Ramadan Tariq, *The Quest for Meaning, Developing a Philosophy of Pluralism* (London: Penguin, 2010).

Ramsey Clark, *War Crimes – A Report on United States War Crimes against Iraq* (Maisonneuve Press, 1992).

Ramsey Paul, War and the Christian Conscience (Durham, N.C., The Duke University Press, 1961).

Randall Kenneth C., 'Universal Jurisdiction under International Law' 66 *Texas Law Review* (1988).

Rawls John, *A Theory of Justice* (2ed.,1999).

Raz Joseph, *The Morality of Freedom* (1986).

Raz Joseph, *Ethics in the Public Domain: Essays in the Morality of Law and Politics* (Oxford: Oxford University Press, 1994).

Raz Joseph, 'Why the State?' in N. Roughan and A. Halpin (eds) *In Pursuit of a Pluralist Jurisprudence* (CUP 2017).

Rehman Javaid, *International Human Rights Law* (London and New York: Longman Pub Group, 2nd ed., 2010).

Reisman W. Michael, 'Legal Responses to Genocide and Other Massive Violations of Human Rights', 59 *Law and Contemporary Problems* (1996).

Reiss Hans Siegbert, *Kant: Political Writings* (2003).

Report of the Independent Inquiry into the actions of the United Nations during the 1994 genocide in Rwanda, *UN Doc S/1999/1257* (1999) [Rwanda Report].

Rinceanu, Johanna, 'Concept and Systematization of the Criminal Offense in Romania' in U. Sieber, S. Forster, & K. Jarvers (Eds.), *National Criminal Law in a Comparative Legal Context*, Vol. 3(1): Max-Planck-Institute Max-Planck-Institute für Ausländisches und Internationals Strafrecht (2011), pp. 73–85.

Rinceanu Johanna, 'The principle of legality (*Nullum crimen sine lege*) in Romania' in U. Sieber, S. Forster, & K. Jarvers (Eds.), *National Criminal Law in a Comparative Legal Context, vol. 2* (1): Max-Planck-Institute für Ausländisches und Internationals Strafrecht, (2011), pp. 89-10.

Rinceanu Johanna, 'Criminal Liability of Legal Persons in Romania' in *Riccardo Borsari, Responsabilita` da reato deli enti* (Padova: Padova University Press, 2016), pp. 407–418.

Rishimawi Mona., 'A Reality or a Mirage: Judicial Review of Detention,' in Charles Riziki Majinge (ed.), *Rule of Law Through Human Rights and International Criminal Justice: Essays in Honour of Adama Dieng* (Newcastle: Cambridge Scholars publishing, 2015), pp. 507-522.

Robertson Geoffrey, *Crimes Against Humanity – The Struggle for Global Justice* (Penguin Books, 3rd ed., 2006).

Roméo Dallaire's, *Shake Hands with the Devil: The Failure of Humanity in Rwanda* (Carroll & Graf, New York, 2003).

Rosen Allen D., *Kant's Theory of Justice* (Ithaca, London: Cornel University Press, 1996).

Rosenstock R., 'An International Criminal Responsibility of States?', in United Nations/International Law Commission (ed.), *International Law on the Eve of the Twenty-First Century: Views from the International Law Commission* (United Nations New York, 1997), pp. 265–85.

Ruth Mackenzie & Philippe Sands, 'International Courts and Tribunals and the Independence of the International Judge', 44 *Harvard International Law Journal* (2003), pp.271-285.

Ruys Tom, 'Of Arms, Funding and Non-Lethal Assistance: Issues Surrounding Third-State Intervention in the Syrian Civil War,' 13 (1) *Chinese Journal of International Law* (2014), pp. 13–53.

Ryngaert Cedric, *Jurisdiction in International Law* (Oxford: Oxford University Press, 2009), PP. 42-84.

Ryngaert Cedtric, 'Territorial Jurisdiction Over Cross-frontier Offences: Revisiting a Classic Problem of International Criminal Law' 9 *International Criminal Law Review* 9 (2009), pp. 187–209.

Sacirbey Muhamed, *International Criminal Tribunal Born as Bastard?' The World Post*, available (https://www.huffingtonpost.com/ambassador-muhamed-sacirbey/international-criminal-tribunals_b_3344169.html.

Sadat Nadya Leila, Custom, 'Codification and Some Thoughts about the Relationship between the Two: Article 10 of the ICC Statute,' 49 *DePaul Law Review* (2000).

Sadat Nadya Leila and S. Richard, 'The New International Criminal Court: An Uneasy Revolution,' 88 *Georgetown Law Journal* 581 (2000).

Sadat Leila Nadya, 'Competing and Overlapping Jurisdictions', Bassiouni, ed., *International Criminal* Law (2008).

Sahovic Milan and William W. Bishop., 'The Authority of the State: Its Range with Respect to Persons and Places' in Max Sorensen, *Manual of Public International Law* (London : Macmillan, 1968), pp. 311-380.

Salter William Mackintire, *Anarchy or Government? An Inquiry in Fundamental Politics* (1895).

Salter William Mackintire, *Ethical Religion* (1889).

Salter William Mackintire, *The Conflict of the Catholic Church with the French Republic* (1907).

Saner Hans, *Kant's Political Thought* (University of Chicago Press, 1973).

Sassoli, 'State Responsibility for Violations of Humanitarian Law', 84 *IRCR* (2002).

Saul, M 'Identifying *Jus cogens* Norms: The Interaction of Scholars and International Judges,' *Asian Journal of International Law* (2014) (forthcoming).

Schabas William A., Justice, 'Democracy and Impunity in Post Genocide Rwanda: Searching for Solutions to Impossible Problems,' 7 *Criminal Law Forum* (1996).

Schabas William A., *The Abolition of the Death Penalty in International Law* (2002 and 2005).

Schabas William A., *The UN International Criminal Tribunals: The Former Yugoslavia, Rwanda and Sierra Leone* (Cambridge: Cambridge University Press, 2006).

Schabas William A., *Genocide in International Law: The Crimes of Crimes* (Cambridge University Press, 2000 and 2009).

Schabas William A., *An Introduction to the International Criminal Court* (Cambridge University Press, 2011).

Schachter Oscar, *International Law in Theory and Practice* (1991).

Schwarzenberger Georg, 'The Problem of an International Criminal Law,' 5 *Current Legal Problems* (1950).

Schwarzenberger G., *International Jus cogens*?, 43 Tax. L. Rev (1965).

Sevrine Knuche, 'State Immunity and the Promise of *Jus cogens*', *Northwestern Journal of International Human Rights (*2011), Vol. 9, No. 2, pp. 149-183.

Shaffer Thomas L., 'The Legal Ethics of Radical Individualism' 65 *Texas Law Review* (1997).

Shelton, D. 'Normative Hierarchy of International Law' 80 *American Journal of International Law* (1986).

Shytov Alexander Nikolaevich, Conscience and Love in Making Judicial Decisions (2001), p.xiv.

Sieber U., S. Forster, & K. Jarvers (Eds.), *National Criminal Law in a Comparative Legal Context*, Vol. 3(1): Max-Planck-Institute Max-Planck-Institute für Ausländisches und Internationals Strafrecht (2011).

Simma Bruno & Philip Alston, 'The Sources of Human Rights Law: Custom, *Jus cogens*, and General Principles' 90 *Australia Yearbook of International Law* (1992).

Simon William H., *The Practice of Justice: A Theory of Lawyers' Ethics* (1998).

Sinclair I., *The Vienna Convention on the Law of Treaties* (1986).

Sliedregt Elies van, Pluralism in International Criminal Law, 25 *Leiden Journal of International Law* (2012).

Sliedregt Elies van & Sergey Vasiliev eds., *Pluralism International Criminal Law* 3 (Oxford, 2014);

Smith Norman Kemp, '*Commentary to Kant's 'Critique of Pure Reason''* (Humanities Press, 1962).

Smith Alic Halford, *Kantian Studies* (Greenwood Press, 1974).

Smith T. S., *Lecture Delivered over the Remains of Jeremy Bentham, Esq., in the Webb-Street School of Anatomy & Medicine, on the 9th June, 1832* (London: Effingham Wilson, 1832).

Sowilet A., *The Problem of the Creation of a Permanent International Criminal Court* (1951).

Spiermann, 'Humanitarian Intervention as a Necessity and the Threat or Use of *Jus cogens*' 71 *Nordic Journal of International Law* (2002), 523.

Spooner Lysander , *Natural Law; or the Science of Justice: A Treatise on Natural Law, Natural Justice, Natural Rights, Natural Liberty, and Natural Society; showing that all Legislation whatsoever is an Absurdity, a Usurpation, and a Crime. Part First.* [1882], available at http://oll.libertyfund.org/titles/spooner-natural-law-or-the-science-of-justice-1882.

Sriram C., 'Wrong-sizing International Justice? The Hybrid Tribunal in Sierra Leone', 29 (3) *Fordham International Law Journal* (2006), pp.472-506.

Stahn Carsten (ed.), *The Law and Practice of the International Criminal Court* (Oxford University Press, 2015).

Stern Robert, *Understanding Moral Obligation: Kant, Hegel, Kierkegaard* (Cambridge, Cambridge University Press, 2012).

Stigall Dan E., 'The French military Intervention in Mali, Counter-Terrorism, and the Law of Armed Conflict,' 223 (1) *Military Law Review* (2015), pp. 1–40.

Strawson P. F., *The Bounds of Sense: An Essay on Kant's 'Critique of Pure Reason'* (Methuen, 1966).

Sugarman David, ed., *Legality, Ideology and the State* (1985).

Suy, E 'Article 53: Treaties Conflicting with a Peremptory Norm of General International Law ('*jus cogens*')' in Corten, O and Klein, P (Eds.) *The Vienna Convention on the Law of Treaties: A Commentary Volume II* (2011).

Talmon S., 'The Duty Not to 'Recognize as Lawful' a Situation Created by the Illegal Use of Force or Other Serious Breaches of a *Jus cogens* Obligation: An Obligation without Real Substance?', in C Tomuschat and J. M. Thouvenin (eds.), *The Fundamental Rules of the International Legal Order* (2005).

Thirlway H. W. A., *International Customary Law and Codification* (1972), pp. 70-94.

Thornberry Patrick, *International Law and the Rights of Minorities* (Oxford, 1991), pp. 57–109.

Thouvenin M. (eds.), *The Fundamental Rules of the International Legal Order* (2005).

Tomoko Yamashita 'Do *Jus cogens* Norms Invalidate State Immunity? International Restorative Justice and Japanese War Compensation Cases' Chinese (Taiwan) 31 *Yearbook of International Law and Affairs* (2013), pp. 160-194.

Tomuschat, C and Thouveinin, JM (eds.) *The Fundamental Rules of the International Legal Order: Jus cogens and Obligations* Erga Omnes (2006).

Tunkin G., "Soviet Theory of Sources of International Law", in *Volkerrecht und Rechtsphilosophet: Internationale Festchrift for Stefan Verosta* (1980).

Turner Jenia Iontcheva, Nationalizing International Criminal Law, 41 *Stanford Journal of International Law* (2005), pp. 1-52.

Tyler Tom R., 'Understanding the Force of Law', 51 *Tulsa Law Review* (2016), pp.507-519.

Van Schaack Beth, Ronald C. Slye, *International Criminal Law: The Essentials* (2008).

Van Schaack Beth, Ronald C. Slye, *International criminal law: intersections and contradictions* (2020).

Vanhullebusch Matthias, 'The Arab League and Military Operations: Prospects and Challenges in Syria', 22 (2) *International Peacekeeping* (2015), pp.151–168.

Verdross, A 'Forbidden Treaties in International Law: Comments on Professor Garner's Report on 'The Law of Treaties'' 31 *American Journal of International Law* (1937), 571.

Verdross, A '*Jus Dispositivum* and *Jus cogens* in International Law' 60 *American Journal of International Law* (1966).

Vest Hans, 'A Structure-Based Concept of Genocidal *Intent'*, *Journal of International Criminal Justice* (2007), pp.781-797.

Vidmar, J 'Rethinking *Jus cogens* after Germany v. Italy: Back to Article 53?' 60 *Netherlands International Law Review* (2013).

Virally, Michel, 'Réflexions sur le *Jus cogens*' ['Reflections on *Jus cogens*'] 12 *Annuaire Français de Droit International* (1966), 5.

Virally Michel, 'The Sources of International Law,' in M. Sorenson, *Manual of Public International Law* (2nd ed., 1968).

Vischer K. Robert, *Martin Luther King Jr. and the Morality of Legal Practice: Lessons in Love and Justice* (2014).

Vleeschauwer H. J., *The Development of Kantian Thought* (Nelson, 1962).

Vyver Johan D. van der, 'Prosecution and Punishment of the Crime of Genocide', 25 *Fordham International Law Journal* (1999), p.286.

Vyver Johan D. van der, 'The International Criminal Court and the Concept of *Mens rea* in International Criminal Law,' 12 *U. Miami Int'l& Comp. L. Rev.* 57 (2005), pp.57-149, at 92. Available online at: http://repository.law.miami.edu/umiclr/vol12/iss1/3.

Waldock H., 'General Course on Public International Law,' 106 *Recueil Des Course* (1962), pp. 39-103.

Ward Keith, *The Development of Kant's View of Ethics* (Humanities Press, 1972).

Watson John, *The Philosophy of Kant Explained* (Garland, 1976).

Weatherhall Thomas, *Jus cogens International Law and Social Contract* (2015).

Weil, P 'Towards Relative Normativity in International Law' 77 *American Journal of International Law* (1983).

Weinrib Ernest J., 'Law as a Kantian Idea of Reason', 87 *Columbia Law Review* (1987), pp. 472-508.

Weisburd M, 'The Emptiness of the Concept of *Jus cogens*, As Illustrated by the War in Bosnia-Herzegovina', 17 *Michigan Journal of International Law* (1995-1996), pp. 1-51.

Weiss T., *Military-Civilian Interactions: Humanitarian Crises and the Responsibility to Protect* (2nd ed., Rowman & Littlefield Publishers Inc, Lanham (MD), 2005).

Weller Marc, *Iraq and the Use of Force in International Law* (Oxford: Oxford University Press, 2010).

Wet De, 'The Prohibition of Torture as an International Norm of *jus cogens* and Its Implications for National and Customary Law,' 15 *European Journal of International Law* (2004).

Whiteman, MM '*Jus cogens* in International Law: With a Projected List' 7 *Georgia Journal of International and Comparative Law* (1977), p. 609.

Wigmore John Henry, *The Principles of Judicial Proof as given by Logic, Psychology, and General Experience, and Illustrated in Judicial Trials* (Chicago: Little Brown & Co., 1913).

Williamson Myra, *Terrorism, War and International Law, The Legality of the Use of Force Against Afghanistan in 2001* (London: Ashgate Publishing, 2009).

Wistrich Andrew J, Jeffrey J. Rachlinski & Chris Guthrie, 'Heart Versus Head: Do Judges Follow the Law or Follow Their Feelings?', 93 *Texas Law Review* (2015).

Wladyslaw Czaplinski, 'Concepts of *Jus cogens* and Obligations Erga Omnes in International Law in the Light of Recent Developments', 23 *Polish Yearbook of International Law* (1997–1998).

Wolff Christian, *Ius naturae et ius gentium* [*The law of nature and the law of nations*] (Halle, 1740–46). Available at http://oll.libertyfund.org/titles/vattel-the-law-of-nations-lf-ed.

Wolff R. P. (ed.), *Kant* (Doubleday, 1967).

Wood Allen W., *Kant's Moral Religion* (1970).

Wood Allen, *Kant's Ethical Thought* (Cambridge University Press, 1999).

Wood David, *Judicial Ethics: A Discussion Paper, Australian Institute of Judicial Administration* (1996).

Wright Quincy, 'Proposal for an International Criminal Court' 46 (1), *American Journal of International Law* (1952), pp. 60-72.

Wright Quincy, 'The Scope of International Criminal Law: A Conceptual Framework,' 15 *Virginia Journal of International Law* (1975).

Wägenbaur B., *Court of the European Union* (Hart, 2013).

Zaman R., 'Playing the Ace? *Jus cogens* Crimes and Functional Immunity in National Courts,' 17 *Australian International Law Journal* (2010), 53.

Zammito Johan, *The Genesis of Kant's Critique of Judgment* (University of Chicago Press, 1992).

Zarembka Paul, *The Hidden History of 9-11-2001* (New York: Seven Stories Press, 2008).

INDEX

C

D

E

F

G

H

I

J

K

L

M

N

O

P

Q

R

S

T

U

V

W

Y